Praise for
The Mother Heart of God

"Well done! *The Mother Heart of God* is brilliant, balanced, and beautiful. What a superb and important contribution to the expanding conversation. I love it! When a brilliant interviewer and journalist wraps her quest and questions inside her "story," humanity is delivered a stunning and important gift! You are holding such a gift in your hands!"

Paul Young, author of The Shack

"A book for all men and women who love God. Trudy touches the heart of what it means to be human and what it means to grow in grace and understanding. Every house of worship must have this book in their library and every woman a copy next to her bed."

*Lynne Bundesen, author and three-time winner of the
"Excellence in Media" Angel award*

"This new book is an amazing example of how a collection of articulate, educated people deeply committed to differing religious faiths can agree on a concept that has never even occurred to most of us. And yet the concept is so obvious."

Vivian Ruskin, a journalist related to Mark Twain

"Draw deeply. *The Mother Heart of God* is what men and women have been waiting for! Emboldened by the Bible Trudy loves deeply, she has captured the true meaning of the verse in Genesis that both the *"male and the female"* are created in the image of God. Self-esteem will be restored as women take their rightful place in the world, as God intended. It's been a long time coming."

Susan Janetti, mental health counsellor

"Trudy has a journalistic passion that knows no bounds—lively writing, unbridled enthusiasm, and a killer instinct to get to the bottom of a story."

Rick Rake, co-publisher,
Click Media Works (former editor of the Abbotsford News*)*

The

MOTHER
HEART

of

GOD

*Unveiling the Mystery of the Father's
Maternal Love*

TRUDY M. BEYAK

New York Boston Nashville

Scriptures noted ASV are taken from the American Standard Version.

Scriptures noted CJB are taken from the Complete Jewish Bible. Copyright © 1998 by David H. Stern. Published by Jewish New Testament Publications, Inc. www.messianicjewish.net/jntp. Distributed by Messianic Jewish Resources Int'l. www.messianicjewish.net. All rights reserved. Used by permission.

Scriptures noted DR are taken from the Douay-Rheims Bible.

Scriptures noted ESV are taken from The Holy Bible, English Standard Version®, copyright © 2001 by Crossway Bibles, a division of Good News Publishers. Used by permission. All rights reserved.

Scriptures noted KJV are taken from the King James Version of the Bible.

Scriptures noted NASB are taken from the New American Standard Bible ®, Copyright 1960, 1962, 1963, 1968, 1972, 1975, 1977, 1995 by The Lockman Foundation. Used by permission.

Scriptures noted NIRV are taken from the Holy Bible, NEW INTERNATIONAL READER'S VERSION ®. Copyright © 1996, 1998 by International Bible Society. All rights reserved throughout the world. Used by permission of International Bible Society.

Scriptures noted NIV are taken from the HOLY BIBLE, NEW INTERNATIONAL VERSION®. Copyright © 1973, 1978, 1984 by International Bible Society. Used by permission of Zondervan Publishing House. All rights reserved.

Scriptures noted NKJV are taken from the NEW KING JAMES VERSION. Copyright © 1979, 1980, 1982 by Thomas Nelson, Inc., Publishers. Used by permission. All rights reserved.

Scriptures noted NRSV are taken from NEW REVISED STANDARD VERSION of the Bible. Copyright © 1989 by the Division of Christian Education of the National Council of the Churches of Christ in the United States of America. Used by permission. All rights reserved.

Scriptures noted RSV are taken from the REVISED STANDARD VERSION of the Bible. Copyright © 1949, 1952, 1971 by the Division of Christian Education of the National Council of the Churches of Christ in the United States of America. Used by permission. All rights reserved.

FaithWords
Hachette Book Group
237 Park Avenue
New York, NY 10017

www.faithwords.com

Printed in the United States of America

RRD-C

First Edition: April 2013

10 9 8 7 6 5 4 3 2 1

FaithWords is a division of Hachette Book Group, Inc.

The FaithWords name and logo are trademarks of Hachette Book Group, Inc.

The Hachette Speakers Bureau provides a wide range of authors for speaking events. To find out more, go to www.hachettespeakersbureau.com or call (866) 376-6591.

The publisher is not responsible for websites (or their content) that are not owned by the publisher.

Library of Congress Cataloging-in-Publication Data
Beyak, Trudy M.
  The Mother Heart of God : Unveiling the Mystery of the Father's Maternal Love / Trudy M. Beyak. -- First Edition.
    pages cm
  Includes bibliographical references.
  ISBN 978-1-4555-2776-2 -- ISBN 978-1-4555-2778-6 (ebook) 1. God (Christianity)--Love. I. Title.
BT140.B49 2013
231--dc23
                              2012045483

Contents

PART ONE

Made in the Image of God

CHAPTER 1

The Journey Begins

This hope we have as an anchor of the soul, a hope
both sure and steadfast and one which enters within
the veil.

Hebrews 6:19 NASB

VINCENT VAN GOGH preferred to paint people rather than cathedrals because he said the eyes reveal the inward soul, whether a poor beggar or a street worker.

As a journalist, I am also drawn to the eyes of the people I interview.

Whether meeting musicians or murderers, scientists or six-year-old children, I not only listen to the voices and wait on the words, but stay on the unspoken in the eyes. What lies behind those transparent windows to the soul?

The first pair of eyes that hold me are my mother's.

I am seven years old, cuddling with Mom in church and running my fingers over and over again in circles across her soft velvety fur coat. I imagine she is a fuzzy mother bear. She is a short, bosomy, fun-loving woman with brown lustrous curls and big blue eyes like Bette Davis.

Sitting on the hard wooden pews and hiding under her luxurious fur coat, I feel totally safe in her warmth. I listen to sermons about the love of God, spending hours with my eyes transfixed on a large wooden cross hanging midair above the pulpit. It is powerful stuff for a young girl looking around at the stained-glass windows with scenes of people being healed and Jesus holding little children on his lap.

I know without a shadow of doubt that God loves me.

My mother prods me to be a missionary when I grow up.

"Well, I don't know about that idea, Mom," I say quietly, already acutely aware in my few years of life there is a nonconforming side to my personality.

She hugs me anyway.

A soft-hearted woman, Mom rescues abandoned children who are in need of a loving home because she believes love conquers all evil.

With arms open wide to embrace the rejected in society, our house may best be described as a noisy multicultural carnival. In addition to raising me and my three biological brothers, my parents open our home to an array of foster kids.

Mom also gives free respite to the weary parents of a severely disabled girl. Little Jody continually screams and bangs her head. Not surprisingly, it is chaos in our kitchen where all the action is.

My parents end up adopting two little boys—Johnny, an Asian youngster, and Louie, a Native American boy who suffers from fetal alcohol syndrome. They are innocent, live-wired boys. While they may not have grown inside her own womb, Mom assures the boys they were formed in a much, much better place.

"You see, my wonderful, precious boys, you're so special I actually chose you to grow in my heart!" she says. "See!" She points under her amply endowed bosom.

"You grew right here inside my heart. Right here!" she says as she kisses the top of their foreheads and elevates their position to the top of the family hierarchy. It is completely fair according to "Mom's Rule of Justice" that these boys, who had been abandoned, would be so luxuriantly pampered in our home.

The whole family buys into that love.

It is the way of God's compassion.

Mom loves these ragamuffin orphans with great kindness, and as I watch her shower them with love, I too feel the exhilarating, liberating power of love.

Little Johnny had been discarded by his real mom and dad and tossed back and forth between three foster homes by the time he was eleven months old. The brown-eyed boy steals Mom's heart as soon as he moves in.

"Never again will you feel alone," she says to him.

We all nod. Johnny is Mom's boy to stay.

She feels every one of his tears of pain. As he grows to be a teenager, she tells the social workers that Johnny needs a good counselor because he keeps getting into trouble with the law. He crashes a car. His teachers kick him out of class. Meanwhile, Mom prays to God to help her be as patient with him as God is.

She never stops loving him.

Mom worries helplessly, year after year, trying to get him help. But she is stymied by a social system that ignores his developing identity crisis and struggle with homosexuality. Finally, at age twenty-five, he is HIV positive and commits suicide.

Anguish now dims the bright blue in my mother's eyes. . . .

Nine months after Johnny died—just about the time it takes to conceive, carry, and deliver another child—Louie, my other adopted brother, dies in a car accident.

Louie, whose heritage includes a long line of alcoholics, is twenty-one years old and drinking beer with a carload of friends, skidding along the Fraser Canyon Highway. Crashing boulders claim the neural endings of his brain, a sensitive, kind young man whose legacy is a fatal brain injury. Mom had tenderly loved this boy too, nurturing him with hefty cheek kisses and hugs, warning him not to drink because his genes carry the alcoholic weakness.

Another part of Mom's all-embracing heart collapses.

Yet she carries on. Still her faith remains strong.

"God knows our hearts," she says as she tries to make sense of the tragedies. She continues to trust in the God of love and justice who will eventually wipe away all sorrow and all tears and make the crooked things of this woeful world straight.

"All things will pass away one day," she says. "We are only here on Earth for a very short time, so while we still have life in us, we must never stop loving others."

As she comforts me, I realize much later in life that she had modeled in her own special way the kindness of God who comforts us in all of our afflictions.

☙

Thus begins this story.

When the pink blossoms fall once more in another season, I am an investigative journalist breaking news stories, exposing political scandals, and writing human-interest stories.

I am continually inspired by "Mom's Rule of Justice."

Pursuing the truth with compassion drives my work as I try to treat people with respect and kindness, and my news stories often rescue victims of physical and emotional suffering, discrimination, and other social injustices. For twenty years, I help shut down dishonest politicians and report evidence that jails criminals and pedophiles, and I play a critical role in closing the doors of corporations involved in unethical practices.

How?

By simply exposing the truth in print!

Words are powerful motivators in the pursuit of justice.

I am faithfully pursuing the passions of my heart as a journalist when God hands me a new assignment—one that seems almost impossible to fathom. It happens one day with no advance notice or fanfare while I am on a winter holiday and too tired to write any more. Relaxing on the island of Maui on a sun-drenched morning, I am looking forward to snorkeling with the yellow butterfly fish and working on nothing more strenuous than my sorry-looking tan.

Political controversies are far from my mind.

Reading the Holy Bible that warm morning during my study and prayer time, I am impressed by Genesis 1:27 in which Moses beautifully portrays how the male and the female together are made in the image of God, *Imago Dei*.

As I think about this, it suddenly strikes me that the woman, therefore, must reflect the nature of God in some mysterious way—no less than the man.

The feeling that washes over me is warm and electrifying.

Why had I not noticed this before?

I think about my father's strength and his enterprising energy and how his paternal kindness is modeled by my kind heavenly Father. Then I start wondering if my mother's compassion might be a hint there is also a maternal side to God's love. Leaning back in an open place, I take a deep breath.

"Take off your sandals, for the place where you are standing is holy ground."

Exodus 3:5 NIV

Placing my sandals by the door, I step into a holy place and remain quiet for a very long time. Months meld into years of prayer as I immerse myself in the study of the Holy Bible that has left me in complete awe of the *God of my salvation*.

It is not humanly possible for a foolish person like me to expand on the common understanding of God. Expand on the Infinite? Impossible! Yet I feel God quietly impressing me to interview leaders from the major Christian faiths of the world. But I resist this idea. I find excuses. *I cannot afford to take time off my job. Who will talk to me about such a controversial subject? Lord, I don't think I'm good enough to do it.*

More than a dozen years pass by. I attend a Women of Faith conference and once again hear that immortal voice as I kneel down in the room with the red-and-white checkered tiles and close my eyes.

"Lord God, I can't approach faith leaders on this subject and write a book. Look at me. Here I am talking to you, carrying nothing but my hiking backpack, a notebook, and a pen. That's me. Not at all stylish like Oprah Winfrey. I really don't think I can do it."

Another year goes by.

One summer day, during a hike on Mount Baker, the grandeur of the mountain peaks and the snow contrasted by the clear blue sky causes such a deep exhilaration to well inside me that I spontaneously break out singing:

"Over all the Earth, you reign on high,
Every mountain stream, every sunset sky,
But my one request, Lord, my only aim,
is that you reign in me again."[1]

The song gives words to the overwhelming happiness I feel inside as I begin hiking down a long, narrow trail on the other side of Table Mountain where the geography always reminds me of the Great Wall of China. This part of the hike is raw and risky because it is basically one huge rock slide covered by small broken stones.

What happens next defies explanation.

Stupid me. Dumb me. I trip over my own two feet, stepping over the ledge into midair, swaying sideways—rolling down the mountainside like a crazy carpet! Heading downward into a frightening 1,500-foot drop to what appears to be certain death with large jagged granite boulders awaiting me at the bottom. No time to think. In a split second of chilling panic, I see one large rock jutting out of the ground, about three feet wide, come into view as I roll sideways.

A voice shouts in my head: *"Grab that rock. Now! Or you're dead."*

With all the strength, energy, and life I have in me, I lunge and splay my body across the rock and grab it as hard as I can with both hands and legs. I grab it hard. I feel solid pain. I grab the pain. The rock holds.

My body stops rolling. Gasping, I hang on to the only rock on this part of the mountain slope large enough to hold me! I don't move. My heart beating, my left knee bleeding, I feel the bones in my hands, fractured and sprained, throbbing in excruciating pain.

"Lord, I know I don't deserve what you just did to save me." Shaking and stunned, I went from singing to screaming; walking to falling; living to almost dying, in less than five seconds. "Thank you dear Lord, Rock of my Salvation!"

"Now, Trudy, are you ready to do what I'm calling you to do?"

"If it's the last thing I do in my short, silly, sorry life, Lord, yes."

The following year, I arrange to take a sabbatical from my job and start setting up interviews to converse with Protestant, Catholic, and Jewish experts all around the globe to sort out the question about the nature of God by asking:

What does the Bible really say?

Are we missing half of the picture of God?

I pursue a global investigation with pen and notebook in hand interviewing biblical scholars and celebrities from North America to the Middle East and spend the next five years researching the Scriptures and meditating on God's Word.

What is God really like? What sacred evidence does the Bible reveal?

What emerged is a new, engaging picture of the God I thought I knew!

The Quest to Know God

In all, more than fifty leaders of faith agree to enter into a conversation about the so-called gender of God. Some theologians, however, decline to be interviewed. And a few critics tell me I should not explore this question because it is too difficult to understand. Others sidestep the question completely.

When I interview Rev. Joseph A. Fitzmyer, a well-respected biblical scholar, he is civil, but quickly dismisses my queries about the possible gender of God. He is the coeditor of the *New Jerome Biblical Commentary* and is professor emeritus of Biblical Studies at the Catholic University of America in Washington, D.C.

He tells me the question is a waste of time.

I feel uncomfortable. He insinuates I might be some kind of a wacko-feminist. I laugh and assure him that I am a devoted believer in God, just like he is. I tell him that I'm definitely not a feminist. But I am looking for answers. That's why I am trying to talk to as many Bible experts as I can.

"You happen to be a scholar I respect, Reverend Fitzmyer."

Thankfully, he continues our conversation.

God has no feminine attributes, he says with an air of certainty. Later during our dialogue, he admits the Lord God's devotion to us is sometimes described in the Bible as distinctly maternal in nature, quoting a verse in Isaiah 66:13.

However, he is reluctant to give much weight to this passage.

"This is clearly a Scripture where God speaks of Himself like a mother," he says. "But that is the exception, not the rule."

Feeling confused, I later try to set up an interview with a well-known biblical scholar in England. She makes it clear that she only wants to talk to me about the world-famous feminist Mary Cady Stanton and the revising committee that wrote the *Woman's Bible*.

Feminism is definitely not my focus, I tell her respectfully.

She hangs up.

Her anger stings me. Feeling dejected, I fear my investigation is going nowhere as I walk along the well-worn pathway in my back woods with my Bible in hand. Sitting down on my favorite fallen birch tree, I read in the Scriptures that God is delighted to answer my questions and to satisfy the deepest spiritual yearnings in my heart to know Him. *Right now, to be honest, dear Lord, I don't understand what I should do next.* He leads me to a promise in the Old Testament.

The secret things belong to the LORD our God, but the things revealed belong to us and to our children forever.

Deuteronomy 29:29 NIV

Making a commitment, I promise God that no matter what happens I will be faithful to His calling and will try not to get discouraged. I write a little sticky note over my computer desk to remind myself that I am working for the *King of Kings.*

I know I will never receive the wisdom of God through my own human power or intelligence. But "the Spirit probes all things, even the profoundest depths of God" (1 Cor. 2:10 CJB) and generously grants to us, mere mortal human beings, the promise of the immeasurable gift of growing in relationship with our Redeemer.

Praying daily for the Spirit of God to lead me, I begin to interview hundreds of people in every walk of life—from scholars to janitors, from the boardroom to the living room—as a powerful spiritual principle starts to emerge.

I am engaged in a deep conversation with Billy Graham's daughter, Ruth, when she does not hesitate to tell me that her study of the Bible convinces her that we have been missing an important aspect of God's love for many centuries. I am surprised. She encourages me to press forward in my quest for answers.

Meanwhile, sociologist Tony Campolo advises me that the answer to the question will bring emotional and spiritual healing for both men and women.

As I interview leaders of various Christian faiths, I discover the teaching throughout history that the nature of God is "only masculine" poses a serious "disconnect" for many faithful believers. To illustrate why the question of the so-called gender of God is relevant and meaningful today, I sometimes ask men to imagine what it would be like if the following what-if scenario came to pass:

"What if you are a little boy or a young man who faithfully attends a church or a synagogue every week? You are taught that you are made in the image of God, just like the girls are. But, you wonder how? The girls can certainly identity with the Creator. But, you ask yourself, what part of you, corresponds to God?"

A Global Investigation

A paradigm shift is occurring all over the world.

"Everywhere you go, the public is raising gender questions about God," says Father Thomas Hopko, a prominent Orthodox scholar living in New York.

"*This is the issue of our day,*" he tells me.

The nature of God is a significant theological question being asked today by many devout men and women of faith, and the people I meet along my journey are recovering ancient biblical truths that have long been forgotten.

They find these truths relevant for today.

I took a journalistic approach to this question with an open mind and from the point of view that God is real, God is love, and the Holy Bible is true, the inspired Word of God, answering the deepest spiritual questions asked by each new generation.

That was my starting point and remained the focus throughout my investigation.

Therefore, this book is unequivocally and unapologetically Christian in tone and content. I also sought the opinions of Jewish scholars to seek the understanding of those who study the same Scriptures. While they may disagree about Jesus, their foundational understanding of God the Father and *Yahweh* start in the same place.

To be sure, what you hold in your hands is not a typical book.

By weaving elements of personal narrative and solid biblical facts with the interviews I had with fifty leaders of faith, my journal highlights many short stories, linked together by the one controversial question.

You might consider this a world-wide panel discussion.

But it is also the story of my own personal journey to know God.

I took a fourteen-month sabbatical in 2007–08 to interview leaders of various faiths around the world, either in person or by phone. When I felt confused on any point, I'd go back to the scholars with phone calls or e-mails as they patiently answered my follow-up questions. I also spent five years carefully studying the Scriptures to make sure what I was learning met the litmus test of biblical truth.

For the reporter in me, I have to admit some questions still remain.

My own spiritual journey is weaved throughout this book—not because I started out to do that, but this is what happened. I share my story, not necessarily in a straight chronological timeline—but more as a montage of experiences, whether good or bad.

The scholars inspired me in more ways than one.

I don't claim to have interviewed an exhaustive list of experts, but I certainly conversed with a relevant sample. Neither do I believe this book will be the last word on such a controversial subject, but I pray it will serve as a valuable resource. The people I interviewed in this book shared their love for God with great enthusiasm and wisdom.

Their stories stand on their own.

To be clear, my investigation does not downplay, neither does it overemphasize the so-called gender of God because our loving, benevolent Creator is infinitely greater than any human mind can ever fully comprehend. All of the sacred titles for God in the Scriptures are to be revered. The will of our majestic Maker is clear in the third commandment:

> "You shall not take the name of the LORD your God in vain, for the LORD will not hold him guiltless who takes his name in vain."
>
> *Exodus 20:7 ESV*

His name is as holy and everlasting as His law is. The stories in this book are in the context that God reveals Himself as our *heavenly Father*, the *King of Kings*, and *Almighty God*, and He instructs us to pray in His holy benevolent name.

But what is the truth about the possible maternal side to God?

I invite you to join me on a journey to find out why the question about the so-called gender of God is suddenly igniting into relevance today.

That is the question I will now turn to.

CHAPTER 2

Benedictine Monks:
Breaking the Silence

Let the wise hear and increase in learning.

Proverbs 1:5 ESV

I WONDER WHO I will meet at the monastery.

Will I feel out of place as a woman?

These two questions are at the top of my mind as I walk into Westminster Abbey Seminary of Christ the King. This is one of only three Benedictine monasteries in Canada and holds the distinction of being the country's smallest university.

Sunshine streams through a window across a solitary chair where a monk in black habit is concentrating on his study of the book of Genesis. A silver crucifix dangles from his neck reflecting the light as it dances around the surrounding cedar beams. The mood is quiet and somber, but not for long.

Laughter suddenly echoes in the hallway as a seminary student sings off-key, his vibrato choir voice resonating cheerfully. Three other young men chime in. The monk looks up from his study and smiles sheepishly.

"They do have a lot of energy, don't they?" he says.

I sit down with one of the seminary students and ask him a question.

"So what inspired you to want to become a priest?"

Even as I ask the question, I think to myself, I had not imagined meeting a tall, handsome, third-year psychology student in his twenties studying theology at the seminary. But here he is in front of me.

"I was feeling empty spiritually," he says. "My life was meaningless, a never-ending round of parties and buying music equipment and cars and other stuff that never really fulfilled me. It slowly dawned on me that I need to find my way back to God."

After he arrived at the seminary, he found the peace of mind he was seeking. During his free time, he loves to watch the latest political debates on TV and play floor hockey with the guys. He is particularly gifted at stopping the puck as a goalie.

I reprimand myself as he is speaking. Never again will I believe that priests and monks simply spend their time being stoic, silent, and generally unsociable. I could not have been more wrong. They teach me to question my religious preconceptions and stereotypes as one of the elderly monks embraces me with a hug every time he sees me and signs his e-mails "ILY," short for "I love you."

The monastery is built like a medieval castle at the summit of Mount Mary, surrounded by rolling hills and lush bigleaf maples. About a dozen cows graze on the hillside like lumbering cartoon figures. I begin my interviews as the ornamental cherry trees vibrate in pink blossom and Canada geese fly across the marshy lake below.

Three monks—Father Nicholas, Boniface, and Placidus—spend hours in dialogue with me. Their names are not made up, and it strikes me as a curious coincidence that their names rhyme in a singsong pattern.

Father Placidus patiently went into great detail to explain why the gender of God cannot be answered simply. Father Nicholas, in contrast, often stops talking and gazes at me in silence. Meanwhile, Father Boniface is chatty.

"God is neither male, nor female," says Boniface,[1] noting how he respects his female friends as *daughters of the King*.

"There always has to be a positive feminine influence in the world. I think that man without woman is unthinkable. Life would be very dull with just one or the other," he comments with a laugh.

The three monks are in consensus that men and women are both made equally in the image of God, and they believe that a harmonious marriage relationship most effectively reflects the balance found in the nature of our Creator.

I ask another question.

"So the husband and the wife together form, in some way, a kind of mirror image of who God is?" I ask. "That would mean, then, that both the bride and the groom would in some mysterious way reflect the face of God, right?"

Silence.

"Well, yes and no."

I return to the solitude of the monastery over and over again for the next several years to study the Scriptures, pray, and to meet with each of the monks individually.

Father Boniface is known by many as a "faithful friend."

He once worked as a hospital chaplain at St. John's Hospital near Hollywood in the happy days when legendary actors James Cagney and Ronald Reagan (who later became US president) served on the hospital board.

A deep thinker, his eyes are radiant blue behind his wire-rimmed glasses. He grew up on a farm in Oregon, and he tells me that he was five years old when he had an accident that changed his life. Playing with matches, his pants caught fire and caused deep extensive burns to his right leg. Young Boniface was unable to walk for ten long, painful months. But one Sunday, out of the blue, he started walking again.

"God made things better," he says with a faith that is matter-of-fact.

His mother had earnestly prayed for him, and when prayers were answered, she was fond of saying: *"God does such things—His wonders to perform."* The boy was destined to serve this God of compassion, in large part, because of her devout faith.

His long-time friend Father Placidus reveals a similar story.

He is leaning back on an old brown velvet couch in front of a picture window and for a moment watches the cumulus clouds float past the snow-capped peaks of the Coast Mountains. He then turns his mind to my question.

"There is no such God as an all-male God or an all-female God," he says with an air of distinction as a seminary lecturer on such subjects as Latin and theology. He acknowledges, however, that both gender roles are important. His mother, for example, was also a godly inspiration to him. One day after she had surgery and was suffering in great pain in her hospital bed, she turned her sorrow over to God by simply saying: *"I've got a bed, but all He [Jesus] had was a cross."*

Placidus never forgot those words.

The faith of a mother seems to be a common theme with the monks.

God has given a woman her wonderful maternal instinct to care for others in a deeply sincere way, Placidus explains, noting this is one of the main reasons why more women have been deemed "saints" by the church throughout the ages than men.

That's interesting, I say. Why in the world would that be?

"I think it's because women have this great, innate capacity to love, and they have an astonishing capacity to forgive," he says and then pauses. "I think of the many women who have been abused, and yet they have such an incredible capacity to forgive their abusers and to love with such sincerity."

The words of Jesus as He hung on the cross come to mind.

"Father, forgive them, for they know not what they do," he told his attackers (see Luke 23:34).

As a journalist I have often written about the sobering fact that one in three women is assaulted during her lifetime. An emotional memory rises in my mind. I think about the survivors of crime who plead with me to use my pen to inform the public about their experiences. They say it is healing to share their stories.

So I listen. I cry, and I write.

I remember interviewing Joan, whose ex-husband killed their four-year-old boy in a rage of jealousy, a brown-eyed angelic boy who did nothing but hold his mom tightly around her legs and cry for her help. Even though her former husband had threatened to hurt their son, a judge decided to give him visiting rights anyway.

Two days later, as the car sped away with her boy waving good-bye in the car seat, she knew she would never see him again. Joan's courage to carry on living with this heavy cross of unending sorrow reveals the fatigued face of a modern-day saint.

A few years later, I meet Ginger,[2] whose best friend "Joy" had been murdered.

Joy's husband strangled her to death with his leather belt in a crack-induced split-second of insanity. I can still see the anguish on the face of the eldest daughter as she weeps in the middle of the street with her arms up in the air, pleading, "Why?"

As coroners wrap the mother's body inside the house, an army of news photographers snap the daughter's picture while a police officer wraps his arms around her to try to comfort her when no comfort can be found. Ginger takes the girl home, as well as her five other brothers and sisters. She holds all of them close to her heart, buying new beds and blankets and meeting their school-teachers.

What compels someone to adopt six motherless kids?

Ginger is a sales professional attending a community church. Some time prior to this tragedy she had made a commitment to love others as Christ so dearly loves us, and now she reflects to the world broken by sin the human face of the image of God.

The monk calls such women "saints."

"I don't think women really set out to be saints, Father Placidus," I say to him. "They just have big hearts, and they ache when others ache, and they care when no one else cares." I swallow hard.

Why do you love with such sincerity? He looks at me with respect.

"Father Placidus, I'm here because I want to know God on a deeper level."

He smiles: "I have no doubt, you will."

Marriage and the Image of God

The marriage union is an important key to revealing the image of God.

"When God created us in His image, in His likeness, He inscribed in our very being—whether male or female—the profound inscription that I am to be a gift to another in a communion of others," says Placidus, as we return to the big question.

How does this roll out in reality?

When a man and woman repeat their marriage vows to be faithful to each other and two people become "one flesh" (see Matt. 19:4–6), their union in a mutually respectful, harmonious relationship has the potential to most profoundly reveal the oneness of the Trinity and to reflect the image of God, he says.

The one true living God is mysteriously represented by three divine persons, the Father, Son, and Holy Spirit. Similarly, as a child of God, we also represent a spiritual mystery, he says, because "each person is a trinity of body, mind, and spirit."

There is deep spiritual significance in marriage.

Considering God's noble goals for humankind, it is devastating when people engage in activities that degrade and disrespect God's image in themselves and others, like premarital sex, adultery, divorce, pornography, and homosexuality, he says.

"The porn industry is all about greed and disrespect, it is all me-centered and defaces people who are made in the image of God and are made to be holy."

God designed us to be spiritual beings, and we will never find true rest until we cast off the corruption of this world and live in harmony with Him, says the monk, noting how deeply the Creator longs to make us whole again.

"Jesus is the perfect image of God. To the extent we allow Him to forgive our sins and to recreate us, we may become a new person, a holy person like Him."

I listen intently. So much to absorb! When I get home that evening, I snuggle into the warmth of my husband's strong shoulders and feel an indescribable sense of wholeness. Joy washes over me just by being with him.

"I love you," I say.

"Love you, too," he replies.

I know it sounds corny, but I love loving him. I feel like we are meant to be together—physically, mentally, and emotionally. I met him when I was a teenager, and we marry when I am eighteen years old. Playing hard and working hard, we learn to water-ski together and to figure out the ropes of running a business partnership as I create advertising flyers and do the accounting while he meets new clients and does much of the physical work.

Most important, we have three beautiful girls together.

When we go out dancing, nothing makes me feel happier than leaning my head on his broad shoulders and stepping into a ballet-like pattern that synchronizes with swaying waltzes such as "Endless Love" by Mariah Carey.

I trust him in the big things and little things in life. He can fix practically anything in the house, armed with his nails and hammer, plumbing tools and paint. Meanwhile, I'm the opposite. I do not even know how to change the fluorescent light in our office. Over the years, unfortunately, his interests start to change, as do mine.

We clash more than once during our marriage.

By the end of my conversations with my three favorite monks, my husband is gone. No shoulder to lean on. No waltz to step to. My heart is broken. They say that divorce is more painful than death. A part of me died that year . . . a big part.

The monks tell me we are to be gifts to one another—and that's what I thought my husband and I were to each other. But sometimes, sadly, gifts are rejected. And even God's gifts go unappreciated and ignored. I had married my husband for life. Now I fall into an abyss of grief.

Counseling helped. Time helped. Friends helped.

One of the monks advises me to ask God to help and to give me strength, and in some mystical way, He would turn the blubbering mess that is "me" into someone peaceful and calm. He looks at me tenderly: "Jesus loved others and was rejected, too."

ℒ♥

I love being married. Still do, even though I'm not.

The following Saturday, I visit my friends who are camping. Their preschool boys are running around playing outside with water spraying from a tap and yelling at the top of their lungs. Such sweet mayhem! Mommy is breast-feeding the newborn inside the travel trailer while Daddy gathers up the kids, scoots them indoors and starts to make lunch.

"Can you hand me the peanut butter?" he says to me with a big smile.

I love that smile. Then he leans over the table and kisses his wife.

"Love you," she says with her eyes closed.

"Love you too!" he replies as he prepares the peanut butter sandwiches.

I'll always long to repeat the experience of the intertwined life, when two become one. Some people become bitter after divorce. I never wanted to be like that. I'm not saying I always accepted the loneliness, rejection, and grief with grace. I was often disappointed, angry, and fearful. But, mostly, I slumped over in deep sadness.

It seemed like forever to work through the grief, but one day I suddenly woke up and looked around the world with eyes wide open—as if revived out of a coma. An interesting metaphor in the Bible describes God's faithfulness to us as a devoted husband. Since I am now single, I start to lean on Him in a way I have never done before and the joy of heaven starts healing my soul.

I still thank God for the gift of my marriage and the opportunity I had to learn to love my husband and to be loved by him. I still think it is true—when a man and a woman marry, two different worlds merge into one. And when there is peace and love in the home, life just doesn't get any better than that. God designed marriage for our personal growth and happiness, and as partners hold hands and hearts together in love, somehow our loyalty, love, and devotion reflects an aspect of who He is!

The monks give me much to think about—unpacking decades of spiritual contemplation into a few conversations. Walking in the abbey gardens in silence one day, I watch one of the monks climb a flight of gray cement stairs leading to the bell tower. It is a misty afternoon. The fog is rolling into the courtyard in a surreal blanket of white—starkly contrasting his flowing robe of black. The scene reminds me of a mystical stairway to heaven. I think to myself, I can only take one step at a time in my journey to know God. Sometimes I fall. But with His help, I get up and walk again.

I spent many more days studying the Bible at the monastery and would often walk along the forest pathway around Mount Mary to pray for guidance. One day a tiny white trillium springs to life as it finds an opening in the dead leaves. Soon the pathway is alive with countless little lilies and the forest is awash in green, overtaken by the energy of budding maple trees and perennial wild flowers.

Feeling dead no longer, I am energized by the appearance of new life.

The words of the monks slowly sink deeper and deeper into my soul.

They obviously love their mothers for inspiring them to grow in faith, and they respect women as "daughters of the King." This is who I want to be—a daughter of the King, a faithful steward, serving God with perseverance and undying loyalty.

The monks explain that each person is designed to reflect the character of our compassionate Creator at every stage of life. At birth, a child is unified in mind, body, and spirit—"a trinity" so to speak. Later, when marrying, two people become one in unity, as they live as "gifts to one another." In another stage of life, as parents, a father's devotion and a mother's love for their children combine in multi-creative ways to form a blessed preview of the divine character and love of our majestic Maker.

As "children of God," each of our experiences in life, whether we are married or single, laughing or crying, buying or selling, living as "a saint or a sinner"—all of this, and more, forms a part of the imperfect mix, the palette in which Christ uses to paint a picture of His love on our hearts and to demonstrate His love to others.

I will explore these concepts more in-depth later.

I meet with a quiet, reserved, silver-haired monk, who decides to speak openly.

He is slowly measuring each word as he stares intently at me after I ask him for the third time the big question about the so-called gender of God.

"Women are made in the image of God," he says. "Just read the Scriptures and you can see there is a female element in God."

I am taken aback.

What did he just say?

Then, as if he regretted the answer he had just given me, he adds: "But we must be careful to accept the limitations of the human intellect when it comes to understanding God."

He looks uncomfortable as he changes the subject.

This is the first time I have heard a credible Christian leader use the term "female" or "feminine" in connection with the nature of God. I'm not sure what to think of this, since I have spent my lifetime envisioning the eternal righteous God with masculine features. As a conservative Christian, I'm comfortable with this view. Men are pastors and priests—God is masculine—end of story.

I am speechless.

But it is as if God is tenderly guiding me to walk to the door of an exciting new art gallery where I peek through a small window at the top of the door to catch a glimpse, here and there, of bright, glorious watercolor paintings hanging on the wall, beautiful portraits of the Creator God I have never seen before in my life.

The monk is silent again, backing away.

I look at the door in anticipation.

CHAPTER 3

Science and Sex

> Humans were created fully formed by God in their
> particular gender right from the beginning of
> creation.
>
> Dr. Raymond Damadian, Inventor of the MRI

WHAT IS TRUTH?

That is the question that always drives my journalistic investigations, but the answer is rarely found by following a straight pathway from Point A to Point B.

One warm summer day, I am pursuing a news story about local industrial farms when, to my dismay, I discover that toxic pesticides are leaching into the aquifer. I immediately begin to worry about the small children living in the area.

One of the government scientists who is studying the water samples quietly and covertly gives me a copy of the raw data. Armed with the facts, I start to interview politicians who, not surprisingly, deny there is a problem and refuse to release the scientific information to the public.

I visit people living around the farms.

Some are sick with unexplainable illnesses. They tell me they buy bottled water because the colorless liquid in their wells is filled with "nasty stuff," as the residents like to put it. They may not know how to spell 1,2-Dichloropropane, the name of the pesticide, but they are smart enough to quit drinking the stuff gushing from their taps.

Meanwhile, a local surgeon starts writing "Enviro-Disease" at the top of the medical records of some of the patients living in the area after he sees their unusual neurological problems. He gives me a phone call six months later. He wants to talk.

This is how an investigative news feature starts being pieced together.

I listen to people as they share their stories and check and recheck the facts with medical experts and scientists. If the answers don't agree, I just keep asking. An investigation may take years before it is published. This method of pursuing the truth may not be perfect, but it is very effective. Often I persist questioning the experts until the facts surface to the top. I know I cannot waver. I persevere and must always be willing to accept whatever the truth reveals to me and make no compromise with error.

I ask myself: Do the facts make sense? Can an ordinary person like me, without a PhD, understand the answer and *really get it?*

Are certain patterns starting to ring true?

The news story about the aquifer took more than a year to research, and when it was published, the public outcry caused the government to conduct a large medical study and a decision to enforce tougher farm regulations to protect the aquifer.

It is immensely satisfying to me to help people live healthier, happier lives.

A similar sort of open-minded, objective, investigative way of looking at life also holds true on my journey to know what God is like. But in this case as I interview biblical scholars and leaders and experts in their field, I add an intense search through the Scriptures and pray to the Spirit of God for clarity.

Genetics and Faith

I decide to speak to Dr. Francis Collins, a renowned scientist and a former atheist. I reach him by phone in Bethesda, Maryland.

This visionary geneticist is the father of a medical milestone. At the time we speak together in 2007, he is the director of the National Human Genome Research Institute. From 1993 to 2003, he led an international team of biologists and computer analysts who mapped the entire human DNA code—the blueprint of life inside the nucleus of each and every cell in our human body.

The DNA is our biological command center.

The genome project was an adventure that beats going to the moon or splitting the atom, says Collins, adding that he believes molecular medicine will soon identify the most fundamental causes of disease at a genetic level.

The scientist, during our conversation together, was outspoken about his viewpoint on the nature of God.

Men and women are most certainly made in the image of God in the sense that we are created with some of the characteristics of God within us, Collins says, noting that one of our divinely appointed qualities is our "wonderful capacity to be creative."

Is there an aspect of God that may be feminine as well as masculine? I ask.

"Being made in the image of God has nothing to do with gender," he replies. "It means that God has endowed us with intellect, and with spirit, and an inner moral compass. . . . We have the moral law written within us; that is, we have the capacity of knowing innately the difference between right and wrong."

C. S. Lewis describes the essence of morality in *Mere Christianity*:

We can find out more about God from the moral law within, than from the universe, in general, just as you find out more about a man by listening to his conversation than by looking at a house he built.[1]

Collins explains that God is gently speaking to each one of us in an inner private conversation by way of our conscience, which helps us to know that He is real.

Although the scientist believes the Creator has no particular gender distinction, he calls God "He" several times during our conversation. He apologizes, explaining that the male pronoun is an ingrained habit in our religious culture, but he is trying not to use any pronoun for God, either feminine or masculine.

"I don't think God has a gender," the geneticist explains. "I think God is more like a mind than a physical body. I don't think God has toe nails, for example, and God certainly doesn't have a belly button. I'm not a theologian, but I think of God as holy, as an immensely great and loving intelligence. God is holier than we can ever imagine."

Throughout history, many people have believed in an all-male God because of the influence of the patriarchal culture around them, Collins says, adding that he believes these outdated concepts will change one day—perhaps sooner than later.

As a contemporary intellectual and the author of *The Language of God*, Collins finds a "wonderful harmony" in the complementary truths of science and faith.

But he hasn't always seen it that way. He was an atheist for many years. The turning point in his life occurred when he was a medical student and observed the grace and strength of Christians, many of whom were going through terrible suffering.

How they handled their pain when stricken by disease inspired Collins to study the religions of the world. As he examined the life of Jesus, he was convinced, at twenty-seven years old, to pursue a life of faith.

"There is ample historical and empirical evidence to support the Christian belief in the life, death, and resurrection of Jesus Christ and his moral teachings—if one has an open mind to investigate the facts," he says.

As a deep thinker who balances his worldview as both a serious scientist and a serious believer, Collins advises people to read the Bible with an open mind because the Creator of all life is not limited by dimension, space, or time.

"The God of the Bible is the God of the human genome," he says. "God may be found just as easily in the science lab as in the holiness of a sanctuary."

Why Sex?

I've always been drawn to facts rather than fiction.

I used to watch McCoy, the famous doctor on *Star Trek*, scanning his crew members in a futuristic-looking medical machine. Today, this science fiction is closer to reality, thanks to the ingenuity of Dr. Raymond Damadian, a visionary scientist.

He is the inventor of the Magnetic Resonance Imaging (MRI) machine—one of the most exciting medical breakthroughs of the past century. A scientist of world renown, Damadian recently joined the legendary heroes of his boyhood—Thomas Edison, Alexander Bell, and the Wright Brothers—as an inductee into the National Inventors Hall of Fame.

Speaking in his New York office at the Fonar Corporation, Dr. Damadian answers my questions about his many awards. But he doesn't seem to care about all the accolades.

"Nothing is more delightful to me than getting a letter from someone thanking me for inventing the MRI because it saved their life," he says, noting that his greatest satisfaction in life is to help patients overcome cancer and other diseases. "For me, it doesn't get any better than that. Saving lives eclipses all of the scholarly acknowledgements and awards I've ever received."

Over the years, he has been honored by numerous US presidents, and he received the National Inventor of the Year Award in 2007 for the upright MRI.

His inventions are a godsend for patients across the world. An

MRI gives physicians a three-dimensional view of soft-body tissues such as the brain and the spinal cord by using magnetic fields that emit no harmful radiation.

Damadian discovered how the MRI noninvasively locates cancers in the human body and filed the first patent in the world in 1972. By 1977, he had built the first human MRI machine in history after overcoming many unbelievable obstacles.

"I created the MRI for the benefit and the health of all mankind."

He answers my questions about the nature of God with succinct clarity.

"All human beings—males and females—are made in the image of God just as the Bible recorded," he says. "Humans were created fully formed by God in their particular gender right from the beginning of creation."

I ask him to explain why he believes this.

Each human being is endowed with forty-six chromosomes, inheriting a gene from each parent to determine whether he or she will be male or female. The ovum (the female egg) has twenty-two chromosomes, plus a female-determining X chromosome, while the sperm contains twenty-two chromosomes, plus either an X or a Y (the male-determining chromosome). When the sperm and egg unite during conception, each cell is endowed with the sexual attributes to determine if the child will be a boy or a girl.

The genetic blueprint is ready to roll at the moment of conception.

"It's a wondrously complex process, and God made it possible right from the beginning for the first humans to procreate the world," says Damadian.

He then poses a question to me, so simple, yet so astute, it is life-changing.

"How could two different sexes have evolved separately without the other?"

No scientist can explain this because a man and a woman must be fully developed, biologically, for sex, and thus conception, to work. You don't have to be a rocket scientist to know that a man needs a female to be born. Likewise, the female needs a man, or she, too, would not be born!

One cannot exist without the other.

The MRI scientist brings to light an amazing insight.

It is a biological truth (which hardly bears repeating) that two fully functioning sexual human beings, male and female, must be present for natural procreation to occur in the first place. Therefore, the sophisticated and complementary design of the first two human beings is living proof a divine Maker created them.

In what way are both genders made in the image of God? I ask Damadian.

God has empowered men and women with wisdom, understanding, and language, he replies, noting that none of the lower life forms on Earth are endowed with the language complexity humans enjoy in communication with each other.

"Why don't we see mountain lions writing music, for example?" he says, adding that God gives the gifts of creativity, music, art, and literature to human beings.

On the specific question of the gender of God, Damadian pauses.

"Since both men and women are made in God's image, and we hear a lot from church pulpits about the masculine qualities of God, doesn't it follow that there must be aspects of God that correspond to such distinguishing feminine qualities as love, compassion, and caring for others—the very reasons that a man is incomplete without a woman?" he asks in a rhetorical statement.

So if that is true, why do we tend to stereotype the gender of God? I reply.

"Being a male, I've naturally only thought of God from the perspective of His masculine qualities," he admits. "But God must be all encompassing for both sexes. . . . You can see God in what He has created—and He has created both man and woman."

If you want to know the Creator, the Bible provides the logical answers.

Scientists cannot explain how life itself came to be.

"The one thing a scientist becomes conscious of—the more he studies and learns about a process, such as a living process or the solar system—the further he is from comprehending how it began."

Exhibit A

Theologian Jürgen Moltmann writes that God's creative activity has no analogy, and it is also unimaginable. The divine act of creation is never dissected into a number of different processes. It is unified and unique.

Creation took place suddenly, as it were—in a moment.[2]

Dr. Damadian explains that the very presence of human beings on this planet is a major scientific indicator pointing to the existence of God. . . . Each gender must be perfectly and intricately formed with all of the complementary organs and biochemical markers in place for procreation to occur in the first place. This leads to an important spiritual question about how we may best reflect a mirror image of our Maker.

Damadian, Collins, and the monks I have interviewed so far explain this has to do with our creativity, our character, and the way in which Christ transforms fallen human beings into moral beings, as God originally designed in the image of the Divine.

Is gender, therefore, a part of the nature of God?

Collins believes God is beyond gender. It is simply a religious habit that many of us picture God as "male," and this is deeply ingrained in our culture. And Damadian candidly states that being a man predisposes him to think of God as strictly masculine.

It is a common pattern. I do the same thing all the time. And so do my female friends. We always call God *He*. I am not sure, at this point, whether this is a problem.

I don't think it is. Or is it?

CHAPTER 4

Dear Lord: Who Am I?

Behold what manner of love the Father has bestowed
on us, that we should be called children of God!

1 John 3:1 NKJV

THE SMELL OF stale curry overwhelms me as he opens the door.

"Hi, pleased to meet you," says Santa Singh Tatlay, an elderly man with a long, gray beard, wearing a turban, a casual suit, and a polka-dot tie.

A blast of warm air hits me when I walk into his small apartment. I see a room with a brilliant orange sheet partially covering a large religious book on a pedestal. The view from his front window is row upon row of older mobile homes with rust-splashed metal roofs. Tatlay is reportedly a revered Sikh spiritual advisor who has published an important series of reference books on the Sikh holy script in Amritsar, India.

"How did you manage to have the time to write so much material?" I ask.

"Well, six years of jail time is a lot of time to have on your hands."

"Yes, well, um, sir, can I ask why you decided to kill her?"

"My seventeen-year-old daughter was young, innocent, and

beautiful," he says, but he disagreed with her decision to marry a man he did not want as a son-in-law.

"His family was not matching mine, socially, economically, or education-wise. That family was too low [in the caste system], in my opinion. What dignity or respect was there? I didn't want my daughter in the ditch."

So he made sure she landed in the grave.

He arranged to send her a gift, a kettle that exploded as soon as it was plugged into an electrical outlet. The memory of the "honor killing" is not a nice one, and Tatlay explains to me that he has since had a spiritual awakening.

"I think it was really bad. I shouldn't have done it," he says. "I was in spiritual darkness. I've changed since then. You know, at that time I thought, 'I am the man. I am always right.'"

The evil of sexism casts a dark shadow across our world.

It just does.

It is an unfortunate reality that women are disrespected in one way or another in practically every culture. In some countries, they are even considered "less than" fully human. In India and China, babies are aborted simply because they are girls. And what about girls enslaved to prostitution in Southeast Asia and the oppression of Muslim women in some Middle Eastern and Third World countries?

These are not trivial facts.

Gender-based violence against women—female infanticide, sex trafficking and exploitation, dowry killings and domestic violence—causes more death and disability among women (15 to 44) than cancer, malaria, traffic accidents, and war combined![1]

Although it is subtler than in many other parts of the world, undertones of bias are a reality of life in North America, where women still earn 23 percent less on average than men;[2] and one in three women is a victim of sexual or physical assault.

Why are many of the world's cultures so hard on women?

Maybe it goes back to my central question: *What is God really like?* Would a better understanding of the nature of God make a difference? If the answer is in the spiritual realm, this has the potential to bring profound healing for half of the human race.

Imagine an analogy, for discussion's sake, that God is blue and white and explicitly informs the prophets that He created blue and white people to reflect who He is. Yet the popular religions of the day, for some reason, teach that God is only white.

Women are the blue people.

"Dear Lord, Who Am I?" That is the question countless girls, teenagers, and grown women struggle to answer every morning as they face the mirror.

One of the reporters in my newsroom, Christopher Foulds, once wrote a thought-provoking column about a conversation he had with his four-year-old girl. *If only we could all be as sweet as she is,* he thinks to himself as he gets ready to tuck his little angel in bed. The political issues he writes about at work are nothing compared to the tough questions she asks him about God before she sails into Dreamland.

How Do I Answer My Little Girl's Questions
by Christopher Foulds
Abbotsford News

It has been the end-of-day ritual since she was able to sit up and help turn the pages of one of those baby books with cardboard-like binding. We would take her out of the bath, and give her a bottle of milk, then sit on the couch and read a bedtime story. Dr. Seuss's *Green Eggs and Ham* was a favorite, but didn't come close to *Are You My Mother?* for the sheer fun of making strange noises with our voices: Choo-choo! Vrooom! Quack! Quack! And Moo!

At two, she moved to a "big girl bed" from the confines of the crib, which also necessitated a graduation in the book department. We traded *Goodnight Moon* for sillier stories, trading point-and-speak pages for honest-to-goodness tales on how Wednesdays can be wacky, not to mention the mess that mounts if you give a moose a muffin.

Then, in the blink of an eye that passes between birth and preschool, esoteric questions began fermenting in her four-year-old mind. One week, she is fascinated with the possibility that there really is a dinosaur who works with Daddy. The next, she's positively indignant at the thought: "Da-deeeeee!" she says, rolling her eyes and her "e's" in exasperation at just how sadly misinformed her pop can be.

"Dinosaurs died a long time ago!"

Preschool arrives and the world explodes with new stuff. Twice a week for an entire school year, she is now a "big girl," going to school like the older friends with whom she plays every day. And, somehow, somewhere within this new world, the question of our very existence, the question that has forever consumed mankind, has entered her sponge-like mind and, as any parent who has been there will attest, it's enough to make you rediscover the wonder that is a smile. At the same time, the naked innocence of the queries is enough to break your heart in two. And, so it was Monday night, following a quick reading of the *Berenstain Bears Adventure* that we turned off the lamp, clicked on the night-light and hunkered down to perform her favorite ritual.

Yes, we are praying.

She and her mom started doing it months ago, so I carry the torch when I become storyteller. She begins each prayer, every night, with the exact same line:

"Dear Jesus . . ." and ends each prayer, every night, with the exact same line: "In Baby Jesus' name. Amen."

In between, she gives thanks for "the sunny day, for playing with her friends, for her baby brother, and for her mommy and daddy."

But on this night, she has questions. Oh, she has questions!

"Is 'Amen' Baby Jesus' last name?"

"No," say I, treading carefully since the big question is far from being resolved in my mind. "It kind of means 'thanks' at the end."

"Is Baby Jesus a boy?"

"Yes."

Of course, the questions only get more difficult for a dad who doesn't quite know what the heck he believes and struggles daily with *the Big Question*.

"Is Baby Jesus God?"

"Um, well . . . yeah . . . God is Baby Jesus' daddy."

"Is God in the sky?"

"Yes, he's in the clouds. He's in heaven. He's everywhere."

"Is God a girl?"

"Uh, er, well, maybe. But I think he's a daddy. Baby Jesus is a little boy and God's his parent, his daddy."

"Then Amen can be the mommy?"

"Exactly!"[3].

Controversy in the Classroom

I am taking a song-writing course from Brian Doerksen, a Christian musician, when one of the men in my class asks me about my work as a journalist. I tell him I am considering some ideas for a book, and he is immediately interested in the topic.

"You should talk to my Bible instructor, Gay Lynn Voth," he says. "She said something in class the other day that I think you'll find very interesting."

Intrigued, I later arrange to meet Voth, a bright, engaging instructor at Columbia Bible College. She has spent two decades thinking about the question of the so-called gender of God. And I am surprised to hear her say that she is planning to discuss the column by Christopher Foulds with her students of religion.

"How do you think they will respond to it?" I ask her.

"Why don't you join the class and find out for yourself," she suggests to me.

Smiling warmly, she is sitting behind her office desk, drinking her jasmine tea, surrounded by books on philosophy and theology, pictures of grandchildren, portraits of Jesus, and posters of orca whales and deep blue ocean.

"Have you ever faced any personal struggles on this question?" I ask.

"I'm a historian, a researcher, and a theologian; I have an inquisitive mind," she says, noting that she "certainly was not" taught anything about the so-called gender of God in Sunday school. This issue, however, became vitally important to her as she pursued a degree in religious studies. Born and raised Mennonite, she often felt like she did not fit into the mold of a typical girl when she was growing up. She was intellectual, analytical, and studious and felt more comfortable doing "boy" stuff.

"I felt like I had a male mind that didn't belong in a female body," she explains, adding that she is heterosexual, but struggled to accept her femininity.

Theology captured her interest when she was a young woman, and she met her husband while attending a Bible college. They married in 1974. Her gender identity as a female, however, did not feel like a "comfortable fit" until she became a mother. Giving birth and raising three daughters helped her to explore her role as a woman and to cultivate the rich, feminine, emotional and spiritual capacities within herself.

"As I prayerfully asked God for wisdom to raise our three daughters, I began to identify my maternal instincts for my daughters with the deep desires that God has for me. Each of my daughters helped expose me to the loving, maternal aspects of God in a deeper way than I would have on my own."

She started thanking God for blessing her with the gift of femininity, the ability to give birth, and the gift that Jesus gave to humankind when he was born of Mary.

While Voth was a busy mom raising children, she conducted Bible studies and taught Sunday school. She was thirty-three years old when she first heard rumblings in her church that the nature of God may not just be exclusively masculine.

It shocked everyone!

"It didn't go over very well," Voth says, noting how the idea confused her.

"It was referred to as a bad thing. Back in the '80s this was thought of as a real problem, a real threat to the church that could lead to goddess worship. I tried to fight it myself," she explains. "I wanted nothing to do with it because I thought it was heresy . . . that is why this has been a difficult journey."

At heart, like many believers, Voth is theologically cautious and conservative. She was interning as a youth pastor when a professor encouraged her to pursue a degree in religious studies. As she studied anthropology and sociology, it struck her that the disdain of ages past has been against her simply because of her gender.

Yet she knew the God of the Bible advocates love and justice for all.

"Both men and women share this basic human equality because we are both made in the image of God," she says with conviction.

After she earned her degree, she started teaching at Columbia Bible College, and one day she read the now legendary column by Christopher Foulds.

"It gave me goose bumps," says Voth, noting how his little girl's questions perfectly illustrate the problem of trying to depict God as exclusively masculine.

"We adults have a lot to learn from children."

The following week, I sit at the back of a classroom and watch Voth pace back and forth, waiting for her students to settle into their desks.

"I really, really need a coffee," says a twenty-one-year-old man as he rubs his eyes and drops his books on the desk with a thud and looks around the empty class.

Without another word, he heads to the coffee shop and returns with a steaming cappuccino in his hands. He is joined by about thirty other students for the "red-eye special," the dreaded early morning eight a.m. class. Right on time, Voth walks to the front of the class and starts to write on the blackboard as the whispering subsides.

She tells the class that most women have been considered a "sex object" at some time in their lives, and she shares a personal story to prove her point.

While attending a missions' festival, she bumped into a man she had not seen since she was in her twenties. She was shocked when he told her he could not believe she had earned a degree in religious studies. All he had seen were her good looks. Unfortunately, his attitude is condescending toward women, a common practice for some men who consciously or subconsciously live with an air of superiority.

"Women have been silenced throughout history," Voth says.

But thankfully, much progress has been made in our Western culture. Elisabeth Schüssler Fiorenza, a professor at Harvard Divinity School, for one, defines feminism as "the radical notion that women are people." That is the starting point for Voth.

"You don't have to be anti-men to be pro-women," she tells her students.

I smile to myself. I love her statement. Having grown up with five brothers and enjoying the companionship of my many wonderful male friends, one of my biggest criticisms of the feminist movement is the negative attitude toward men.

Voth captures my feelings exactly. We are pro-women and pro-men!

To spark class discussion, she shares a comment from an essay called "The Subjection of Women" written in 1869 by British philosopher John Stuart Mill. He writes that the subordination of one sex over the other is wrong and is one of the chief hindrances to human improvement. This practice, according to Mill, ought to be replaced by the principle of perfect equality.

The Bible, in fact, supports the ideal of perfect equality, Voth says, because both men and women, in their complementary strengths and talents, represent our Maker.

"You are you—and you matter to God! Your gender qualities deserve the highest regard and respect," she says as she hands out a discussion paper featuring the work of Jürgen Moltmann, a well-known Protestant theologian in Germany. He teaches that the model of the family is a good way to better understand the mystery of the Trinity and author Neill Q. Hamilton also makes this point.

"If Christianity continues to emphasize God as only a father-figure, this makes us deprived children of a one-parent family," states Hamilton, who writes that within the Trinity, the Holy Spirit performs a type of mothering role by comforting us.

In this respect, God "parents" us in both father and mother modes.

"What do you think of this idea?" Voth asks her Bible students. "Why do we always use the male pronoun [He] for God? Does that mean God is male?"

Some of the young men and women look around at each other with puzzled expressions and turn up their eyebrows as the instructor stirs their thinking.

"If God is referred to exclusively with the male pronoun, people just assume that our Creator God is only masculine," Voth says, noting this may not be the entire story.

"The male is not any more closely identified with the image of God than the female. The love of God is expressed in both feminine and masculine qualities."

This statement causes some male students to feel like their self-identity with God is unraveling before them. *What? Are you kidding me? Masculinity is supreme because we're like God.* The reaction of young women is even more interesting. They have no idea what to think. *You mean something about me corresponds to God?*

Voth explains that it is true that God is our kind heavenly Father and this is a time-honored religious truth because fathers are our source of security, protection, and strength in the family. So, in many respects, the pronoun "He" is appropriate.

But what about a possible mothering side to God?

David plans to be a pastor, and he tells me that the Bible class has broadened his thinking. And Alex Wiens, a student in his second year of Biblical Studies, agrees: "It helps me wrap my mind around God to think of the Trinity like a family," he says, adding that he finds the early morning Bible class "fascinating."

He is learning things about the Creator he had never heard before.

"It makes sense to me that God would have both sets of gender characteristics and perspectives," says Wiens, who is considering a career in engineering, a profession that requires a keen ability to view tough challenges from many different angles.

If having an open mind and a thoughtful interest in learning new facts—even when they don't fit our preconceptions—is vital for success in the engineering field, isn't that the least we can do to try to understand the most holy God who created us?

Men and women around the world are seeking wholeness.

A healthy sense of community requires love and justice at the foundation. Since we are all children of God, we need to work together, as partners in peace, writes Rev. Felix Chingota as he gives the overarching reason to appreciate both genders.

A healthy self-identity "helps us to understand the core of why we do what we do, and how we live . . . and what it is that gives life its deepest meaning," says Chingota, a Presbyterian minister, in a publication called *Created in God's Image: From Hegemony to Partnership.*[4]

What Is True Femininity?

Dear Lord, who am I? It always seems to go back to that important question.

People who have a positive self-image are comfortable in their own skin, but this often poses a serious challenge for most women at some point in their lives.

What does it mean to be female?

"An infertile woman may feel disabled, but she is just as much a woman as any other woman," says Gay Lynn Voth. "We have to be careful about arguments that claim if a woman doesn't have a womb or if she doesn't bear a child, she's not a woman."

And menopause does not mean the end of a woman's femininity either.

Being feminine is *who a woman is*: Inner beauty, gentleness, and compassion are gifts of femininity that God has placed in the heart of every woman. The Scriptures proclaim that the "splendor, majesty, and glory" of God are expressions of His indescribable beauty and magnificence! And there are no fewer than thirteen words in the Hebrew language of the Old Testament to describe "beauty."

> *One thing I have desired of the LORD,*
> *That will I seek:*
> *That I may dwell in the house of the LORD*
> *All the days of my life,*
> *To behold the beauty of the LORD . . .*
>   Psalm 27:4 NKJV

Voth shares much in common with Fulata Mbano Moyo, who lives halfway across the world. She also struggled with her self-identity when she was younger.

It has been a long journey to gender wholeness for Fulata.

"Inner healing, and reconciliation to my gender, did not come easy for me," says Fulata, the program executive for Women in Church and Society.

Raised in Malawi, Africa, her father had five wives and she grew up as a "tomboy" at odds with her own gender. She believed, then, that women had little value and seemed to be worth a "mere fraction of men." This idea formed early in her mind as she grew up in a polygamous culture where her five mothers were relegated to the role of simply being the "cowives" of her father. She was not happy she was born a girl, and her femininity was a confusing issue for many years.

The world church leader shares a humorous story to illustrate.

Her aunts instructed her not to play with boys after she had gone through the transition of "being a woman" at the arrival of her menses. As a naïve fifteen-year-old teenager, she took her aunties' advice very seriously. So when she received a nice letter from a boy, she believed with all of her heart this meant she was now pregnant!

In tears, she confided the astounding news to her mother who told her with a straight face: *Fulata, now do not get pregnant again!*

Laughing about this experience today, Fulata, of course, has grown wiser over the years about her gender and sexuality. The facts of life were soon abundantly clear to her when she became pregnant by her first boyfriend two years before she graduated from university. She married him after their first baby was born, when she was twenty-five years old. Together, the couple raised three sons.

Fulata is a devout Christian and earned a PhD from the School of Religion and Theology at the University of KwaZulu-Natal in South Africa, with grounding from the Yale Divinity School and School of Medicine in the US.

Although she grew up halfway around the world, her story resonates with Voth and countless other women and teenagers who have been crushed by a crisis in self-confidence at one time or another in their lives.

I can also relate to these women because I too was a girl who grew into a confused teen, heading for trouble.

When I first interview Dr. Elizabeth Johnson, past president of the Catholic Theological Society of America, she talks to me about Jesus, our Redeemer.

"Jesus changed the worldview of women, you know," she says to me.

"Yes, I know—he changed me too," I reply.

I remember the exact moment—as if it were yesterday.

A *"Bruised Reed,"* He Will Not Break

Humming along with the car radio, a twenty-three-year-old man uncorks a bottle of rye whiskey in the front seat of the convertible. A lopsided smile betrays no foreboding of the rape he has in mind.

I am in the backseat.

As we drive along the freeway, I watch wistfully as thousands of leaves dance in the air like confetti thrown at a wedding. After swigging back half the bottle, I feel unsteady and groggy as I meet an older woman, who appears to be a prostitute. She is nameless, weary, and wiry with tangled black hair falling around her white parchment face.

She and I see in each other's eyes the pain of a wordless shame.

I find myself falling into a queen-size bed in a skanky nondescript motel room—darkened by navy blue Venetian blinds, paralyzed by my inability to push away the twenty-three-year-old man beside me.

I am fifteen.

A few days later, a police officer escorts me into his police car and asks me questions. I am silent as I sit in the backseat of the vehicle. He asks again. I turn my head to the window. I turn away from the God of my childhood, only to sink into a black hole of alcohol and drugs, darkness and despair.

Years later, when I am twenty years old, I open the Holy Bible for the first time in my life and read about Jesus, who does not shame or condemn, but heals the brokenhearted by wrapping His arms of love around them. Maybe that is why His encounter with a certain young woman caught in adultery resonates with so many. His kind words of reassurance are among the most comforting in all of Scripture.

"Neither do I condemn you; go and sin no more."
                                    John 8:11 NKJV

I walk away forgiven in the sunlight of God's Spirit—the gift of God's love living inside me like treasure in a jar of clay. I finally find rest, knowing I am loved and healed by my Savior, confident He does *not break a bruised reed, nor extinguish a smoldering candle* (see Matt. 12:20). I am gratefully drawn to the *Holy One* who leads justice to victory.

That was a crucial turning point in my life, leading to complete healing. I now fast-forward to today as I quietly work as a journalist asking a contemporary religious question: What does it mean to be made in the image of *Almighty God*?

It seems to me, the most sensible approach is to start with the basics.

Not only is God the Creator, as Francis Collins and Raymond Damadian explained earlier, He is our Savior who rescues us from sin and is "recreating" us. As we open our hearts, the Spirit of God reshapes our lives according to His original design and sculpts in us a reproduction of the character of Christ.

The "unruly one" begins to reflect the Holy One in a transformation every bit as shocking as seeing a pig wear pearls. The pig is becoming a princess. I once read the classic story *Pygmalion*, written by George Bernard Shaw. In this story, Henry Higgins, a phonetics professor, meets Eliza Doolittle, a girl who is living in "the gutter." He rescues her off the streets, teaches her how to speak and to walk gracefully, and inspires her to reach the pinnacle of poise. Over time, she becomes *My Fair Lady*.

It occurred to me that if it is true that the Bible reveals masculine and feminine metaphors to give us a picture of the nature of God, this may inspire a worldwide wave of healing for women and free them to rise to their true stature in the Creator's design as daughters of the King. It is an exciting possibility, which I will address later.

But first things first.

I have learned through much trial and error that the two most important basic steps to know God and to live honorably as His follower is to worship Him as my Creator, and second, to commit my life to Him as my Savior.

Why should I trust Him?

One day I meet a nameless woman in the pages of my precious Bible who appears to be very much like me. She is working and minding her own business when she suddenly meets a prince of a teacher and her life is forever changed. She tells her story in her own words in the following chapter.

Her voice speaks to me. . . .

CHAPTER 5

Jesus, Women, and Faith

Women may not have fared well in the world's religions, but they are greatly loved by God. The discrimination that women bump into, does not come
from the heart of God.

Anne Graham Lotz, Speaker and Author

*CURLING UP ON my living room sofa, I (Trudy) open the Scriptures to
the book of John and find myself taking a walk beside a busy woman who
is preoccupied with her long list of things to do. Not much unlike me . . .*

She hardly notices him.

But he's had his eyes on her for some time.

Walking in the sweltering midday heat, Jesus is weary and
thirsty as he stops to rest his dusty, aching feet. Finding a spot to
sit near Jacob's well in Sychar, he gazes in interest as a Samaritan
woman approaches the well.

She is looking forward to drinking the cool water bubbling up
from the underground spring feeding the well. Avoiding his gaze,
she is amazed when this Jewish man starts to talk with her, despite the long-standing religious and cultural tradition to refuse
to have anything to do with Samaritan people.

Much less an immoral woman like her!

But all He sees is her potential. If you knew the gift of God,
Jesus says gently to the woman, you would ask for the "living water" that would give you eternal life.

Touched by the kindness in His voice, a desire surges within her for the soul-nourishing water Jesus offers. But she feels unworthy. Her sins weigh heavy on her heart as she cringes inside. She lives with her lover. She is immoral, and she knows it.

Yet for some inexplicable reason, she is drawn to the love in the Savior's eyes, the comfort and the charisma, the certain restful reassurance written all over His face.

> The woman said to him, "Sir, give me this water, that I may not thirst, nor come here to draw." Jesus said to her, "Go, call your husband, and come here." The woman answered him, "I have no husband." Jesus said to her, "You are right in saying, 'I have no husband'; for you have had five husbands, and he whom you now have is not your husband; this you said truly."
>
> *John 4:15–18 RSV*

She could have lied. But she didn't. Though He lays out her sins before her, she feels no condemnation. His gentleness makes her feel comfortable. She continues the conversation as the Spirit of God awakens in her a wordless craving for inner peace.

Jesus accepts her confession "I have no husband" just as He uplifts every humble sinner who comes to Him. As He looks at her with compassion, He knows full well she will not follow Him from a sense of religious legalism or drudgery of duty. She is bubbling with enthusiasm. He is keen to transform her life with His gift of redemption and bless her with energy that will revolutionize the religious world.

So He speaks again with those immortal words: "God is spirit, and those who worship him must worship in spirit and truth."

The woman replies: "I know that Messiah is coming (he who is called Christ); when he comes, he will show us all things."

Jesus looks at her intently: "I who speak to you am he."

The woman is speechless in the presence of the Prince of

Peace. When the disciples see them together, they marvel He is having anything to do with a despised Samaritan woman like her. But no one says, "Why are you talking with her?"

Feeling energized by her conversation with Jesus, the woman suddenly drops her water jar, runs back to her village, and tells all of her friends and neighbors, "Come; see a man who told me all that I ever did. Can this be the Christ?"

Inspired by her testimony, the Samaritans ask Jesus to stay, and He happily spends the next two days teaching these beloved people. When they hear the voice of the merciful Messiah for themselves, they thank the woman for her faith:

"It is no longer because of your words that we believe, for we have heard for ourselves and we know that this is indeed the Savior of the world."

John 4:42 RSV[1]

The Samaritan woman, so despised by the religious elite, is chosen by God to inspire an entire city to kneel at the feet of the Savior of the world. This story is convincing proof of the high value God places on women.

In this conversation, He showed the world that His love embraces all, regardless of nationality, age, class, or gender, explains Dr. Elizabeth Johnson, a distinguished Professor of Theology at Fordham University in New York City.

"It is incredible how a woman with a checkered past became the first successful missionary [in Samaria]," she says. And the rest of the story is even more interesting! As Christ pressed forward into the humility of His death on the cross to secure salvation for all, His devoted female followers did not abandon Him, like the others.

So He honored them among the first to celebrate His joy.

"They were the first to see Him alive and the first to preach to others that He was resurrected from the dead!" Johnson says.

"They did not run and hide when Jesus was crucified. In fact, the only person named in all four Gospels who stood by the cross was Mary Magdalene."

Mary Magdalene

Mary is weeping.

In tears, she watches a Roman Centurion pound iron spikes into the hands and feet of the compassionate Healer. Every sickening thud of the pounding, pounds His pain into her broken heart. Mary cannot believe her beloved Jesus, the kindest, most powerful religious teacher ever to walk on Earth, is being crucified.

She adores Him as she would an older brother.

Earlier in her life when her soul was dead, He delivered her from the evil within, forgiving her sins. Now she is alive, and He is the one dying! This pierces her heart as she stands in front of her blessed Redeemer bleeding on the cross.

Crying uncontrollably, she watches the Savior breathe His last. Three days later, tears still pour down her face. Sobbing near the tomb, she suddenly hears someone talking to her behind her. She turns around, believing the man is the gardener.

But then He says the one word that makes her stop in her tracks.

"Mary."

Her heart beats faster. He says her name. She knows that sympathetic voice. She turns and says to Him in Hebrew, "Rab-bo'ni (Teacher)!" You're alive!

She turns to cling to Him as Jesus says fondly, "Do not hold me, for I have not yet ascended to the Father; but go to my brethren and say to them, I am ascending to my Father and your Father, to my God and your God."

One of the most powerful means by which Jesus invites each

one of us into a relationship with Him—both then and now—is His intimate understanding of who we are. He created us and recreates us. He loves us and knows us by name.

When He says her name "Mary" and tells her He will ascend to *"my Father and your Father, to my God and your God,"* He fully identifies himself with all of humankind.

And we rest assured of the love of God because His Father is our Father![2]

Jesus Transformed Worldview

Equality and respect for women finally arrived on this planet in the life and teachings of the Savior, says Johnson.

He had no favorites, and he didn't use an army to demand obedience, but showed love to all as He drove a stake into the prevailing patriarchy. Dorothy L. Sayers (1893–1957), a renowned British author, puts it beautifully:

> It is no wonder that the women were first at the cradle and last at the cross. They had never known a man like this man—there has never been such another. A prophet and teacher who never nagged at them, never flattered or coaxed or patronized, who never made jokes about them . . . who rebuked without querulousness and praised without condescension, who took their questions and arguments seriously.[3]

Jesus enthusiastically included women in His ministry, not as subordinates, but as sisters, equal to His brothers in the community of faith, explains Johnson.

As He traveled throughout Galilee with the twelve apostles and female devotees, a number of wealthy women even bankrolled His ministry out of their own pockets.

Soon afterwards he [Jesus] went on through cities and villages, proclaiming and bringing the good news of the kingdom of God. The twelve [apostles] were with him, as well as some women who had been cured of evil spirits and infirmities: Mary, called Magdalene, from whom seven demons had gone out, and Joanna, the wife of Herod's steward Chuza, and Susanna, and many others, who provided for them out of their resources.

Luke 8:1–3 NRSV, bracketed words added

The New Testament was written by courageous male leaders in the early Christian era, but women also fulfilled an important role. They were highly valued in the early church, Johnson says, noting they worked very hard to transform their culture as missionaries, teachers, and leaders of house churches.

In Romans 16, for example, Paul praised numerous women of faith, such as Phoebe and Junia, an apostle.[4] He also recognized that Priscilla (Prisca) risked her life, along with her husband Aquila, when Christians met in their house for worship during the first century era when believers were persecuted. Men and women worked, side by side, holding key leadership positions.

"In fact, today scholars are trying to figure out why the church would end up later scorning the ministry of women," Johnson says, adding that she hopes the long tide of gender bias is finally turning.

Anne Graham Lotz also expresses strong opinions on this topic. Anne is the founder of AnGeL Ministries and travels the world sharing the gospel, like her father Billy Graham. An award-winning author, she graciously shared her column on how God views women, first published in the *Washington Post*.

The Bible Is Crystal Clear on Equality
by Anne Graham Lotz

The Bible states that in the very beginning: *God created*

*man in his own image, in the image of God he created him; male
and female he created them. God blessed them and said to them,
'Be fruitful and increase in number; fill the earth and subdue it'*
(Gen. 1:27–28). In other words, the biblical record is clear:
God created men and women equal. Period!

Dominion over everything was given to the woman, as
well as to the man. The woman was not created inferior
to the man; nor was the man greater than the woman.
However, when sin entered the human race, one of the
consequences was that men and women became separated
from God.

That basic broken relationship distorted the divine order
in many ways, one of which was that men began to rule
over women.

A vast variety of religions have been established in a vain
attempt to reach God, to bridge the gap between God and
man that sin opened up. But the attempts have been fu-
tile. Man has remained a sinner, separated from God. And
this sinful state has been very evident in the way women
have been treated throughout human history by various religions.

Religion down through the ages has been hard on
women, in general.

From ancient times when their babies were sacrificed to
the gods, to Greek times when they were used as prostitutes
in the temples, and to a lesser degree, in modern day practices
where women are discriminated against or oppressed, the im-
plied message has seemed to be clear: Women are second-class
citizens, objects of scorn or sex or service. Generally speaking,
they have not been highly valued in religious circles, nor in
the cultures those religions influenced until Jesus came.

God Himself elevated the status of women forever when
he chose to send his own Son, Jesus Christ, to be born of
a virgin. The words and actions of Jesus underscored his

elevated opinion of women, as did the early church that was established in his name following his return to heaven. Note the evidence:

- His first miracle was performed at his mother's request (John 2:1–11).
- His first revelation of himself as Messiah was to a woman (John 4:25–26).
- He did his greatest miracle at the request of two women (John 11:1–44).
- His death was memorialized by a woman (John 12:1–8).
- Women were included in his expanded group of disciples (Mark 15:41).
- They stayed with him when he was crucified (Matt. 27:55–56).
- Women observed his burial (Matt. 27:61).
- Following his resurrection, he appeared first to a woman (John 20:1–16).
- He called women to be the first evangelists (Matt. 28:1–10, John 20:17).
- Women were included in the group of disciples who met daily for prayer after the ascension of Jesus (Acts 1:14).
- Prophecy was fulfilled when the Spirit was given equally to men and women at Pentecost (Acts 2:17).
- Women were among the first believers who made up the early church (Acts 5:14; Acts 8:12; 17:4, 12).
- The first church in Europe was begun with a group of women and actually met in the home of a woman (Acts 16:13–15).
- The early church was staffed by women (Rom. 16:12, Phil. 4:3).
- At least one early church was co-led by a woman (1 Cor. 16:19).

The very fact that the Bible goes out of its way to carefully record all of the above reveals the intentionality of God's purpose to reestablish the position of women to that of equality with men. His son, Jesus Christ, not only bridged the gap between God and humans through his death on the cross that made atonement for their sin, he removed all barriers including that of gender, race, and nationality. This was confirmed by the apostle Paul:

There is neither Jew nor Greek, slave nor free, male nor female, for you are all one in Christ Jesus. If you belong to Christ, then you are Abraham's seed, and heirs according to the promise. (Gal. 3:28–29 NIV)

Today, when the Bible, which is God's Word, is read, applied, obeyed, and lived out, women are treated with respect and honored as co-heirs with Jesus Christ in the kingdom of God (1 Pet. 3:7).

In summary, women may not have fared well in the world's religions, but they are greatly loved by God who, in the beginning, created them equal to men. The discrimination that women bump into does not come from the heart of God.

He created them in his own image—with a capacity to know him in a personal relationship. When sin destroyed that relationship, God redeemed them through the death of his own son. One day, he will welcome into his heavenly home every woman who has claimed Jesus Christ as her personal Savior and Lord.

And the equality, respect, and status she has longed for, will be hers.

Forever![5]

A Journey of Hope

I am wandering around an old stately house one day, watching in awe as three troubled teenage girls learn to make designer clothes on their new sewing machines.

Lynn Ned, their mentor, encourages them not to give up on their projects as she reflects inwardly on the fact that she herself has come a long way in her life journey to this land of promise. She was only fourteen years old when she left home and never returned. To make a long story short, she knows all too well the crushing sorrow of drug abuse and the despair felt by victims of sexual abuse.

"They say that your life's journey is someone else's hope," she says quietly.

She emerged from her years of pain with one goal in mind—to do everything in her power to help other girls escape the agony of living on the streets. She dreamed of providing a loving, safe, addiction treatment home for Aboriginal teens.

Ned not only dreamed big, she set big goals for herself.

The shy quiet-spoken woman started taking counseling courses and went to work in a big inner city to plead with homeless kids to go home. But more than a few ended up in coffins. She was devastated. Yet in the middle of her despair as she tried to rescue runaways, Ned discovered the powerful love of the one true God—the one who suffered and died on the cross and rose from the dead to give all of us new life.

Her faith in this great God of the Bible began to move mountains.

With prayer, passion, and perseverance, doors started to swing open as she got a job with the government and, in the process, learned how to request financial grants. Then she made friends with politicians who caught the excitement of her vision. She prayed earnestly, and more than $1.6 million dollars in donations started miraculously pouring into her goal to build an addiction treatment center for teen girls.

Soon carpenters were spiffing up a large old Tudor-style house, installing new floors, and painting walls with the latest decorator colors—her years of pain now bearing the bountiful and abundant benefits of being redeemed.

Today teenage girls are taking a holistic one-year substance abuse treatment program in a beautiful home where they are loved and supported twenty-four hours a day. They eat three nutritious home-cooked meals a day, sew their own clothes, tend flower gardens, and learn skills to help them overcome their past of violence and addiction.

Ned serves as executive director for the Spirit Bear Center.

Her deepest prayers have been answered.

She explains to me that the story of Jesus and the power of His forgiveness and love inspired her with an overwhelming inner longing to serve God and humanity.

"God's presence, power, and peace is like nothing else. God has a purpose for every person, and this gives people hope," she says.

"This is the hope that inspires!"

CHAPTER 6

Complementary Design

Neither gender is either good or bad because we
complement each other.

Ravi Zacharias, Evangelist

"WE WALK BY faith, not by sight."

These words from the Bible are meaningful to Jennifer Rothschild, a contemporary vocalist. This is how she has learned to
live ever since her fondest dreams were shattered when she was
diagnosed with a rare, degenerative eye disease as a teenager. To
her it almost seemed like a death sentence.

Her goal was to be a commercial artist and a cartoonist. But
what could she do since she didn't have her eyesight? Rothschild
carefully considered her options: She could either stay depressed
and feel sorry for herself or trust God with her future.

Praying for help, she says she suddenly found herself walking
toward the piano and without even thinking about it, sat down
and played a song she had never played before. She was overwhelmed with emotion as she started singing from the depths of
her soul the words in that glorious classic hymn called "It Is Well
with My Soul." God had miraculously blessed her with the gift

of music and the extraordinary talent of being able to play music by ear.

"The real miracle was that it was well with my soul," Rothschild says.

Even though she is blind, her eyes radiate with beauty as we begin our interview. Today she is a popular public speaker and vocalist working with the Billy Graham evangelistic team, and she also appears on talk shows such as *Dr. Phil.*

"God loves us deeply and completely just the way we are," she explains. "He is the inspiration of the authentic woman!"

Women need to resist the false media illusions played all around us in our culture because God did not design us to be sex objects or sex symbols.

"Clearly, women have to stop looking in the mirrors held up by others and look into the mirror of God's Word—our true mirror. We are made by the hand of God, and He's crazy about us. Our true value and our true identity are found in the fact that we were created by God."

The Bible states that God "made" man from the dust of the Earth, but He "fashioned" the first woman from Adam's side. The two Hebrew words that translate into "made" and "fashioned" in English are different, Rothschild explains.

"I like to think that we are God's fashion statement!" she says with a smile. "Females are not the same as men . . . we're more intuitive and compassionate and we have a different body shape. I think men and women reflect the image of God and the differences [in the sexes] speak to God's creativity and His desire to add zest to life!"

The Greatest Book Ever Written

Like millions of believers, Rothschild reveres the Bible as the Word of God.

The Holy Bible is like a historical library, a compilation of books written by more than forty inspired authors over a period of more than fifteen hundred years. It is a holy book like no other, as the authors continuously highlight the wondrous theme that "God is love."

The way Jesus honored men and women reveals the will of the Father.

A good example of this is when Jesus healed a woman who was bleeding, despite the fact that according to Orthodox Jewish law, both then and now, a man was prevented from touching such a woman. This poignant story occurs in Mark 5:25–34.

A large crowd is jostling against one another and pressing around Jesus.

In the middle of this confusion, a woman who had been bleeding for twelve years is anxious to speak to Jesus. But her hopes sink as the crowds prevent her from reaching him. If only she could touch the hem of his garment, she believes she will be healed.

Desperately reaching out with all the energy she has inside her, she just barely touches the hem of his cloak as he walks past her in the crowd. The very moment she feels his garment brush against her fingers, she feels his healing power flow over her.

He looks around and suddenly asks: Who touched me?

The disciples cannot figure out why he would ask such a ridiculous question since so many people are pressing around him. But the woman knows and tells him the whole truth. Stepping forward, she kneels at his feet trembling, not knowing what he will say. Will he criticize her? Jesus has no such intention.

He looks at her with compassion and says to her,

"Daughter, your faith has made you well; go in peace, and be healed of your disease."[1]

She gladly exchanges her hurt for His healing!

Daniel Ayuch, a Middle East biblical scholar, explains that Jesus Christ was a revolutionary spiritual leader who worked against the prevailing tide of Roman prejudice that stifled women. The pagan world treated women worse than cattle.

But the Savior denounced all such human oppression.

Some theologians believe that a key turning point occurred in history when Jesus established the rite of baptism. This did away with the former gender-specific Jewish ritual of circumcision in which only men could participate. The following passage explains how we may all identify ourselves as children of God:

> For in Christ Jesus you are all children of God through faith. As many of you as were baptized into Christ have clothed yourselves with Christ. There is no longer Jew or Greek, there is no longer slave or free, there is no longer male and female; for all of you are one in Christ Jesus. And if you belong to Christ, then you are Abraham's offspring, heirs according to the promise.
>
> *Galatians 3:26–29* NRSV

The love of Christ, His gift of redemption, and the rite of baptism eliminates the former barriers of religious exclusivity because of gender, culture, or race.

To be sure, the status of women has come a long way in the past two thousand years. The Woman's Christian Temperance Union and the National Council of Jewish Women, for example, both fought for the right of women to vote, and this was accomplished in the US in 1920. Other countries soon followed suit.

Yet it is an ongoing challenge in every culture to uphold the value of women. And religion is no exception. The way language is used has created some challenges in the translations of the Bible, says Christl Maier, a leading European scholar.

Many biblical versions, for example, use the word "man" to define "human beings," rendering the presence of women practically invisible, she says.

However, changes are afoot in both Judaism and Christendom. The Jewish Publication Society, for example, published an English translation of the Hebrew Bible in 2006 called: *The Contemporary Torah: A Gender-Sensitive Adaptation of the JPS Translation*. In this biblical version, the word "man" is translated as "human," when this is what is meant. Numerous Christian publishers are also taking this approach.

In the meantime, when believers read the King James Version (published 1611) and other literal biblical translations, such as the NASB, it is understood that the term "man," in its proper context, means the entire human race, both men and women.

In One Accord

A man is more than the sum total of his determination and strength. And a woman is more than the picture of her beauty and grace. When a man and woman work together as a team, two different worlds merge into one.

C. S. Lewis in his book *A Grief Observed* writes that God designed marriage to heal the inherent loneliness in each gender and bring peace between men and women.

"Jointly the two become fully human . . . thus, by a paradox, this carnival of sexuality leads us out beyond our sexes."[2]

In another book, *Mere Christianity*, Lewis observes that when a man and a woman marry, the couple become as "one organism," just as a lock and a key operate as one mechanism, and a violin and a bow are played together as one musical instrument.

Combining the strengths and talents of each gender creates a healthy wholeness to bless the family, church, synagogue, school, and workplace with a synergy rarely seen when only one gender dominates.

This ability to work together "in one accord" brings glory to God, says Ravi Zacharias, an international evangelist, noting that God uses the genius of "complementary design" to further the work of the gospel.

"Neither gender is either good or bad because we complement each other," the evangelist explains, adding that it is a false teaching to identify women as "emotional" or men as "intellectual" and to divide people along gender lines.

"When missionaries go overseas, women have shown their genius for learning new languages. God has blessed women with the ability to excel in communication with others as well as expressing what is deep in their hearts and minds."

They are effective communicators of God's grace.

A prophetess, according to *Smith's Bible Dictionary*, is a woman who speaks up for God as an "interpreter" of His word and she clearly shares the truth with others. She is His spokesperson—a valuable member of heaven's PR team, so to speak.

Huldah, a prophetess in the Old Testament era, is a prime example. King Josiah commanded the restoration of the temple in Jerusalem after he listened to her judicious advice. She not only verified that a scroll with the law of God was authentic (621 BC), she also warned the people to obey the commandments and reassured the repentant king that God had heard his humble prayers (see 2 Chron. 34).

A woman may also lead public worship to praise God. After Aaron and Moses led the Israelites through the Red Sea, their sister Miriam, a prophetess at the time, led a victory celebration as the women played tambourines and danced for joy (see Ex. 15:20). Her outburst of joy is not surprising. It is innate in the heart of femininity to celebrate the milestones of life, the birthdays, weddings, and anniversaries.

Godly women leave a trailblazing record throughout history.

When men and women prayed together on the day of Pentecost, God fulfilled His promise to the patriarchs that "your sons and daughters will prophesy" (Acts 2:17 NIV).

And daughters, no less than sons, continue to prophesy today at God's command.

Ezer Kenegdo, The Helper

Where does the inner strength of a woman come from?

God named Eve the *ezer kenegdo*—a lovely Hebrew word that means "helper, lifesaver, and the giver of life," explains author Stasi Eldredge, noting this is how God's own role as our Help and Deliverer is described more than twenty times in the Bible.

Imagine that!

And isn't it amazing that Jesus also describes the Holy Spirit as our "Helper," according to literal biblical translations such as the New King James Version and the English Standard Version?

Therefore, the woman is obviously in good company!

Author Ruth Graham explains that God specifically designed the first woman to be a "lifesaver" for humankind, which is an important role.

Dr. Hyveth Williams, professor of homiletics at the Seventh-day Adventist Theological Seminary in Michigan, concurs with Graham and Eldredge.

"When God created man and woman in His image, you can't just give a picture of the man because that would only reveal half of the face of God. We have a relationship with an invisible God, and both men and women represent the human face of God—you need both faces for God to be seen!" explains Williams.

She emphasizes that Adam and Eve were created with great love by God, and both bear the attributes of the Creator. The first woman was designed to alleviate the deep emptiness and loneliness that Adam was feeling.

The Hebrew word *ezer* often refers to the help and strength of God.

In Psalm 121:2, for example, David, in his weakness, discovered the secret of living a life of supernatural strength when he prayed: "My help [*ezer*] comes from the LORD, the Maker of heaven and earth" (NIV).[3] The Creator gave Eve a fascinating title. In other words, God created Eve to be comparable or suitable to Adam as a strong equal partner, and her role reveals how highly God values women.

The Scriptures disclose yet another noteworthy fact.

Many translations state that the Lord God took one of Adam's ribs to fashion Eve in the secondary creation story in Genesis 2. Recent biblical scholarship, however, reveals the little-known fact that the word "rib" may be understood in a deeper way.

Interestingly, the use of the term *tsela* by Moses, the author of Genesis, indicates that he intended for it to be understood that God did not just take a little rib of Adam's side. The Hebrew word *tsela* is an architectural term, which literally means a "half room or a half building,"[4] explains Williams.

"Created together, Adam and Eve were formed by God as the first human being—not just the man. This creates a beautiful and gracious mental picture—as the two halves form a perfect photograph of the God of love!"

Eldredge concludes that it is important for each person to know that he or she is made in the likeness of God. Thus, the Creator is not only reflected in the strength of a man, but in the beauty of a woman, her tenderness, gentleness, and kindness.

In the egalitarian order of heaven and earth, a man is said to be the head of the household, but it is also true that it is the woman who gives birth to the man:

But here is how things are for those who belong to the Lord. The woman is not independent of the man. And the man is not independent of the woman. The woman came from the man, and the man is born from the woman. But everything comes from God.

1 Corinthians 11:11–12 NIRV

Compassionate Caregivers

The role of the *ezer* is not for the weak of heart.

My friend Helen was working as a care-aide for Paul, an energetic ninety-two-year-old, when he surprised her with an invitation to come to his house for a barbecue to celebrate the World's Best Wrestler and the country's Top Male Athlete of the Year.

Helen laughs.

"I guess he asked me to come over because I always clean his house and do his windows." She pauses for a moment of irony. "And the other day I had to go there at three a.m. to take him to the hospital! That was funny. Well, maybe not so funny."

Paul called her in the middle of the night because he had a headache and was feeling sick. He pleaded with her: "Could you please come over and help me?"

Helen, who is one of the nicest persons walking on this planet, is always ready to help others, especially if they are sick and elderly. So she shimmies out of her pj's, puts on her jeans and blouse, washes her face, and drives over to Paul's house.

When she arrives, he sheepishly says: "Well, maybe I should take an aspirin."

She gives him a loving, but firm ultimatum: "You have two choices at three in the morning. You can choose to go in my car or your truck—right over to the hospital!"

Helen insists because he had earlier complained so bitterly

about how sick he felt. So she figures it is time he is checked by a doctor. But it's a big waste of time.

"We went to the hospital and the doctor gave him two Tylenols and a Gravol pill 'cause his tummy was upset," Helen says. "So back home we go."

By now it is 5:30 a.m., and she is feeling frustrated. What to do now? She decides it is the perfect time to clean his house. And dear Paul goes back to sleep in the comfort of knowing his house, his health, and his heart are in good hands.

His faithful helper, Helen is loyally walking by his side.

Whether it is this funny story of the day or next week's serious incident, this sort of experience is repeated over and over again in a woman's life.

According to a recent study, a typical family caregiver in the US is a forty-nine-year-old woman caring for her widowed, sixty-nine-year-old mother who does not live with her. Not only is she helping her aging parent, she is married and holds down a job. About 66 percent of family caregivers are women, and more than 37 percent have children or grandchildren under eighteen years old living with them.[5]

Talk about being busy and feeling pressure!

There is nothing wimpy about an *ezer*. In this generation, one only has to think of the tough-as-nails politician, former Prime Minister of England Margaret Thatcher or the prophetess Deborah in the Old Testament to balance the picture.

Deborah was a prophetess—a legal expert called, as it were, to the Israeli Bar Association. As a wise judge and a savvy political leader, she advised the military commanders of the army of Israel to go out and fight a just and winnable war.

"Go!" she tells Barak. "Has not the LORD gone ahead of you?" (Judg. 4:14 NIV).

But Barak would not leave unless she went with him. So Deborah fearlessly helps lead an army of ten thousand men to have confidence in the great Commander of heaven as they win the military victory against the Canaanite leader, Sisera.

Women need to see themselves and their gender in the positive light in which the Creator God views them. Then they will relate to God in a healthier way.

Think of another brave Jewish woman named Esther.

She was a humble woman who radiated beauty inside and out. Yet she didn't believe she was a person of much worth until her uncle Mordecai encouraged her to step outside her comfort zone. When the King of Persia put on a beauty contest to decide who would become his new bride, his eyes lit up as he watched Esther walk toward him. She was crowned queen within the year.

Esther became exactly the gracious leader the king had envisioned her to be.

Not only was she beautiful, but intelligent, courageous, and wise. And God eventually called Queen Esther to save her nation from genocide.

Luci Swindoll: *True Freedom in God*

Contemporary women of faith wield a positive influence in today's society.

Thousands of women break out clapping as Luci Swindoll strides on stage in a black pants outfit at a Woman of Faith conference in Seattle. She steps forward with the confidence well-honed after a thirty-year career at Mobil Oil.

"A life of adventure is ours for the taking whether we're seven or seventy," she says to the crowd. "It's all about keeping our eyes and our hearts open."

Sitting backstage, Swindoll explains to me that it was easy for her to fit into the corporate petroleum world. She worked hard to earn her leadership stripes as a top-ranking executive for the company now known as Exxon Mobil, an oil giant that has recorded a net income of more than $25 billion in sales annually.

She asked God to help her each day to be a blessing on her job.

"I enjoyed it. I could be me—without having to fit in like I was one of the guys."

During her first twenty-five years at Mobil, she moved up the corporate ladder, so to speak, but was unaware of this because she had never set out to be a manager. She simply worked hard to try to do a good job and then one day, out of the blue, "boom," it just happened, she says with a laugh.

"I was asked to be in management. It was never my goal to become an executive. It was my goal to be a good employee."

When she became so busy writing and speaking, she decided to take early retirement and commit her life to full-time Christian ministry. An accomplished writer, she is the author of such books as *I Married Adventure: Looking at Life through the Lens of Possibility*. She is also a past member of the executive team for *Insight for Living*, a popular Christian radio ministry featuring her brother Pastor Chuck Swindoll.

Luci lives in Texas, has never married, and walks a spiritual journey that is not well-traveled. A woman who moves to the top of a high-rolling petroleum company is an anomaly in the world of business, but a devout Christian woman who makes it to the top is—well, this is newsworthy.

She is a no-nonsense go-getter.

Although she worked as an oil executive, she managed to escape the flighty politics of "Big Business and Big Money." But it would have been ever so tempting. She avoided the spiritual pitfalls that are often experienced in the "world of power" by making a concerted effort to continually devote her life to God.

As a woman of faith, Luci prays to God daily and asks Him

to guide her in every activity of her day, whether singing opera, writing, drawing, or speaking in public.

She advises women to engage in the awesome possibilities of today.

"Take risks, strike out on your own, try something new," she suggests. "And most important, define yourself by no one else's definition. . . . Whether you feel joy or sorrow, you will grow through all of your experiences."

She is inspired by such authors as Hermann Hesse, a Nobel Prize winner, who taught that everything in life is transitional and encouraged people to live life to the fullest every moment of the day. Gertrude Stein may have popularized the feminist movement, but Luci believes it is more important to be engaged in the spiritual path of human liberation.

"There's nothing like the freedom you'll find in God."

Luci is excited about the Revolve Tour for teen girls, which travels across the nation helping youth find their purpose in life. These conferences pass the torch of faith to teens struggling to establish their true feminine identity in a media-saturated culture.

"There is so much pressure on girls to compromise the true essence of who they are as females," she says. "But God has a plan for their lives that is far more fulfilling than they can sometimes imagine!"

The media pushes women to be super thin, wear goofy expensive designer clothes, and be sexually promiscuous to be a "somebody."

But there is a much happier and healthier way to live.

"You don't have to be any of those things; you simply have to be yourself."

Feminine Mystique

One day I give one of my grown daughters a nice new T-shirt.

But I discover the gift, the next day, lying on our driveway, covered in dirt. She had dropped it on the asphalt by accident and had driven over it with her car. There it lay on the pavement, rain-splattered and pathetic, plastered and caked in brown tire marks. Smiling to myself, I pick it up and wash it, but it remains a mangled mess.

Arriving for a visit later, I ask my daughter how she likes her new T-shirt.

"Oh, I really like it."

Have you worn it yet? I ask in feigned innocence.

"No, no, not yet, but I will soon," she assures me.

I bring a white bag out of the kitchen and pull out her bedraggled, tattered T-shirt and ask her how she likes the tire marks. She bursts out in laughter seeing the status of her shirt and the twinkle in my eyes.

She had no idea she had run over her gift.

"It's okay, I'll get you another one. Watch how you drive, okay." I smile.

Unfortunately, and on a more serious note, personally and collectively in our culture and in our religion we tend to devalue the Creator's gift of femininity.

Francis Schaeffer writes that "people should see a beauty among Christians in the practice of the centrality of their personal relationships—in the whole spectrum of life and in the whole culture."[6]

Author Philip Yancey in his book *Reaching for the Invisible God*, reveals that it was not a sermon that encouraged him to have faith. He was drawn to worship God, in large part, because of the beauty he found in music, literature, and his wife's love.

"I turned to God primarily because of my discovery of goodness and grace in the world through nature, through classical music, through romantic love."

As Yancey contemplated the good in the world, he began to seek the Giver.

"Full of gratitude, I needed someone to thank."[7]

"A gracious woman attains honor . . . and she smiles at the future" (Prov. 11:16, 31:25 NASB).

God empowers women to bring forward their many talents and skills.

The beauty in a woman nourishes, comforts, and inspires others, says author Stasi Eldredge, noting how a woman has a certain feminine mystique to unveil because she bears the image of God. When a woman is comfortable in her femininity, this communicates to all within her circle of influence that she is at rest with herself because of who she is in the unspoiled framework of God's wonderful design.

Her life radiates to everyone that "all is well."

This reminds me of a conversation I once had with my eldest grandchild. I was playing on the living room floor with my granddaughter Amie, who was five years old at the time, when I casually ask her if she likes being a girl.

"Uh-huh," she replies, moving her toy pony to the big Fisher-Price barn as I decide on the spur of the moment to test her comfort level with her gender.

"Do you ever think it would be nice to be a boy?" I ask as I brush her hair.

"No," replies the little girl, with great emphasis on the N-O.

"Do you *really* like being a girl?" I probe again.

"Uh-huh." Now the preschooler is getting impatient with me.

"Don't you like being a girl, Grandma?" She looks at me with big blue eyes.

"Yeah, but sometimes I wanted to be a boy when I was younger," I say.

"Well, Grandma, why would you ever want to do that? Because Jesus made you a girl!" she says in dramatic exasperation.

I smile. She definitely made her point.

Basic interpretation: *Jesus made me who I am. That's it. All settled.* It took Amie six seconds to figure out one of life's biggest questions. She's comfortable and happy that Jesus made her a girl—with all of the beauty, affection, and sensitivity that being female involves. Her self-confidence is perfect in who she is. Life is great! This is true whether you're Luci Swindoll or my five-year-old granddaughter.

CHAPTER 7

Masculine, Feminine, and Beyond

When God created men and women to be like him, women are half of the equation. We are half of the picture.

Ruth Graham, Author

MOST OF US are fascinated by gender issues.

It often begins in the home listening to our son yell "vrooom" as he pushes around his little truck in the living room, in contrast to our daughter who sings softly and pretends to be "Mommy" to her dolly. No one has taught either of the children how to behave. In childlike innocence, the goodness of their gender flows outward from deep within themselves as natural as breathing.

Children are born with their individual nuances.

Scientific research shows that the language area in a girl's brain develops earlier than the area that specializes in spatial relations and mathematics. In boys, it is the other way around. They also respond differently to social pressures and stress. Boys tend to perform better under stress than girls.

Moms and Dads who affirm and celebrate the goodness of a child's distinct "maleness" or "femaleness" give them the security and confidence to be themselves as created in the holy image of God.

The differences denote divine dignity.

Dr. Robert Hiebert is smiling as he gazes at a photo of his two beautiful daughters, one with a violin cradled on her shoulder, the other with a flute in her hand.

They are the epitome of beauty, grace, and innocence.

The photo is placed on his desk at Trinity Western University (TWU) where he is the Director of the Septuagint Institute, a new research center of biblical scholarship—the only one of its kind in North America. The Septuagint Institute, like TWU's Dead Sea Scrolls Institute, is gaining an international reputation for cutting-edge scholarship.

Language and translation are his specialties.

He translated the book of Genesis in conjunction with more than thirty scholars who translated the Septuagint—the Greek version of the original Hebrew Scriptures—to produce *A New English Translation of the Septuagint*, published by Oxford University Press.

The deep-thinking scholar is also a devoted dad.

Hiebert is proud of his daughters' musical talents, and his eyes soften as he fixes his gaze on their faces in the photo. His warm smile says more in that short pause in our conversation than a million words. When he speaks about his wife and his daughters, he reveals a quiet devotion and a profound respect for the feminine gender.

As a loving father, he envisions the Creator as a kind, loving God.

He says Christians need to be open-minded about exploring the feminine qualities of God that are hinted at in the Bible, particularly in some of the metaphors.

The Warrior and the Woman

The prophet Isaiah, for example, combines the metaphors of both a mighty warrior and a woman in childbirth to describe the Lord God's passion for justice.

The LORD will march out like a mighty man,
like a warrior he will stir up his zeal;
with a shout he will raise the battle cry
and will triumph over his enemies.

For a long time I have kept silent,
I have been quiet and held myself back.
But now, like a woman in childbirth,
I cry out, I gasp and pant.
                              Isaiah 42:13–14 NIV

This picture discloses a sacred balance in the *Lord Most High,* first, as a powerful military leader who pursues justice in the cosmic battle against evil and prevails over His enemies; but then also as a woman who lives in remarkable self-restraint, keeps still for a very long time, and then suddenly moves into action as one going into labor.

I (Trudy) hesitate to comment further on this powerful metaphor.

It seems more reverent, somehow, to let the words speak for themselves.

I sit back quietly and read the whole book of Isaiah and then return to this chapter. I notice that just before the prophet pictures God as a warrior and a woman in childbirth, he prefaces these metaphors by advising the people to give glory to God and to "sing to the LORD a new song" (Isa. 42:10 NASB).

This takes me to the leading edge of eternity.

Personality, Not Biology

Why does the prophet juxtapose a mighty male warrior in this metaphor with a woman going into childbirth to describe God's passion for justice?

In one mysterious way He may be seen as masculine in personality, the *Holy One* who exhibits divine *power to lead*, commands our obedience as *God Almighty*, and rescues us with creative initiative, justice, and authority, saving us in supreme power. In another sense, the great and awesome *God of Mercy* is tenderhearted, deeply protective, and displays feminine personality with divine *power to nurture* us.

To be clear, the holy eternal God is beyond gender.

But He relates to us, at times, with the characteristics of a wise parent who cherishes and nurtures a growing relationship with His children. The prophet Zechariah also presents a poignant portrayal of the nurturing love of God:

> *The LORD your God is with you,*
> *he is mighty to save.*
> *He will take great delight in you,*
> *he will quiet you with his love,*
> *he will rejoice over you with singing.*
>   *Zephaniah 3:17 NIV*

This passage takes my breath away on so many different levels.

I am reminded of an experience I had with one of my granddaughters. I was unable to hold her until she was three months old, and she was frightened when she first came to my house.

Everything was new to her, and she did not know me.

Holding her gently on my lap in my rocking chair, I tenderly sing a song that I compose especially for her. She is soon comforted by my soft humming voice, and she lays quiet and still, resting warmly as I wrap her in my warm arms of love.

Now she is starting to trust me and relax in our new relationship.

As she closes her eyes, she feels so beautiful to me.

This is how God must feel when I rest in the arms of amazement.

Imagine . . . the Creator of the cosmos takes great delight in me, quiets me with His love, and soothes my spirit with song. The Lord of the Sabbath, who composes the magical melodies of the birds in the forest, the intelligent songs of the whales in the vast ocean deep, and inspires the creative genius of musicians to write the most harmonious symphonies and love songs ever heard—actually rejoices by singing over me!

Ruth Graham: "Feminine Side of God Is a Fact"

When I catch up with Ruth Graham, a vivacious woman of faith living in Virginia, she does not hesitate to tell me that her study of the Bible convinces her there is a maternal side to God's love. I am amazed by her outspoken honesty as she encourages me to press forward in my quest for biblical answers.

"Don't ever give up on this one," she said. "This is really important."

Ruth is a survivor who shares from her heart.

The youngest of three daughters of legendary evangelist Billy Graham, she is a popular public speaker and the author of such books as *A Legacy of Love: Things I Learned from My Mother*. No stranger to heartache, she is open about her struggle with divorce, a teenage daughter's pregnancy, and a son's battle with drugs and depression.

She is learning to trust God, even in the tough times.

It is an honor and a privilege to pray to God, she says, and she has often felt the loving arms of the heavenly Father wrapping around her to sustain her through her many trials.

Graham always prays to "our Father," although her study of the Bible inspires her to conclude that God loves us with both masculine and feminine attributes, even though the feminine elements are not often preached about in church.

"The feminine side of God is a fact," she says.

"There are a number of references in the Bible about the feminine qualities of God. To deny this is to deny who God says He is. . . . When God created men and women to be like Him, women are half of the equation—we are half of the picture."

God named Eve the "helpmate." Translated from Hebrew, this word means the "lifesaver," but unfortunately, women have long been relegated to a low position in the world. This is not according to God's perfect plan, Graham explains.

"We are not second-class citizens. Women have always been held in high esteem by God. There were strong men in the Scriptures, but there were also examples of strong godly women."

She points out that the Bible clearly records stories of women who were extraordinarily brave, including Rahab, a prostitute, who risked her life in Jericho to save two Israeli spies. She could have been executed if she had been caught, and the apostle Paul praises her actions as "righteous" in the Hall of Faith (see Hebrews 11).

Even though Graham is candid about the feminine dimension in God, she is definitely not going to start calling God *she*.

"I still think and pray to God as my Father, but I know God has feminine qualities," Graham says, noting that it is important for women to enjoy the fact that God made them with their unique feminine qualities.

She is "very happy" being a woman, and her sisters are too.

"My mother raised us to be strong women and to enjoy our femininity."

She believes that Bible translations should be more "gender

accurate" because "man" is often used to mean "human." However, she is not worried about such contentious issues because the most important goal in life is to know and to serve God.

"I think you need to find value in who you are in Christ and to do what God has called you to do in life."

Touched by an Angel

When I walk into my newsroom some time later, telephones ring offbeat to the tempo of male voices blaring on the police scanner. Above this background noise, one woman's husky laugh is so contagious that when she phones me in our crowded newsroom, the other reporters hear the echo of her booming voice.

"Is that Della Reese?" Vikki Hopes, another reporter, whispers to me.

I nod my head, cradling the phone under my ear. The other reporters are suddenly quiet, trying to eavesdrop on our conversation.

"I like what you wrote," Della tells me.

"Oh, that's great, Della. Hopefully we'll be able to talk again."

Legendary actress and singer Della Reese-Lett is a household name. She is featured in Hollywood's Walk of Fame for her role as a costar in *Touched by an Angel*, the only religious TV show to hit the Top 10 in ratings. She played the big-hearted personable angel named "Tess," the angel who saved people from dying in car accidents and cheered up lost children. In real life, she also has her eyes on heaven as the founder of an independent Christian church in Los Angeles called UP Church. As a pastor, she teaches her congregation to put their trust in God.

"If there is a feminine aspect in all that there is in life, then there is a feminine aspect to God," Della says to me, noting that God certainly made women differently than men for a good reason.

"I feel I was designed by God to have different functions than a man; I was designed to replenish the Earth and to carry a child."

Della's mom Nellie was a magnificent woman of faith who often prayed to God as a close friend. One of her mom's prayers was for Della to be healed when she was gravely ill with rheumatic fever at three years old.

"My mom made God an important part of our lives," she said. "My mother felt like God was her friend."

Her legacy of kindness left a lasting spiritual impression on Della as the first person to teach her to lean on God's wisdom during every upheaval in life. Like her mother before her, Della loves the Lord with all her heart.

"My mother would never say that God was up there somewhere in the clouds with a big book in His hand checking off all your mistakes.

"God wants the best in life for all of us!"

Danae Dobson: *The Nurturing Side of God*

As Ruth Graham and Della Reese so aptly point out, a mother is usually the first person in our lives to encourage us to trust in God. And Danae Dobson's life is also positively influenced by her mother's faith.

She is the only daughter of Shirley and Dr. James Dobson, a popular American psychologist, founder of Focus on the Family and *Family Talk*. A public speaker in her own right, Danae is the author of more than twenty books—most of which are aimed at children.

Her mom, Shirley, modeled the love of God to Danae by gently teaching her to pray and to obey the Lord God even during life's toughest times. Shirley Dobson was raised in a home with an alcoholic father and a faithful mother. In the midst of this chaotic life, her mother, Alma Kubishta worked at a fish cannery and an aircraft factory during the war, which often required her to get up at four a.m. Though her burdens were many, she always made sure her children went to church every Sunday.

"My mom [Shirley] was only five years old when she started to ask God to help her to meet a good Christian man whom she could marry one day," explains Danae.

"Isn't it amazing that she met my dad?"

Who would have imagined that a humble, praying five-year-old girl would one day become the chairwoman of the US National Day of Prayer and rub shoulders with presidents and first ladies and earn the Christian Woman of the Year award?

"Never in a million years would my mom have ever imagined being in the position that the Lord has called her to," Danae says. "It's mind-boggling what the Lord can do in your life when you surrender to Him. There's no limit!"

Her mom and dad form a wonderful couple with qualities on both sides of their marriage who have taught Danae to grow in her faith in God.

The Bible records that God made both males and females in His image, she says, noting that God also displays qualities that are both masculine and feminine.

The Creator loves His children in perfect balance.

"The feminine qualities that come to mind are God's compassion and His nurturing side," she says. "There's also the sensitive side of God. He's sensitive to my needs, which is more of a feminine quality of relating than a masculine quality."

God Embraces and Transcends Gender

A woman's heart is uniquely designed to reflect the beauty of the Creator.

Stasi Eldredge, coauthor of the best-selling book *Captivating*, helps women feel blessed in their femininity.

"God's love is healing, comforting, gentle, and kind, just like a mother's love. The Bible uses beautiful imagery to depict God's tenderness as a mother nursing, weaning, and caring for her children."

Therefore, women may certainly discover their true identity in God.

Eldredge points out that although it is true that God transcends typical male and female gender distinctions, our Creator's love is also expressed in both masculine and feminine ways.

"It is a mystery that God both embraces and transcends gender."

Academy award-winning musician Buffy Sainte-Marie also notes that there is a "sacred feminine aspect of the loving, nurturing, omnipotent Creator."

Excitement about this issue is sweeping across the world.

"We live in an era when the first generation of female theologians are being educated in biblical knowledge," says Dr. Janet Soskice, Professor of Philosophical Theology at Cambridge University, England.

A number of innovative theologians are discovering the maternal dimensions of God's love. And they're not afraid to proclaim it. It is like they are bringing new eyes to the Word of God.

"It's very important for churches to teach that women are made wholly in God's image—none of the denominations have gotten it quite right for thousands of years."

The question about how God relates to women did not bother Soskice when she was younger, but it became increasingly more important as she and her husband raised two daughters and she interacted with her seminary students. It deeply troubled her to learn, for example, that people used to refuse to accept a communion chalice if it came from a woman's hands, an attitude that has now changed.

"From the ancient world until now, females were deemed inferior to males," she says. "But this was a misguided belief that all churches would now like to distance themselves from."

The theologian is the author of scholarly books, such as *The Kindness of God: Metaphor, Gender, and Religious Language* and *The*

Sisters of Sinai. She embraces the Christian faith as profoundly meaningful for life and explains that God wondrously designed the world by using the "paired differences"—the light and the dark, the sea and the dry land, the male and the female—to display the fecundity of God.

"Together the two genders are made one, and they complete each other," she says, adding that, in her opinion, "it is appropriate to identify masculine and feminine qualities in all three persons of the Godhead."

✒❤

I take my Bible in my hand and climb up the wooded hillside behind my old country house, where bigleaf maple trees are draped in rain-soaked leaves and the sound of robins singing. The soft brown dirt is well packed from my walking in the rain forest. The path is steep and challenging.

Finding my favorite knoll in the mossy cradle of three grand old maples, I hang my feet over the edge, thanking God for everything He is doing in my life. As I look around at dozens upon dozens of massive moss-covered deciduous trees, my breath is taken away as powerful beams of sunlight—like exquisite unique sails of white—move down through the woods from the sky to the forest floor like giant pillars of white light.

If we follow Him, we will not walk in darkness.[1]

It is my daily routine to study God's Word in the quietness of the forest. A bald eagle and a resident red-tailed hawk often fly overhead. With heartfelt affection, I name the woods "God's holy hill" one day after I read the following passage in Psalm 99:9: "Exalt the LORD our God, and worship at his holy hill; for the LORD our God is holy" (KJV).

Climbing higher to the very top of the hill, I kneel and close my eyes:

"Dear Lord, remember when our book wasn't a book yet, but it was just an idea you planted in my heart? Thank you for opening the doors for me to interview scientists and scholars and many other wonderful people who have become my friends. You impressed me right from the beginning I should interview one of Billy Graham's daughters. What Ruth told me the other day was powerful."

Try to define femininity. He prompts me to dig deeper.

"Strength is the essence of a man—just as beauty is the essence of a woman. These powerful attributes are designed into our DNA at conception—to reflect your image, dear God. Your divine nature is a sacred balance of strength and beauty."

You're moving in the right direction, keep going. . . .

"A woman nurtures her husband, her children, her parents, and her friends by binding others to herself with tenderness. She alleviates the loneliness and sadness others feel. The softness and beauty of a woman comforts, attracts, and inspires, just like the beauty in your creation awakens in me a spiritual yearning to belong and to be one with you. The loveliness of the white lily, the song of the robin, I could go on and on. I love feeling the intensity of your divine, creative love."

A woman who follows me is among the most beautiful of creatures, He says.

I am unable to move from that thought. "Even me?"

Yes, you.

"Lord, I'm nothing like the rain forest or the stars."

Trudy, even better! Masculine and feminine ways of relating to others defines an aspect of who I am, that's what Ruth Graham explained to you. Keep following me, and you will see.

It is a big spiritual *aha* moment for me to discover that a big part of who I am—my gentleness and femininity, my maternal instinct—corresponds to my Creator God!

One day, sometime later, I am sailing through the wild waves of the wind-churning, glacier-fed Harrison Lake, completely soaked by waves of freezing cold water splashing over me as I brace myself in the back of the pontoon. It is as if I am covered from head to toe by cascading waterfalls of crushed ice—all at once shocked, yet refreshed by a wordless take-my-breath-away excitement. Today I have never felt more alive as the Spirit bears witness that I am a child of God.

"A gift opens doors; it gives access to the great" (Prov. 18:16 NRSV).

My gift of gender gives me access to commune with the great and awesome God on an intimate level. What joy this brings me! I am finally able to fully identify myself as a daughter of God, as precious and beloved as a son.

Later that week I visit my daughter. Her voice is animated as she smiles widely with a grin stretching from ear to ear. She has a great sense of humor, like her father, but she has my big, infectious smile. Uniquely herself, she is an amalgam of her mom and dad's features. Children need to know their origin because the characteristics of their parents inform them who they are. Ideally this gives them meaning in life.

How much more important is it for us to know the nature of our Creator.

And here's another thought: If I choose to ignore an important side of God's character, don't I cause Him to endure great suffering because of this neglect?

Dr. Jürgen Moltmann gives us a good starting point to contemplate:

"Do we have to conceive of the Creator . . . as indifferent towards his masculine and feminine image on earth? The God who can allow his glory to appear at one and the same time in male and female form cannot, at all events, be a merely masculine God."[2]

A Timeless Conversation

"Before I formed you in the womb I knew you, and before you were born I consecrated you. . . . Everywhere I send you, you shall go, and all that I command you, you shall speak (Jer. 1:5, 7 NASB).

God designed His sons and daughters for nobility.

He knows where we reside and exactly how long we will live. We are alive because of who *He is*. In a divine conversation at the beginning of time, recorded in the first chapter of Genesis, *Elohim* simply stated: "Let *us* make humankind in *our* image, according to *our* likeness" (Gen. 1:26 NRSV, italics added).

Clearly, the words "us" and "our" reveal a powerful clue about our Maker.

One of the most holy names for God, *Elohim*, is plural in form, but singular in meaning—or sometimes referred to as "uni-plural" or a "plural of majesty." In other words, God—the Father, Son, and Holy Spirit—form a divine Trinity who interchange together, one in purpose and unity. (More on the Trinity in Chapter 15.)

And, somehow, as a child of God, I am also integral to the creation story, as Father Placidus explained earlier: Each one of us is a "trinity of mind, body, and spirit."

Dr. Robert Hiebert, a professor of Old Testament Studies at the Graduate School of Theological Studies at Trinity Western University, has this to say about the significance of the creation of the first man and woman:

"The relationship between Adam and Eve—who were not identical in gender, yet complemented one another in their love relationship in community with one another—somehow, according to Genesis 1, is a reflection of *who God is*," he says.

"In what way this is to be understood in terms of reflecting the image of God is a theological question that is not easily answered."

Meanwhile, Dr. Elizabeth Johnson explains that God is a transcendent mystery.

"God cannot be captured in either one of the genders. . . . Neither male nor female is more divine than the other. In fact, both taken together are in the divine image."

Moltmann asks the same question raised by many people of faith: "What is the nature of God, whose image appears in both male and female form?"

He also finds the answer in the first chapter of Genesis.

"Both genders proceed from the essence of *who God is!*"

PART TWO

The Nature of God

CHAPTER 8

The Mercy of God:
Protective and Womb-Like

As a mother comforts her child, so will I comfort
you. . . .

Isaiah 66:13 NIV

As I BOARD a plane heading to Beirut, I am thinking about Ann
Penner.

Her vivacious thirty-one-year-old daughter, Bonnie,[1] was providing nursing care to pregnant Palestinian women at a prenatal
clinic, south of Beirut in Sidon. One morning Bonnie, a devout
Christian, went to the clinic forty minutes early to pray for her
patients. When she answered a knock on the door, she was shot
to death.

It was a devastating shock to all who knew her.

"There are no guarantees in life," Ann tells me as I write a feature story commemorating her daughter's brave ministry to give
medical care to Muslim women.

"She really cared a lot for them," says Ann as she encourages
people to have faith in Christ and to courageously follow their
convictions no matter what.

Little did I know I would end up later landing in the Middle
East myself. I arrive in Beirut, overwhelmed by the noise of

motorists continually honking their horns to the cacophony of loudspeakers blaring Islamic prayers. Soldiers carry rifles under their arms, while large army tanks are posted at strategic street corners. Larger-than-life Hezbollah placards decorate the skyline, above the streets in some districts of the city, as people move into a mosque to gather together. Although there is a continual threat of car bombs, any time, any place, I feel surprisingly safe.

Once I get over my jet lag, I set out to interview a notable Bible scholar.

Religious controversies may abound, but I have no desire to cause a war of words over the so-called gender of God. I am here to study the Scriptures and to seek a peaceful resolution to the ongoing debate about this question.

Theologians in the Middle East are shaking their heads over the controversy raging in Judeo-Christian circles over the gender of God. These wise sages question why anyone would believe the imaginary plots of best-selling suspense novels such as *The Da Vinci Code*.

"There has never been a cover-up of the sacred femininity of God, as alleged in *The Da Vinci Code*," says Dr. Daniel Ayuch, a world-class Bible scholar at the St. John of Damascus Institute of Theology. The seminary is operated by the Greek Orthodox Church of Antioch, which traces its roots to the days of Christ and the early apostles.[2]

Although violence breaks out sporadically in the "war with no end" in the Middle East—it is peaceful today. A warm breeze rises from the Mediterranean Sea and blows across the narrow road winding up Balamand Mountain as I head to the seminary. The sea spreads across the horizon below, like mystical turquoise satin.

The professor smiles widely as he greets me with a warm handshake.

"I'm so glad you made it. Did you have any trouble getting here?"

Wearing a blue suit, Ayuch appears professional yet casual as he walks beside me in the hallway of the theological institute, an austere building set high on the edge of a plateau on Balamand Mountain. We talk about the ongoing political unrest.

Several monks in black attire pass by, and he nods his head to them.

As I enter the theologian's office, the first thing I see is a crucifix of Jesus hanging on the wall and a pair of white sheer curtains billowing in the breeze across the open patio doors. The outer courtyard is filled with red roses in bloom. Nearby, a meandering pathway leads past a lemon grove and an ancient monastery built in 1157 with massive beige stones bleached by centuries of sun.

This is the place where Ayuch finds himself—a country steeped in religious history and the pivotal point of prophetic predictions for the future. Jesus spent time teaching and healing in the nearby city of Tyre, and the apostle Paul set sail from the picturesque port of Sidon on his way to Rome. A mystical feeling pervades the air in the Middle East, where the major monotheistic religions of the world have their roots.

The Spirit of God is here, always has been here.

My conversation with Ayuch is reverent, open, and honest, leading comfortably to the paternal and maternal qualities of the Creator God.

Even though God is widely known as "our heavenly Father," the scholar explains that it is also true that He loves us with tender maternal characteristics, such as mercy and compassion.

"He's not just a macho God," he says, adding that most theologians do not view God with only masculine attributes.

The Bible is clear—the maternal qualities of God were never a secret. Quite the contrary! The Scriptures reveal many wonderful maternal aspects about God, Ayuch says, with a confidence honed by years of biblical research.

He is a professor of New Testament courses. His heritage is Syrian, but as a multilingual specialist, he is fluent not only in Arabic, but Spanish, English, and German. The theologian is well-known for his expertise on the Gospel of Luke and the Book of Acts, using narrative analysis. He leafs through his Bible as he puts together facts of archeology, history, and scriptural evidence to place each piece of the puzzle exactly where it needs to fit to start making perfect sense to me.

"One of the most important words in the Bible about the feminine aspect of God is the word 'mercy,'" Ayuch explains, noting that the Hebrew root of the word is *racham*, which means "womb" in the Hebrew and Arabic languages.

"Mercy is an amazing word—an extremely important word," he says.

"The Bible repeatedly describes the mercy of God in the original Semitic languages as womb-like—protective and nurturing—just as a mother's womb protects and nourishes her baby until delivery."

The mercy of God is ever-faithful, like a devoted mother who never gives up on the child of her womb and always shelters her beloved offspring.

I stop writing and stare at the scholar in astonishment.

But he does not stop speaking. He continues to share the wisdom of the ages, and it comes at me in soothing drafts as if billowing across the white sheer curtains from heaven itself. An inaudible voice speaks deep within my soul: *Trudy, this is what you need to know to understand me better.*

The scholar wearing the blue vest smiles and quietly proceeds.

"The deepest desire of God is to create new life and to protect children from injury, to nurture them until they are mature, and for their lives to ripen, so to speak, and to bear good fruit," Ayuch explains. "God's mercy surrounds the human soul like a womb carries a child, which is a very profound female function."

This was revealed to the prophet Isaiah in the eighth century

BC when he used the most sublime words possible to unfold God's maternal love for us.

> *Listen to me . . .*
> *You who have been borne by me from birth*
> *And have been carried from the womb.*
> *Even to your old age I will be the same.*
> *And even to your graying years I will bear you!*
> *I have done it, and I will carry you.*
> *And I will bear you and I will deliver you.*
>
> Isaiah 46:3–4 NASB

"This was an astounding revelation for that era," the scholar says to me.

"It still is," I say as I lean back in the chair, enthralled by it all.

The professor explains that the deep mercy of God for the people of Israel was an attribute that was generally not acceptable to the surrounding nations during the Old Testament era when the people demanded their false man-made gods be militant and macho. But the Scriptures graphically reveal God's maternal love as verifiable fact.

"The God of love and compassion and protective mercy depicted in the Bible actually does display the loving role of a mother!"

The theologian finds it interesting that the writers of the Old Testament had absolutely no problem stating that God is not only strong and powerful in nature, but merciful and loving, which were recognized as "typical feminine activities."

This is illustrated in yet another metaphor highlighted by Isaiah:

> *Can a woman forget her nursing child,*
> *or show no compassion for the child of her womb?*
> *Even these may forget,*

yet I will not forget you.
See, I [God] have inscribed you on the palms of my hands;
your walls are continually before me.
                    Isaiah 49:15–16 NRSV, *bracketed word added*

No love on Earth is more committed to another human being than the love of a mother. She carries her baby in the warmth of her own body as her womb expands one thousand times its original size to accommodate the child growing to full-term. Then, on the day of delivery, she goes through the anguish and pain of labor to give life to her precious offspring. The new mom is overjoyed with excitement as she cradles her baby close to her heart and comforts and nurses her beloved child with maternal tenderness.

These texts by Isaiah present a powerful illustration of the maternal love of God, the Middle East scholar concluded.

"This ancient truth is as profound today as in times past."

✏

Never have I felt more awestruck by the mercy of God as I am today.

God loves me in a sacred balance like a kindhearted father and a merciful mother! And the proof has always been there, neatly tucked away as hidden treasure in the Holy Scriptures, just waiting to be discovered.

This is big news to me. This is the page-stopper.

I thank Dr. Ayuch for his expertise and his time because I know he has a class to teach this afternoon, but I am in no hurry to leave the seminary grounds. I walk slowly past the lemon trees and a tree heavy with ripe oranges and head toward the ancient monastery on the property that seems to be calling out my name.

With a bounce in my step, I start humming the song "Glory

Be to God on High" when I see an elegant looking steeple come into my view. It is the only surviving stone church tower of its kind in all of the Middle East.

The courtyard is vacant as I feel an impulse to go higher.

Climbing the stone stairs to the upper level of the monastery, I am surprised to find a row of cedar doors built into the massive stone walls. Each door has a key that turns a lock, leading into a small private prayer room. Charles H. Spurgeon once wrote about a "great bunch of keys" that are hidden in the good old book, the Bible, and "there is a key for every lock, and if it were not so, there are one or two promises like master-keys which will fit all."[3]

I feel like I've just discovered a great master key.

"As a mother comforts her child, so will I comfort you" (Isa. 66:13, *NIV*).

I know the feeling of being out of my comfort zone, feeling like a fish out of water. Labeled a slow learner as a child, I worked hard with my hands as a young woman. I cleaned offices as a dutiful janitor for ten years, and the next thing I knew, I was watching the movie *Good Will Hunting* and it was coming true in real life as I earned one writing award after another as an investigative journalist.

Rising from janitor to journalist was discomforting.

Then, out of the blue, the hands that wrote the golden stories broke down into hands that could not even hold a pen. A failed surgery, disability, insecurity, going from a journalist to a "nobody." Again I floundered, out of my comfort zone.

"First days" are like that too—both scary and stimulating.

My first day married. My first day buying a house. My first day having a baby. Going to university. Working as an editor. Interviewing top politicians. Meeting judges, accepting awards. Undergoing hand surgery. Unyielding years of pain. Learning to dress again. Finally being able to clap my hands together again after a choir concert for the first time in three years, and to feel the blessed warmth rising in my hands applauding together, rising higher with each emotion of the clapping.

Oh God, I can clap my hands again. . . .

"As a mother comforts her child, so will I comfort you. . . ."

I know that feeling.

I am kneeling in a small prayer room in a foreign country with the fragrance of aromatic cedar, ancient stones, roses, and lemons filling my senses as I close my eyes in a whisper of wonder.

"Dear loving God, thank you for reminding me today that I am not a nobody. My identity is fully developed in you. My femininity corresponds to an aspect of who you are. This is the first day in my life that I have solid evidence from your Holy Word that you have a maternal side! It's unbelievable, really. I had no idea your mercy shelters and surrounds me like a mother's womb."

The applause of heaven like a distant song gently grows in volume as I meditate on what Isaiah must have heard when "the mountains and the hills will break forth into shouts of joy before you, and all the trees of the field will clap their hands" (Isa. 55:12 NASB).

"My Father God, you have a mother's heart of mercy!

"A mother's heart, imagine that!"

Although I am halfway across the world in the Middle East, in my mind I am transported back in space and time to the west coast of North America and a memorable scene as I hold my mother's hand when I am five years old.

Walking into the Grade One classroom on the first day of school, I am horrified by clocks and walls that trap me, words I cannot read, and colors I cannot identify. I tightly hold her hand, wanting to run home and chase the butterflies and the gentle bumblebees on my parents' flower farm.

I am at home in the woods, not a wooden desk.

My mom tends to rescue me, and she lets me stay home more than once to escape this torture called school. She softly whispers to me some mornings that I can sleep in her large oversized bed and cuddle in her soft, fluffy comforter.

To me, this is pure bliss.

My comforter makes me feel warm inside, the same way King David must have felt when he wrote that God's comfort brought joy to his heart. I always feel happy in my mom's presence. She protects me even when I get into trouble; actually, in those moments she really shows the world her true compassion colors.

I am an energetic eleven-year-old girl when my friends and I decide to be entrepreneurs and hike up the price of the Girl Guide cookies. At the end of the day, we take our lucrative profits to the Bradner Store and proudly buy a pocketful of orange popsicles and Crispy Crunch chocolate bars.

Mom is sad when the neighbors ask about the real price of the cookies. The Guide leader later comes to our house and wants to kick the little thieves out of the Girl Guide pack. Mom hugs me and asks, with tears, for our punishment to be waived as she urgently claims a promise from Scripture.

> Therefore, there is now no condemnation for those who are in Christ Jesus.
>
> *Romans 8:1 NASB*

There is no censure in Mom's voice. She convinces the leader to soften our punishment. So I write over and over again, one hundred times on white-lined paper, our Guide motto: "Be prepared and always do a good turn to others." I stay a Girl Guide in good standing because moms are just like that.

One early morning when I am in my teens, Mom discovers me sliding into the house at 5:45 a.m. after I spent the night partying and falling asleep on a friend's couch. Looking unkempt in her pink pajamas, she sleepily rubs her eyes and stares in unbelief as I walk sheepishly through the front door.

There is no lecture as she motions to my room.

"You'd better go to bed right now," she says, visibly annoyed, and then pausing, she quietly assures me, "I won't say anything to your dad."

I whisper in shame, "I'm . . . I'm really sorry, Mom."

She gently pats me as I walk past her. "Sleep tight."

My mistake is forgiven and never mentioned again. Her mercy—it makes no sense to me after I have caused her such grief, yet to Almighty God, it does because the Most Merciful One entreats me in gentle tones: *"I have loved you with an everlasting love; I have drawn you with loving-kindness"* (Jer. 31:3 NIV).

"God's Best Ideas" in India

Millions of people in Mumbai watch the riotous Bollywood (Hindi) movies on TV for entertainment while others live in squalor, leading desperate lives in slums surrounded by open sewers.

Where can one find peace in such a hectic, crazy world?

Visitors to Mumbai travel by rickshaw and fast train to a Jesuit community where young people play cricket in the courtyard and study the Bible in a classroom. Father Fio Mascarenhas is kneeling down with his head to the carpet, praying earnestly that *the word of the Lord may speed on and triumph.*

He is the chairman of the Catholic Bible Institute in Mumbai when he tells me that he is worried about the rapidly changing culture in India, where 80 percent of the people are Hindu, 10 percent are Muslim, but only 2 percent are Christian.

His faith must never fail.

The Jesuit priest is a popular international speaker. Father Fio, as he likes to be called, helped establish the International Catholic

Charismatic Renewal Services in Rome in dialogue with Pope John Paul II, and then returned to India where he has been the rector of several Jesuit institutions. He is the author of best-selling books such as *The Holy Spirit, Co-Heirs with Christ,* and *God's Best Ideas.* His books have been translated into three Indian languages, Japanese, Chinese, Indonesian, Italian, Spanish, and Polish.

I can hardly wait to ask him about his biblical research.

He is a keen communicator and tells me he was "very excited" when he first learned about the tender heart of God's maternal mercy, a discovery that was reinforced again for him in 2003. Visitors who attend his spiritual retreats are taught about this great spiritual truth, and the Vatican is well aware of this.

"I worked in Rome for eight years, and you bet the pope has personally experienced God's maternal loving care," Father Fio says to me.

Not only is God's love paternal, strong, loyal, and steadfast (*hesed*), but his love is merciful, compassionate, tender, and womb-like, according to the root of the Hebrew word for "mercy," which is derived from the root word *rehem.*[4] Since *rehem* means womb, this means God actually has the same tender feelings a mother has for the child of her womb, he explains.

A mother does not just have pity for her child, she feels for the child.

We matter to God—a lot!

"God's love is not frightening, nor is He a hard taskmaster. . . . God's love is tender, like the beauty and tenderness of a mother's love."

This womb-like protection is a feminine feature.

Divine Deliverer

Have you ever felt like giving up in life?

Are you frustrated? Anxious? Or feeling worried?

"Sometimes, when life is very hard and we don't know what to do, and the way seems very dark, indeed; we need to wait patiently for God's delivery," advises Fio.

During any transitional waiting period, we are very much like an embryo that is growing and developing and being nurtured in the darkness by the nutrients provided by our mother. We are completely dependent on her for our delivery.

Not one iota of effort is expended by the unborn child.

All of the work is done by the mother!

The child abiding in the mother is safe, warm, and protected. We must trust our great Deliverer to rescue us from evil. When we are feeling helpless in the darkness, we are a mere embryo of what God intends for us to be. But we can always be assured of the womb-love, or the mother-love, God has for us.

In fact, spiritual growth often happens slowly, silently, and quite dramatically through the darkest periods of our lives as we learn to trust fully in God's providence. So it is with all of life. A seed must be planted deep into the dark, airless soil before a flower springs into colorful bloom. In a similar way, the Spirit gives us new birth in a burst of creative energy, moving us through the darkness of our difficulties—into the warmth of God's light and love.

When we experience our *"aha"* moment about the power of our Creator's maternal love for us, Fio says it will change us, and we will begin to have the fruit of the Spirit in a way we have never experienced before.

I pour myself a cup of Earl Grey tea. It feels good to be home.

As I add a touch of peppermint to the steaming brew, I look outside my kitchen window expecting to see the usual serene view of the western red cedars, the maples, and the overgrown bushes in the woods.

But my heart skips a beat at what I see dangling in my tall purple rhododendron bush. A Swallowtail butterfly, magnificent in its bold black and yellow stripes, is spinning and fluttering out of control in panic.

It is caught in a spider web.

I grab my sandals and race out the door as fast as I can, hoping to free the butterfly. Can I save it? As I pull away the sticky silk threatening to kill this beautiful creature, the butterfly floats to the grass and shakes itself, trying to restore its balance, moving its delicate wings slowly to the front, then to the back.

I am worried. Will it die?

"I just want you to fly," I say to the butterfly, thinking: *Why in the world am I talking to a butterfly as if my words have some kind of healing power?* But I can't help myself. "Come on, get up, you can do it, get up and fly."

I am desperate for this creature of indescribable dignity and beauty to fly. And then, suddenly, it lifts off . . . graciously winging up and away into the air, fluttering high above the trees, home where it belongs.

To the afflicted and the needy, the divine Deliverer does not delay. I have never before freed a butterfly from a spider web. But I know God has.

Arise, your sins are forgiven. . . .

One day Anne Lamott steps inside a small Presbyterian church. She's been through a lot. Atheism. Abortion. Alcoholism. And today she's suffering another excruciating hangover when she feels a yearning for . . . something.

What? Delivery? Freedom?

Compassion, maybe?

CHAPTER 9

God of Infinite Compassion

God's love for us is like the deep love a mother has
for her newborn, like the protective love a mother
has for her sick three-year-old child, and like the unconditional love a mother has for her cantankerous
eighteen-year-old.

Anne Lamott, Author

"JUST CALL ME Annie," she says with her trademark infectious
laugh.

Anne Lamott shares her life like an open book with a zany
sense of humor as she describes herself as a left-wing, born-again
Christian with "attitude." The author is renowned for her gut-
wrenching honesty.

Raised by atheistic parents, she got into drugs and alcohol
as a teenager, heading full-speed ahead into the path of sexual
promiscuity. An alcoholic who didn't want to be a Christian, she
says she was drawn to the love of Jesus shortly after she went
through the trauma of having an abortion. She found forgiveness,
love, and true spiritual peace for the first time in her life when
she gave her life to the Lord.

Lamott is a *New York Times* best-selling author of such nonfiction religious books as *Travelling Mercies*, *Plan B*, and *Grace
(Eventually)*. After finishing a recent book tour, she conversed
with me about the topic of the gender of God.

To begin our discussion, the author tells me she believes that Mary, the mother of Jesus, exhibited some of the deepest maternal expressions of divine love ever expressed in human form. When Lamott was going through the despair of drug and alcohol withdrawal, she experienced deep spiritual comfort by singing the lyrics of one of her favorite songs "Let It Be" by the Beatles.

"I believe one of the greatest pieces of spiritual advice anyone has ever given another person is to just *let it be*," she says as she shares a memorable experience.

One late night, she was unable to sleep because she was suffering in the throes of alcoholic psychosis and paralysis. During those dark hours, she felt "the maternal presence of God," right there beside her, stroking her forehead and calming her down. Later when she was very hungover, she says she decided, at thirty-one years old, to wander into a little church in one of the poorest communities in California.

"This little Presbyterian church was Spirit-infused. It was a very powerful experience to come to God. Without this church I don't think I would have survived the last few years of my drinking."

The compassion of God is a profound reality in her life.

We all need courage to be kind and compassionate, she says, adding it is so sad that we live in a world where all the people we love are going to die. That is why the compassion of a mother is such a powerful illustration of the generosity of God's love. Think about it. When Jesus was bleeding and dying on the cross, His mother did not abandon Him. She stood beside Him and comforted Him in His pain.

Who can fathom what went through her mother's heart of love as she knelt at the bottom of the cross where her beloved son was hanging? Nothing could separate Mary from Jesus—not even the terror of the Roman guards could separate her from her son. That's a mother's commitment of love! And this is a great picture of the way God loves us and forgives us every step of our amazing spiritual journey, says Lamott.

We are never left alone in our frail, fallen, foolish human condition. The ministry of the Spirit of God, as Lamott explains it, is something like a heavenly birth coach saying, *"It's okay. You're okay,"* when we go through hard times.

"God's love is profoundly maternal to me," she says. "God's love for us is like the deep love a mother has for her newborn, like the protective love a mother has for her sick three-year-old child, and like the unconditional love a mother has for her cantankerous eighteen-year-old."

Lamott, however, does not think of God in either male or female terms.

"God is much bigger than gender."

Another Side of Compassion

After my interview is over with Lamott, I ponder her comment that God's compassion is like the "unconditional love a mom has for her cantankerous teenager."

That makes me smile and takes me back a few years.

It is three a.m. one early morning when I hear a light tapping on a window which seems to be coming from downstairs. Then I hear nothing. After another half hour of listless dreams and tossing to one side and the other, I hear something like pebbles tinkling down our roof. I perk up my head and listen with both ears.

It's not the cat running down the stairs or the rabbit chasing moths in its cage. It is something else. I stumble out of bed, slink to the bedroom window, and peek over the ledge. I am not sure what I will find. For ten years I have checked all manner of strange noises of what I suspect to be bandits, prowlers, or would-be attackers, but I have never nabbed one. So I do not expect to see anyone. But what a startle!

There before my very eyes is a boy, maybe sixteen years old, wearing cutoffs and a red shirt and he's throwing rocks at my teenage daughter's bedroom window. He does not see me, and my daughter sleeps so soundly she can sleep through a hurricane.

My mind whirs in panic. *Okay, okay, what do I do, what do I do?* I'll surprise him, that's what I'll do.

Quietly, I turn around in the dark and reach for my housecoat. I plan a face-to-face encounter! Softly pitter-pattering down the stairs, I get to the bottom and grasp the doorknob of the front door as I gaze through the gold opaque glass window to see a shadowy figure of the unsuspecting teenager. As quickly as humanly possible for a woman who is half asleep and rather un-coordinated, I swing the door open so fast, I almost jerk my right shoulder out of place.

"You get in here, right now," I say to him.

The young man steps in. He is handsome and surprisingly calm. Considering he is facing a woman with two big eyeballs and a head of hair looking like an abandoned starling nest, he appears rather unruffled. He is well groomed. I am not a pretty sight.

I give him a twenty-second interrogation, not quite sure what I am supposed to say to the trespasser. It's not like I do this every night or have had any sort of practice.

What do you say to a kid who falls in love with your daughter in the berry patch?

I tell him he needs to go home.

Well, that's the last I'll see of him, I think to myself. But I am wrong.

He returns in the light of day to apologize. Why? Apparently his mother is encouraging her son to live up to a certain code of honor. Since integrity and character are in the formative stages, she wants him to live up to his potential and a high standard of ethics. If she has anything to do with it, he will mature into a man of integrity.

Mom's "tough love"—as is often the case—is simply an expression of another side to her compassion, longing to help her child develop good character.

⁂

Mercy and compassion are often misunderstood, says Leslie Chambers.

"It's interesting—I used to think that mercy meant you were overemotional or too mushy and that it would mean that someone could get away with doing anything," explains Chambers, Director of Ministry Events for Exodus International.

Life has taught her that mercy is not a sign of weakness, but strength!

Raising two children gives her and her husband numerous opportunities to see the effectiveness of mercy, and this principle guides them in their discipline decisions. Parental choices are similar to the way God deals with us, she says. When a child is doing wrong, sometimes the best way to win his or her heart is to show compassion.

"When someone shows you mercy and is extremely giving and understanding to you, it draws you to them and allows them to truly help you. When our children misbehave, do we love them any less? Of course not! Though our children may deserve punishment for what they do; it's not always going to help them. Sometimes they are too young to understand that what they're doing is wrong."

In the same way, our God of infinite compassion understands our level of maturity, our human frailties and failures, and disciplines us with perfect love.

"As God's children, we are corrected for our own good."

Notes in Indonesia

I am impressed by women of compassion who are able to resolve conflict.

And I am about to introduce myself to a world-caliber peacemaker.

Rev. Dr. Margaretha Hendriks-Ririmasse is a global Christian leader, dean of the Indonesian Christian University in Moluccas, and also a respected Bible scholar.

She lives on an island in Indonesia where harvesters are melodiously singing a cappella as they pick coconuts and cloves in the plantations. But all is not sweet and nice on the Spice Islands, as the Moluccas in Indonesia were once known.

Like the volcanoes in the Ring of Fire that created these fertile Southeast Asian islands in the first place, violence recently erupted, seemingly out of nowhere. Rioters, wild with fury, burned down the university, where Hendriks-Ririmasse was teaching theology, and they reduced the campus to ashes.

Newspapers reported that Muslim militants were forcing Christian families to accept the Islamic faith or be shot to death, beheaded, or killed by machete. Thousands of people in the province of Maluku died the cruelest of deaths, including innocent children and a pregnant woman whose baby was cut out of her womb with a machete.

Some estimated the death toll, from 1999 to 2004, to be in excess of ten thousand.

"It was terrible. Snipers were shooting people; you could hear the sounds of the bullets and the mortar exploding; and then you'd see the bodies floating in Ambon Bay," says Hendriks-Ririmasse.

The university students are meeting in temporary quarters when I interview Hendriks-Ririmasse, after I had read about the carnage and her courage. I believe she will bring a unique perspective to my exploration on the gender of God.

Her family has worshipped Jesus in peace for many generations.

She continues to attend the oldest Christian church in Southeast Asia called the Protestant Church of the Moluccas, which is located on the island of Ambon. I am amazed by her optimism about the future, despite the recent devastation in her country.

This devout woman literally battles the sword with the Word of God.

About 88 percent of the people in Indonesia are now Muslim, the largest Islamic population (180 million) in the world. This is a major change from the past when about half of the people on the islands of the Moluccas were Christian. The people of these two world faiths lived together peacefully, side by side until their idyllic islands ignited into flame and human terror when a radical Islamic group called Laskar Jihad (Warriors of Holy War) decided to convert all of Indonesia into an Islamic state. Political analysts cite religious, economic, and political reasons for the violence.[1]

With her faith on fire in the vortex of unspeakable brutality, Hendriks-Ririmasse and several other heroic women stepped forward to the front lines carrying only the flag of the impossible, a green flag for peace.

These humble Christian women initiated an interfaith "peace and reconciliation" group to come up with a nonviolent solution to stop the spilling of blood around them. With the help of female politicians, they contacted like-minded Muslim women who also wanted peace. The women started meeting together and called themselves the Caring Women's Movement in the Moluccas.

Hendriks-Ririmasse was named the coordinator for the Protestants.

The women's peace movement played an important role in ending the conflict, she says, as their tears eventually moved the hearts of the warlords.

There has been relative peace in Ambon since her university was destroyed. But sporadic outbreaks of violence continue to plague the Moluccas. Indeed, the entire country of Indonesia has been hit by natural disasters, earthquakes, and tsunamis.

"We've lost so much," she says.

The wounds of her world caught in four succinct words.

Yet Christians remain faithful to this day, and she is looking forward to the day when "we ain't going to study war no more" as proclaimed in a favorite gospel song. Walking in the footsteps of Jesus, Gandhi, and Martin Luther King, she feels God is calling his faithful people to pursue peace, justice, and equality for all.

"I think our world today needs peace, and we need to promote a culture of peace," she says. "Our biggest challenge is to live in a pluralistic society and to put down our swords and guns and to live in peace in the sisterhood and brotherhood of our different religions. Otherwise we will continue to encounter violence."

Pursuing peace is where women can shine. God has given women the gift of reconciliation and the ability to bring together warring factions to a place of understanding and peace, she says, as attested by her experience.

Yet women, themselves, need justice. They suffer discrimination around the world, being subject to political, economic, and religious oppression, and she believes it is important for men to step up to the plate to free them from oppression.

She promotes the goal of equality at her university.

"God gave women dignity because He created us to be like Him in character. God is just and loving, and He loves women for who they are. We are all children of God," she explains. "Our God of love demands no less than that we stand up for justice."

This commitment to justice relates to the question of the gender of God.

It is important to teach the public that God has a feminine side, metaphorically speaking, the scholar says. As this spiritual breakthrough becomes more well-known around the world, this truth will bring about a profound sense of dignity for half of the human race, currently marginalized.

"If you read the Bible carefully, you will see a feminine aspect of God there," Hendriks-Ririmasse explains, noting that God is basically saying in the Book of Isaiah, "*I love you* like a mother loves her children and has loved you from the womb."[2]

Why hasn't this concept been more widely taught in Christianity?

The Indonesian theologian sighs.

The problem throughout church history has been that the liturgies tended to be very masculine because the Bible was usually read through the eyes of men. But that is no longer the case, she says. Female theologians are discovering the maternal aspects of God in the Bible, which had been long forgotten in the past. And a new appreciation for these metaphors is happening in Indonesia, as it is all across the world.

I am moved by her courage, her willingness to express her Christian views, despite fears of persecution and feeling her life may be threatened. She walks a fine line. She is careful not to criticize, yet speaks the truth.

View from the Vatican

A few months later, I phone the Vatican, requesting an interview.

Father Federico Lombardi, director of the Vatican Press office, explains to me that Pope Benedict XVI has some definite opinions about the topic in question, and Pope John Paul I also gave an eye-opening sermon about the maternal side of God's love.

Lombardi and I have a frank and open discussion.

An interesting sermon—once preached by Pope John Paul I— was both "unusual and important," says Lombardi, but the world knows very little about it because it was spoken entirely in Italian.

He graciously provides me an English translation of the sermon for the purpose of our interview.

What did Pope John Paul I say?

He was speaking at Saint Peter's Square in the Vatican City on Sunday, September 10, 1978, when he prayerfully asked God to bless three politicians who were anxious, at the time, to sign a peace agreement at Camp David to stabilize the war-torn countries of the Middle East. The pope acknowledged that Egyptian President Anwar al-Sadat was a religious man and US President Jimmy Carter was a Christian. He also noted that Israeli President Menachem Begin prayed to the Lord in difficult times, recalling how the Hebrews had unfairly complained that God had supposedly "forgotten" about them when they were wandering in the wilderness for forty years.

This complaint, of course, was not the case.

God is always faithful, just as a mother never forgets the child of her womb as depicted in Isaiah 49:15, said Pope John Paul I, adding that we are all prone to suffer anxious feelings at times. But our God of compassion is with us—always!

Here is the pope's quotable statement:

"We are an object of an endless love of God. We know that He always has His eyes fixed on us, also when it seems to us, that it is at night. God is Father, even more, is mother. He does not want our evil; He only wants to make us the good to all."

The pope then asked the congregation this question: "When children are feeling sick or weak, doesn't that give their mother even more reason to love them more?"

His words were encouraging then. And they still are! While this sermon was hardly a theological discourse, his statements, nonetheless, record a historical moment when a Catholic leader used such plain language.

"This is the most famous occurrence of a pope talking about

the word 'mother' for God," Lombardi explains during our interview, adding that the prophets in the Bible also painted consoling word pictures to describe our Maker's maternal love.

In the meantime, when Pope Benedict XVI was known as Cardinal Joseph Ratzinger, he led a commission for the Catechism of the Catholic Church, which gave the following spiritual advice to believers:

> "By calling God Father, the language of faith indicates two main things; that God is the first origin of everything and transcendent authority and that He is at the same time goodness and loving care for all His children. God's parental tenderness can also be expressed by the image of motherhood (Isaiah 66:13, Psalm 131:2, and Isaiah 49:15), which emphasizes God's immanence, the intimacy between Creator and creature . . ."[3]

Pope Benedict XVI also revealed a remarkable insight in a sermon he gave to priests and pastoral assistants in Loreto, Italy, on March 7, 1988, when he was still a cardinal.

The revelations in the Bible upset everything the world had formerly thought about God, he said, as the Scriptures unveil the mystery of God's maternal mercy.

"In the Hebrew Old Testament, God's pity for men is not described in psychological terminology. Rather, corresponding to the concrete manner of Semitic thought, it has been given a title that basically is the name of a bodily organ, namely *rahamim*, which, in the singular, means 'the womb,' " he explained.

The Old Testament prophets used the analogy of the mother's womb to disclose how God's mercy gently shelters us, carries us in love, and gives us life.

"As heart stands for feeling . . . so the womb becomes the term for being with another. It is the most intense reference to the faculty of a human being to exist for another, to take him within oneself, to bear him, and in the bearing to give him life."[4]

"Being with Another"

Mercy is mentioned more than 250 times in the KJV Bible.

It is also true that mercy is at the heart of God's justice. (See Appendix 1.)

The Bible teaches us the virtue of being merciful to orphans, widows, and strangers. It is a fact that both men and women show compassion to others, but as the *Jewish Encyclopedia* states: "Women are recognized as prone to pity or mercy."[5]

The feminine heart of mercy is true on a global scale.

To illustrate, one day an Egyptian pharaoh's daughter discovers an innocent Jewish baby wailing in a basket boat floating on the Nile River. It is in her power to drown him or to deliver him. Will she follow the law of the land that gives her permission to kill the child, or will she listen to her heart and save him?

And when she had opened it [the basket], she saw the child: and, behold, the babe wept. And she had compassion on him . . .

Exodus 2:6 KJV, bracketed word added

Her heart is smitten with pity at the sound of the baby's cry.

Though the boy is obviously Hebrew, a race despised by the Egyptians, she immediately adopts the child as her own and calls him Moses. He is thereafter treated as royalty. In myriad ways more meaningful, the merciful heart of God also melts at the sound of our cry. We may plead as this man does, with head bent low:

The tax collector stood at a distance. He would not even look up to heaven, but beat his breast and said, "God, have mercy on me, a sinner."

Luke 18:13 NIV

And so God has mercy on us and treats us as royalty, especially when life is heavy and trouble hits us out of nowhere. But no place in the world is safer than when we are being carried, as it were, in God's womb of mercy. We need not feel afraid. Jesus comforts us in some of the most sublime words recorded in all of Scripture:

"It is not the healthy who need a doctor, but the sick. But go and learn what this means: 'I desire mercy, not sacrifice.' For I have not come to call the righteous, but sinners."

Matthew 9:12–13 NIV

It is the pity and the power of God to save and to heal us, not because we are good, but because we are weak, sick, and prone to sin. This is God's gift of compassion—to be one with us and to carry us into eternity. The apostle Paul writes that we exist because of the will of our Maker, and "in him we live and move and have our being." As some of the poets have said, we are God's offspring (Acts 17:28).

I think about the first time I feel my baby move inside my womb. I marvel how the warmth of my body shelters my little one from danger, threat, and injury. *"Being inside me"* is my guarantee, my seal of safety to my baby. All of my child's tomorrows are wrapped inside my today. And in some mysterious way, I *live and move and have my being,* divinely sheltered in my God's infinite heart of mercy.

David also learned to trust God in this way:

I have calmed and quieted my soul, like a weaned child
with its mother; like a weaned child is my soul within me.[6]

Psalm 131:2 ESV

The pope discloses an innovative idea when he writes: "As
heart stands for feeling . . . so the womb becomes the term for
being with another." But it makes perfect sense. When someone
is "being" with me, their presence is always practical, positive,
and powerful.

Here, in a few word pictures, is how I experience this:

*My mother hugs me when I go to the funeral home to prepare
the eulogy for my brother. My dad plants flowers in the garden
as I stand with a rake in my hand and a smile on my face. My
best friend invites me to swim in the Pacific Ocean on a blistering
hot day to be refreshed and rejuvenated. This is a taste of what
it means to "be with me." One of God's most gracious names,
the "Comforter," expresses His intimacy of always "being present"
with me, carried in the heart of Infinite Mercy!*

CHAPTER 10

"As a Hen Gathers Her Chicks"

Jesus referred to His deep compassion for us by using
the metaphor of Himself as a mother hen.
Dr. Gary Chapman, Author and Counselor

WHAT IS IT about the psychology of love that always grabs our
attention?

Dr. Gary Chapman devotes his life to helping married couples
stay in love and connected to one another. A prolific writer,
speaker, and pastor, Chapman is known for his popular book
called *The Five Love Languages*, a best seller that has sold more
than seven million copies worldwide. The book has been translated into forty different languages, such as Spanish, French,
German, Dutch, Hindi, and Arabic.

Love, acceptance, and physical touch are universal human
needs.

When I meet Chapman at the Ten Crows Studio, he looks re-
laxed in his dark green suit. He is preparing for the next segment
of the popular television show called *Marriage Uncensored with
Dave and Christie*. His background as a trained anthropologist and
social researcher helped him to discover the interesting phenom-

enon of the five love languages after many years of counseling couples.

He explains that he was studying his counseling notes when he first discovered several distinct patterns of expressing love. Testing out his theories, he received overwhelming positive response from the public when he started lecturing on the topic.

"People really get it!" he says.

How can you win someone's heart and inspire their continual devotion?

Simple! Find out their primary love language and make an effort to love them in the way they feel is most important, the author explains, noting that everyone has a primary love language, followed typically by a secondary one.

According to Chapman, there are five fundamental love languages: words of affirmation, acts of service, giving gifts, physical touch, and quality time.

Knowing how to love others is not only an effective skill for every couple to have, it also helps your children and your friends to feel loved. People feel the greatest satisfaction in life by loving others. It's pretty fundamental, Chapman says.

Does he believe God has a particular love language?

"God speaks all of the love languages fluently. God is love, and the deepest and most heartfelt need for all humans is to feel love," he says, noting some examples.

The life of Jesus was devoted to acts of service when He healed people. And He forgives with loving words of affirmation and gave us the "gift" of His life to forgive our sins. He healed lepers with the touch of His hands and sensitively taught spiritual truths by spending quality time with both children and adults.

We all respond to God in our primary love language, Chapman explains.

A person whose love language is physical touch will have a dramatic conversion when they feel the arms of God embracing them. Other people whose love language is quality time will read the Bible for some time and then give their lives to God.

Similarly, people who love gifts are convicted when they learn how God gives them the gift of salvation. In Martin Luther's case, words of affirmation transformed him as he was moved by the powerful words in Scripture that "salvation is by faith."

There is no specific love language preference in either men or women.

ℒ❧

Is it possible God may have a maternal as well as a paternal side to His love? I ask Chapman.

He gives the question considerable thought, noting how Jesus referred to His deep compassion for people by using the concept of Himself as a mother hen:

> "O Jerusalem, Jerusalem, you who kill the prophets and stone those sent to you, how often I have longed to gather your children together, as a hen gathers her chicks under her wings, but you were not willing."
>
> *Matthew 23:37 NIV*

The author cautions, however, that we should not read too much into the use of this feminine imagery because it is strictly a metaphor. When Jesus lived on Earth, He displayed some qualities of character that may be viewed as feminine, such as tenderness and empathy, but he also exhibited strong masculine qualities.

People are able to relate to both the masculine and feminine qualities of God's love, but in Chapman's opinion, the Creator is beyond any gender constraints.

"I believe that God is Spirit."

꧁꧂

A mother hen's natural maternal instinct is to protect her young. This is true of females in practically all bird species as the following factual story illustrates.

One day, ten unlucky little ducklings fall into a storm sewer near Mill Lake.

The mother duck loudly starts sounding the alarm as she patrols the manhole cover with all the skill of a savvy soldier and quacks away at potential predators. A couple of conniving crows circle above. City crews soon arrive on scene, and they listen to the sound of much peeping below the metal grates as ten tiny, fuzzy ducklings huddle together in a ball of feathers, floating on the storm water.

"I've pulled a lot of things out of sewers—but never one of these," says the city worker as he gently pulls out each of the little ducklings, who then waddle in unison to make a straight B-line for their mother hovering several feet away.[1]

Isn't that the way of God?

Almost before we utter the words *Dear God, please help me*, He rescues us as eagerly and tenderly as a mother hen responds to the fearful peeping cries of her young and gathers them into the shelter of her wings. The story about the ten ducklings caused many people in my city to smile, but another story, this one ending in tragedy, also reminds me of the biblical analogy.

The Fire and the Sacrifice

It is a cold, blustery winter morning when it sounds like a bomb is exploding at a local farmhouse. As firefighters race their fire-engines to the farm to save a large two-story house, they arrive to find it fully engulfed in flames.

The roof is blown off the top of the house. Clouds of smoke

swirl ominously out the windows as the vinyl siding melts away from the black plywood underneath, like butter slips off charred toast.

In the middle of the frightening mayhem, a little girl is blindly running through the smoke in the house—scared out of her mind! Her grandmother grabs her, tightly clutches her sweet little cherub, completely surrounding her body with her own body as a human shield to try to protect her from the flames.

Meanwhile, it is a crazy war zone outside.

Family members are yelling and screaming and jumping from the windows, just barely escaping the fire. Inside, the inferno churns out still more clouds of choking acrid smoke. It seems like forever before water starts pouring into the walls.

Sometime later, firefighters find the deceased grandmother crouched down in the hallway, completely enveloping her granddaughter's body with her own. The look on her face is unforgettable—almost peaceful. And the little girl still looks like a little princess, her skin and hair still beautiful.

Both died of smoke inhalation.

While the inferno raged around her, the last thing the frightened little girl felt in her life was the comfort of her kindhearted grandmother's arms of love.

"They were huddled together. Grandma was on top of her and had extensive burns on her back. The little girl basically had no burns on her. . . . She must have loved her so, so much. . . . ," said a man who was privy to this moving scene in the house.

When Jesus said He longs to gather His people around him like a "hen gathers her chicks under her wings," He used a powerful feminine analogy to illustrate His deep yearning to protect us. And He certainly paid the ultimate price by sacrificing His life on the cross to offer salvation to all—to cover us, save us, and rescue us from sin.

I find the New Testament in perfect orchestration with the Old Testament.

The Old is the spiritual bedrock for the New. These two holy books are not separate entities, but a continuum of the powerful truths inspired by the Spirit of God. In my mind, there is no contradiction, but only a continual confirmation of ancient truths, relevant for today. I believe we owe much to our spiritual forefathers, the faithful scribes and scholars of the Jewish faith.

·

Studying the Good Book in Jerusalem

Dr. Yair Zakovitch teaches courses on the Bible at the Hebrew University of Jerusalem in Israel with his trademark quick wit and charm.

The happy-go-lucky professor recently shot to public fame as coauthor of a book that stayed on the best-seller list in Israel for more than thirty weeks called *That's Not What the Good Book Says*. A leading scholar in the literary analysis of the Bible, Zakovitch is the former Dean of the Faculty of Humanities at the Hebrew University. He is also the past chairman of the Mandel Institute of Jewish Studies where he is currently teaching.

He tells me that he "enjoys stretching the minds" of his students, and the scholar enthusiastically tackles my questions about the possible matriarchal side of God's love.

First of all, the professor explains, it is important to note that the ancient Israelites did not worship male or female gods as the people in the surrounding polytheistic cultures and religions. The Israelites worshipped the one true living God.

The language they preferred to use for God was mostly masculine. But feminine terminology, although uncommon, was also used.

Would you say, then, that there is a feminine element to God's love? I ask.

"I can go with that," Zakovitch replies, noting how the patriarch Moses describes the love of God in the following powerful feminine metaphor:

> *Like an eagle that stirs up her nest,*
> *hovers over her young,*
> *spreads out her wings, takes them*
> *and carries them as she flies.*
>
> *ADONAI alone led his people;*
> *no alien god was with him.*
> *He made them ride on the heights of the earth.*
> *They ate the produce of the fields.*
> *He had them suck honey from the rocks*
> *and olive oil from the crags.*
> Deuteronomy 32:11–13 CJB

The language in this analogy is uplifting and gracious.

The compassion of God is like a doting mother eagle that hovers over her young, spreads her wings and bears her fragile, fearful eaglets on her wings as she flies above the heights of the earth and swoops along with them on the air currents.

Scientists report that a mother eagle incubates her eggs and hunts for food to feed her little eaglets. She bears her young on her wings when they fearfully leave the nest and hovers nearby to rescue them when they become too tired to fly alone. This is a heartwarming analogy of the way God supports believers who are weak and gently nudges them to spiritual maturity.

Something unfortunate, however, happens to the "mother" eagle in some biblical translations, which depict the eagle as *"it"* and in some cases even as *"he."* The Complete Jewish Bible—like the King James Version—retains the original feminine pronoun.

In the original Hebrew language, these texts also show how God nourishes His people in a distinctly maternal fashion, Zakovitch explains. In this passage, the young suck honey and olive oil from the rocks and crags for nourishment, which is the same notion in the Hebrew language as a child nursing.

Other Scriptures also denote the maternal elements of God's love, said the professor, quoting Isaiah 49, when God called Isaiah to be a prophet and a servant before he was born. The Creator named him while he was yet in his mother's womb.

"Like a tenderhearted mother, God never forgets us," says the scholar.

The Holy Scriptures are clear that God comforts us as a mother encircles her children with compassion. Believers should allow these profound promises to sink deeply into their hearts and to rest fully in the love of God, he says.

The Israeli scholar provides other biblical passages to ponder.

When God spoke to King David in Psalm 2:7, many English translators assert that God had "begotten" or "fathered" David. But this is not an accurate translation, according to Zakovitch. In the original Hebrew language, the Creator God actually said to David that *"I gave birth to you"* which is a maternal attribute.

The professor is comfortable with the beautiful truth presented in the first chapter of Genesis that both males and females are made in the image of God.

That's what the Good Book says!

The Dove

When I decide to stay at my Aunt Bep's house in Holland, I sleep upstairs in her loft, which gives me a panoramic view over the deep blue skyline.

In the morning I wake to the sound of a dove cooing to me in her swaying "woo—woo—woooo" as she rests on a branch overlooking my aunt's garden.

I enjoy looking out the window to admire the resident dove in her incandescent colors of blue, gray, and mauve. Her presence exudes a comforting ambience for me until she decides to fly away at a speed of up to forty-five miles an hour.

Doves are irresistible, gently cheering us with beauty and song.

Is it any wonder that this lovely bird is often seen as a messenger of healing and happiness in the Scriptures or that the Spirit of God is depicted as a gentle dove? I turn to the Holy Word once more to find out how the cosmos was created out of chaos:

> The earth was without form, and void; and darkness was on the face of the deep. And the Spirit of God was hovering over the face of the waters.
>
> *Genesis 1:2* NKJV

Rabbi Laura Duhan Kaplan explains to me that the "hovering" activity of the Spirit is a vibrating energy. In the Torah, this word is the feminine form of the verb.

"The Hebrew word for hovering or *mirachefet* is the same word used to describe a mother bird hovering over her nest. This is very much a motherly image," she says.

Oxford scholar Sebastian Brock explains that this term is also grammatically feminine in the Peshitta (the Syriac Bible), noting the Spirit was "hovering" (*mrahhefa*) over the surface of the waters. The verb (*rahhef*) also describes a mother eagle gently hovering over her chicks (see Deut. 32:11). In addition, the Arab people use this verb to describe a mother soothing her child. Some Bible versions denote the Spirit "brooding" over the earth at creation like a mother bird broods over her nest.

A dove is typically the bearer of great blessings.

After the worldwide flood devastated the antediluvian world, a female dove gave Noah an olive branch to assure him that the danger was past and it was safe for him and his family to come out of the ark.

Then the dove came to him in the evening, and behold, a freshly plucked olive leaf was in her mouth; and Noah knew that the waters had receded from the earth.

Genesis 8:11 NKJV

The dove and the olive oil represent the Holy Spirit as our *Custodian, Guardian,* and *Deliverer.* When the Spirit overshadowed Mary, the mother of Jesus (see Luke 1:35), this was similar to the way the Spirit of God "hovered" over creation.

It is noteworthy the Spirit, in the form of a dove, also rested on Jesus at the very moment of His baptism when a voice from heaven stated: "This is My beloved Son, in whom I am well pleased" (Matt. 3:17 NASB).

Is it a mere coincidence that the Holy Spirit's activities in the Scriptures are sometimes portrayed in the protective hovering motions of a female bird?

The Eagle

It is mid-May, and I am enjoying a welcome "holiday" at home.

I'm excited to see the endangered Pacific waterleaf plants "blooming" all over my hillside. When I say "blooming," it is a bit of an inside joke. These strange-looking wildflowers develop no dainty blossom. Instead they grow these unique "bizarre" soft balls of greenish-purple, fuzzy-wuzzy "cat-like" whiskers.

They always bloom at the same time as the bumblebees wake up from their winter hibernation and begin to forage along the wooded trails in my backyard. I find it immensely entertaining when the hillside comes alive with thousands upon thousands of soft fuzzy balls forming a thick green carpet on the forest floor, surrounded by the symphony of bustling bumblebees, like energetic little buzzing trumpets.

This morning I am lost in thought, walking up the pathway as the bumbles accompany me in surround sound. It is a wonderful symbiotic relationship the fuzzy flowers and the buzzing bees enjoy together—dependent on the other for survival.

Suddenly, I am shocked as a majestic bald eagle swoops about twenty feet in front of me in all of her glory. She dodges around the cottonwoods and just barely misses the dozens of maple trees in the forest. Rushing over me is not only the blush of shock, but I bask in the wind of her wings sweeping across my face.

Is she crazy, taking such risks?

I have seen many an eagle sailing on the currents high above in the sky. But this is a first. What in the world is she doing flying so low in my densely overgrown forest?

I wonder if a young eaglet has fallen out of its nest and landed in the underbrush of stinging nettles on the east side of the hillside. Stinging nettles are my scourge.

When I can't stand them any longer, I put on my leather gloves and go on a rampage to pull out as many as I can. The strapping stingers can grow up to seven feet tall. Crazy things! I also find myself, at times, falling into the stinging nettles of sin and then feel remorseful, fearful, and fragile. The analogy of God caring for me as a mother eagle teaches me to trust my Deliverer who is always nearby to lift me when I fall.

CHAPTER 11

A Baker, a Midwife, and More

> Jesus spoke all these things to the crowd in parables;
> he did not say anything to them without using a para-
> ble. So was fulfilled what was spoken through the
> prophet: "I will open my mouth in parables, I will
> utter things hidden since the creation of the world."
>
> *Matthew 13:34–35* NIV

WE ALL COME to the stories in the Holy Bible with our own personal stories.

When I first read about the untimely death of Martha's
brother, Lazarus, a flood of emotions transports me back to the
side of an ER hospital bed with my heart breaking into pieces. I
stare in unbelief at Louie, my twenty-one-year-old brother.

He is barely hanging on to life.

The young man in the bed doesn't even look like Louie. His
black hair is stuck to his forehead, and the natural olive tone of
his face now reflects the eerie purple and yellow shadowing of
multiple bumps and bruises.

The room smells of nausea and antiseptic ointment. The ven-
tilation machine gasps in and out, filling his lungs then emptying
them of oxygen as my eyes question the lines and graphs on the
EEG. I desperately search for brain-wave activity. I hold his cold
hands and speak into his vacant brown eyes that open and close
at random.

"Louie? Louie. Hey, buddy, how're you doing?"

I sigh. "I love you, Louie."

With my tears flowing over his pajamas, I gently touch his arms, caress his skin, pray and agonize with God to please help him live. I beg for Louie's gentle voice to speak to me, even if he would just give me a groan. I plead for my little brother to give me a clue that he is conscious, that his brain is okay, maybe even give me a weak smile.

"Please, Louie, please tell me you can hear me—I just want you to be okay."

But no movement—nothing!

In the past, we had shared many quiet conversations together. He spoke with a slight lisp and often gave me a hug with a tight embrace. I slump down crying on the white bedsheets, cradling his hands in mine. Those soft beautiful artistic hands! He once built a miniature wooden boat intricately designed with white linen sails and beige pine moorings.

Will his ship ever touch water again?

His life hung between life and death for a little more than a day or so and then, unceremoniously and unalterably, he was gone, another drunk-driving statistic. I cannot describe the grief of losing my little brother.

When he died, my life closed in on me like the cold, wooden casket that held him. Only God's precious promise of eternity assures me of the blessed resurrection reunion morning when I hope to hug Louie once more.

Many years later, when I interview Dr. Elisabeth Moltmann-Wendel, a leading European scholar, she begins our dialogue by sharing a profound life-and-death story about a sister who also lost her brother to the terror of the tomb.

I often nod in agreement during our conversation.

The theologian, who lives in Germany, is the author of inspirational books, such as *A Land Flowing with Milk and Honey* and *As a Woman and Man of God Talking*. In 1997, she was honored with the Herbert Haag Award for Freedom in the Church.

She tells me that it took the untimely death of Lazarus to drive his sister, Martha, a hardworking capable Jewish woman, to her knees. But after her amazing encounter with Jesus, she became a bold, powerful preacher—second to none.

"Martha put it very clearly in her confession that Jesus is the Son of God, and her story holds an important clue," says the scholar, "about the worth of a woman in the eyes of God."

Martha Is First to Profess Jesus as Lord

Martha's brother, Lazarus, is dying and then he slips into heart-searing silence.

She desperately seeks the healing touch of Jesus. But He arrives too late. In fact, four days too late! When Lazarus is buried, Martha is overwhelmed by anger, sorrow, and despair. When she sees the Lord Jesus walk toward her, her faith causes her to take action.

"Lord, you can ask whatever you want from God, and God will give it to you," she says to him. Such hope! Such courage! Such a daring statement! She has faith because Jesus makes blind men see. He makes the skin of lepers healthy again. He can raise the dead to life. Can't He?

"Your brother is going to rise again," Jesus tells her.

"Yes, yes, of course," Martha replies somewhat impatiently, figuring He is talking about some far-off future fanfare at the end of time, when trumpets call the dead to rise from death.

"I know Lazarus will rise at the resurrection on the last day," she says.

Jesus looks at her. "No Martha, this is big stuff—listen carefully. Lazarus, your brother, is going to rise again—today!"

What did I just hear? Martha is puzzled as Jesus now has her full attention.

"I am the resurrection and the life; he who believes in me, though he die, yet shall he live, and whoever lives and believes in me shall never die," He says kindly to her.

She is speechless for a moment.

"Do you believe this?" Jesus asks. "Do you have faith, Martha, that I am the author of all life? Do you believe?"

His question is one of the most profound spiritual questions of all time.

Martha now gazes at Him in complete faith. *"Yes, Lord; I believe that you are the Christ, the Son of God, He who is coming into the world."*[1]

This bold statement (in John 11) is an astounding confession of faith. In fact, Martha is the first to profess Jesus as the Son of God after He had started His public ministry, when His closest disciples had not yet figured out who He was—not even Peter or John, says Moltmann-Wendel.

Jesus not only raised Martha's brother from the dead that day, He did something even more significant. He treated her with as much respect as a male apostle. This is a great story, this conversation between Martha and Jesus, because He inspired a woman to make a powerful liberating statement—one of the most important in the Bible.

Good for Martha.

She got it right.

Jesus is *the Son of God*—the source of all life.

The Gospel according to Bread

The Bible is full of blockbuster short stories.

"The New Testament contains many lively stories about

women which promote new and original ideas to the world about the value of women," says the scholar.

Moltmann-Wendel notes that Jesus was not afraid to use maternal metaphors to describe the Father's heart. In fact, He shook up the religious world when He described His nurturing patience not only as a man sowing seed, but a woman baking bread!

Is there anything more welcoming than walking into the kitchen where your mom is baking bread and the mouthwatering aroma fills the air?

The heart of Infinite Love draws us ever so sweetly. Interestingly, just before Jesus shares the analogy of the "baker woman," He heals a disabled woman who had been unable to straighten her back for eighteen long, pain-grinding years. In this healing, I like to think He also straightened out the debilitation of sexism. As He places His loving hands upon the woman, Jesus blesses her and tells her that she is free.

Suddenly the bent-over cripple stands straight and tall!

The healing should have caused the religious leaders to rejoice, but instead they criticize Him for healing on the Sabbath. But the rest of the people cheer on the Prince of Peace as He joyfully gives us a new way to view the Kingdom. Just as He healed the woman stooped over in pain, He helps every man and woman to walk tall.

> "What is the kingdom of God like? And to what shall I compare it? It is like a grain of mustard seed which a man took and sowed in his garden; and it grew and became a tree, and the birds of the air made nests in its branches." And again he said, "To what shall I compare the kingdom of God? It is like leaven which a woman took and hid in three measures of flour, till it was all leavened."
>
> *Luke 13:18–21 RSV (See also Matthew 13:31–33)*

Does anything appear to have less potential in life than a small, hard seed or a tasteless mound of bread dough?

So unbecoming both!

The masculine side of God's grace is revealed in the male gardener who patiently plants a little brown seed in the soil and cares for it until it grows into a tall tree. The homemaker, likewise, with feminine finesse forms ancient grains into bread.

With painstaking patience, the energizing power of the Creator pulses through the little seed, pressing it up through the soil to reach the sunlight, just as the leaven of the Spirit of heaven transforms listless dough into pure, life-giving bread. Without the addition of leaven, the bread is flat, unappealing, and lifeless, but the yeast generates the transforming power to make it mysteriously rise, as Christ says:

> "I am the living bread which came down from heaven; if any one eats of this bread, he will live forever . . ."
>
> *John 6:51* RSV

Though I am fallen, foolish, and fragile, the Spirit of the living God invites me to partake of the *Bread of Life* and then to rise from the table, nourished, energized, and spiritually satisfied, knowing I am loved and transformed by Christ.

This parable unlocks one of the best-kept secrets about the kingdom of God!

The message is simple, yet so practical.

Though I am spiritually dead inside, the sanctifying Spirit of Christ infuses the light of the Kingdom into my former godless, joyless life. It is my privilege to pray to my precious Redeemer for daily bread each morning not only to sustain my physical body, but to nourish my soul for the needs of the day.

The parable of the gardener and the homemaker are equal in merit.

God is the *Holy One* who gives us life and helps us grow.

A Midwife to the Rescue

The parable of the homemaker baking bread creates a heart-warming portrait of the love of God. Another is the gracious midwife featured in the Old Testament.

Midwives have been helping families ever since time immemorial.

About 597 BC,[2] the Babylonian military forces started to besiege Jerusalem and abducted, as one of their prime captives, Ezekiel, a young man in his midtwenties, the son of a Jewish priest. In this terrible time of terror and treason, God calls Ezekiel to be a prophet and unveils the mystery of His maternal love in the following story.

One day a midwife discovers a squalling newborn baby girl covered in filth and grime, abandoned in a farmer's field. She is filled with pity for the crying child:

> On the day you were born your cord was not cut, nor were you washed with water to make you clean, nor were you rubbed with salt or wrapped in cloths. No one looked on you with pity or had compassion enough to do any of these things for you. Rather, you were thrown out into the open field, for on the day you were born you were despised.
>
> *Ezekiel 16:4–5* NIV

Have sadder words ever been written?

On the day you were born, you were despised. . . .

Upon the sorriest of scenes imaginable, the merciful midwife comes to the rescue, picks up the crying baby girl, cradles her in her arms, and whispers words of comfort as she gently cuts her umbilical cord and wipes away the blood.

How tenderly the baby is adored and adopted as the midwife's very own!

"I made you grow like a plant of the field. You grew up and developed and became the most beautiful of jewels . . . and you became mine," the midwife says (Ezek. 16:7–8 NIV), hugging the child with a devotion unequalled by any other.

Lavished with gifts, the girl is bestowed with the finest food of the land, the sweetest honey and the richest olive oil. She is attired in the fanciest clothes.

> I clothed you with an embroidered dress and put leather sandals on you. I dressed you in fine linen and covered you with costly garments. I adorned you with jewelry: I put bracelets on your arms and a necklace around your neck, and I put a ring on your nose, earrings on your ears and a beautiful crown on your head. So you were adorned with gold and silver; your clothes were of fine linen and costly fabric and embroidered cloth.
>
> *Ezekiel 16:10–13* NIV

Tenderly describing the beloved daughter as *"the most beautiful of jewels,"* the midwife exalts the girl's loveliness with all the pride of a doting parent: "Your fame spread among the nations on account of your beauty, because the splendor I had given you made your beauty perfect, declares the Sovereign LORD" (Ezek. 16:14 NIV).

The Lord is doing it all—freely bestowing upon the daughter the blessing of majestic splendor, making the girl's beauty absolutely perfect. The child, once despised and detestable, is now a glorious princess! Yet, despite all of this heaven-borne attention, the adopted daughter turns her back on the *Holy One* who had so lovingly rescued and loved her. Becoming proud, snooty, and arrogant, the young woman is beguiled by the dizzying dalliance she sees in the mirror—the beauty that God, in fact, had given to her in the first place.

As many of us are inclined to do, she forgot where she had come from.

The cherished daughter then does what is shocking.

She works the streets as a prostitute and breaks the heart of her adoptive midwife as she sinks deeper and deeper into the depravity of sin, evil, and perversion.

The ending of the story is short.

Succinct!

Stunning!

Despite the daughter's abuse and betrayal, the midwife signs a covenant of salvation and forgives her sins in an amazing display of divine compassion!

Who is this merciful midwife?

Who is this supreme being of infinite love?

The prophet Ezekiel makes it obvious the allegory can only be about God.

Matthew Henry in his complete commentary writes that Ezekiel's metaphor about the midwife is full of warnings about God's coming judgment, yet Divine mercy is remembered and reserved for the return of the penitent.

"Every generation of believers finds within the Bible something relevant for them," explains Dr. Yair Zakovitch, a Jewish scholar. He also notes two other texts in the Old Testament that compare God's compassion to a midwife.

But you are the one who took me from the womb;
you made me trust when I was on my mother's breasts.
Since my birth I've been thrown on you;
you are my God from my mother's womb.
                                        Psalm 22:9–10 CJB

"Would I let the baby break through
and not be born?" asks ADONAI.

"Would I, who cause the birth,
shut the womb?" asks your God.
                    Isaiah 66:9 CJB

"Deliver Us from Evil"

There are many different ways to look at a "delivery."

Bill's a truck driver and delivers all kinds of interesting items. Once he had a load of thousands of round, black, steel mining balls rolling around on his flat deck. When he delivered those noisy steel balls—all fifteen thousand of them crashing to-gether—I noticed how proud he looked for having come through on time for the mine owners.

One of the weirdest materials he transports in a tanker is a super-stinky, man-made feed supplement for chickens and cattle. It smells gross. But he loads it. No complaints, no matter how bad it smells. Bill delivers the feed as he promises to do.

Truckers deliver loads. Women deliver babies.

One of the most exciting births that I witness, in a supportive labor role, is my grandchild Amie. I pray for her mom and hold her hand. I cry. I laugh. I make a fool of myself. I hold the baby. I stare. I fall in love right there on the spot. All that pain, all that anguish her mom went through and now this beautiful child is in my arms.

So I ask myself: Did Amie give her mother specific directions on how to do the delivery? Or was it the mother's labor alone that delivered the child?

I think about my tendency to sin, sometimes forgetting there is, in fact, an unseen Deliverer directing this little drama called "my life" with plans to deliver me from evil. Babies don't decide the day they're born. That is in the hands of someone greater.

I cannot say it is due to any noble motive that I open the Bible for the first time in my life when I am twenty years old. No, not at all! In fact, all I want to do is keep my pantry well-stocked with good white wine and fire-water rum and Coke.

All I plan to do is win a heated argument I am having with someone about religion. That is why I start to search the words in the large black leather book that is buried at the bottom of my bookcase. I intend to dig for facts, win the argument, and maintain my free-spirited lifestyle without complication or change.

I tell no one I am reading the Holy Bible.

I have no idea there is hidden in these sacred words a mysterious leavening agent. A year later, I am sobbing on my knees on my living room floor, giving my life to Christ. I lose the religious argument that prompted me to read the Scriptures in the first place. But a spiritual war is won. Or as Ezekiel puts it, this filth-covered, unwashed daughter becomes a child of the *Holy One*. And my Deliverer says those celebratory words: *You became mine!* Thankfully, the mercy of God continues to melt my heart into sorrow for sin, and I pray I will never forget where I came from.

The Lost Coin

I look forward to my interview with Viviane Haenni, a European scholar.

She listens to the voice of God as she heads to the mountains to pray as the Sabbath is about to begin. Surrounded by the majestic hills girding the historic city of Geneva, Switzerland, she prays for spiritual revival.

Haenni is planning to open the first Life Purpose Coaching Centers International® in France and French-speaking Switzerland. Her goal is to help women discover God's mission for their lives. She is excited about this new adventure.

Where the Spirit of God leads, she goes!

The theologian is a gifted Seventh-day Adventist scholar, and she is now working as a life coach for LPCCI®, a ministry founded by Katie Brazelton, a former leader in Saddleback Church, one of the largest nondenominational churches in the US.

Haenni is pursuing a journey that appears to me to be rather unique.

"Spiritual life is not about following religious traditions," she says, "but about following God with all of your heart, soul, mind, and strength."

What does this actually mean to you? I ask the gracious theologian.

God is holy and unlike us, she replies, yet our Creator also unveils His wondrous compassion in both feminine and masculine metaphors.

"If you have eyes to see—you will see!" Haenni says, noting how Jesus uses the powerful parable of a woman searching for her lost coin to illustrate the Father's love.

> "Suppose a woman has ten silver coins and loses one. Does she not light a lamp, sweep the house and search carefully until she finds it? And when she finds it, she calls her friends and neighbors together and says, 'Rejoice with me; I have found my lost coin.' In the same way, I tell you, there is rejoicing in the presence of the angels of God over one sinner who repents."
>
> *Luke 15:8–10 NIV*

When the woman suddenly discovers her priceless treasure missing, she must have felt just as anxious as I do when I misplace my credit cards or a wallet full of cash. Driven by the goal that is at the top of her agenda, the homemaker in the parable is determined to find her precious lost coin if it's the last thing she does.

She lights a lamp, sweeps her house, and diligently searches!

The homemaker is putting in all the effort, just like God does in His rescue mission. The coin has no clue of its lost condition. And when the homemaker finds her precious coin, she throws a party and invites the neighbors to celebrate.

Her excitement is over the roof, so to speak.

Similarly, the God of all grace searches for me when I have fallen offtrack and is completely focused on returning me to safe-keeping, driven by a relentless love to restore me to the place of solace and safety in the bosom of the Savior.

Jesus openly places this parable about the woman searching for her lost coin in the middle of His sermon about the Good Shepherd and the father of the prodigal son.

"We have no problem seeing God as a shepherd and a father, but somehow we don't see God as a woman searching for her lost coin," Haenni says.

"Why is that? This is a beautiful Bible story!"

✌

Elisabeth Moltmann-Wendel also teaches the public to view the metaphor about the woman and her lost coin as powerful evidence of the maternal side of God's grace.

"Women need to relate to God just as we are—as women with dignity."

The mercy of God is also exquisitely depicted in the metaphor of the nursing mother in Isaiah 66. Listen to the aching question whispered by God in these sacred passages: "*Do I close up the womb when I bring to delivery?*" (Isa. 66:9 NIV).

As infants, we may nurse in the solace of Jerusalem's consolations and "drink deeply" of the overflowing riches God freely provides to us (see Isa. 66:11). And then the *God of all Comfort* says the most intimate, softest words ever spoken to humanity:

"As a mother comforts her child, so will I comfort you . . ."

Isaiah 66:13 NIV

How tenderly our Provider consoles us.

Some may have difficulty accepting this divine maternal imagery. But we need to open our minds and overcome our prejudices. The Godhead includes feminine and masculine features, and, of course, qualities that are totally beyond human understanding, Haenni says as she concludes our interview.

"For me, there must be a total balance in the Godhead."

Love That Kisses and Scolds

What is love?

One day I find myself making a tadpole garden, an amphibian observation pool, complete with rocks, grass, and water and all things natural for my granddaughter Amie and her best friend Janelle. As I get my fingers all mucked up and dirty, transporting buckets of rich brown soil to our mini-froggie fantasy world, I hear Amie singing: "This is the best day of my life. This is the best day of my life."

I feel the same way. This is a super great day!

We are all excited about the tadpoles.

But suddenly the horizon darkens, hail falls from the sky, and the children run for shelter into the house. But I, the invincible frog lady, on the other hand, am in far too much bliss to run for cover! I am in the middle of designing a magical green world for my beautiful eight-year-old granddaughter.

Nothing can stop me now.

When the sound of the smoke alarm shrills into my ears, it quickly ends my serenity as I run into the house as fast as I can to find the rooms filled with gray smoke so dense I can hardly breathe.

Choking, coughing, and frantic with fear, all I want to do is find Amie and Janelle and make sure they are safe. *Where in the world are they?*

"Amie! Janelle! Are you okay? Are you okay? Where are you?" I yell.

It turns out Amie had put a half cup of dry cocoa into the microwave oven, hit the high button, and ran upstairs. The cocoa exploded and caught fire. And the kids were nowhere to be seen or heard as I run around the house full of smoke.

I yell very loudly at that moment.

It turns out they are upstairs, innocently wondering what had happened.

I am later reminded of a comment Pearl S. Buck once wrote: "Some are kissing mothers and some are scolding mothers, but it is love just the same and most mothers kiss and scold together."[3]

When cocoa explodes into flame, Grandmas do the same.

"Amie, please answer me right away the next time I call your name," I say with no small amount of exasperation as I kiss her on both cheeks.

"Yes, Grandma. Sorry, Gram."

Later that evening, she and Janelle make me a little handmade card with a funny looking little green frog, perfectly colored with Crayola crayons.

The frog is smiling at me.

"Amie, you're incredible, you know that? Listen, sweetie, I was very scared that you might have been hurt when I saw all that smoke! I didn't know if you were okay. That's why I yelled. You know I love you! You know I don't want you to get hurt."

I smile as I hug her. "Is this still the best day of your life?"

She gives me a big bear hug right on the spot, holding me ever so tightly. When she squeezes me really, really tightly, I like to make it a game and pretend that she's so super strong I cannot breathe. So I cannot breathe this particular moment.

"Gram, the frogs are going to be awesome. . . ."

The Fogbow

Tadpoles grow into frogs. They never go back in time to being eggs.

Children grow into college students; never go back to coloring frogs.

Life is a series of irretrievable, unrepeatable moments.

I think back to the day my mother brought little Johnnie home. I was thirteen years old when I walked over to his crib and quietly stared in amazement. I could not believe this cute little eleven-month-old cherub, dressed in a bright red fleece sleeper, had been abandoned by his own mother. She didn't want him. But my mom and dad did, and they were soon in the process of adopting him. As I stood by his crib, I assured him he would be safe, that we would take good care of him.

"Sweet Johnnie, you're my little bro' now. Don't worry, we'll always love you!"

Knowing God's mercy is like a kindhearted midwife who adopts an abandoned child, and all of the other comforting maternal metaphors in the Scriptures—to my mind, these are among the greatest of spiritual ideas, a sort of *grand finale in theology*.

Pope John Paul II in "Evangelium Vitae" once wrote that the gospel of life "has a profound and persuasive echo in the heart of every person—believer and nonbeliever alike—because it marvelously fulfills all the heart's expectations while infinitely surpassing them."[4]

Isn't that the truth!

It is now a cold damp November afternoon. The fog is thick as I bundle myself into coat, scarf, and mittens. My legs are rather stiff and unyielding as I get on my mountain bike and pedal along Clayburn Road on my way to the Fraser River.

I'm certainly not getting any younger, I groan to myself.

I zip past Monique and Frank's farm where the cows are grazing in the grass and one wise goat likes to jump the fence and lead his two bearded friends to greener pastures. My sorry limbs bump and grate across the unruly railway tracks at the corner of Riverside Road as I casually cycle past the blueberry fields. I breathe deeply the vaporous frost hanging in the air, sweet and fragrant.

Turning my handlebars to the left, I pedal past the harvested cornfields. I hear the trumpeter swans bugling to one another as they graze for the yummy corn leftovers in the fields. I cannot see them. I simply hear them chatting together in the heavy white mist. Evocative! Haunting! And sonorously so sassy!

I am thrilled by their arrival each fall. The trumpeters are the largest waterfowl in North America, yet these pure white lilies of the wind fly so gracefully, migrating more than one thousand miles all the way from Alaska to spend their winters here.

My eyelashes are wet with dew.

Then I see something in the fog I have never seen before. I wonder if I am seeing some kind of a mirage. I blink. I blink again. I stop and get off my bike.

I stand there and stare. There are weird things hanging in the air!

What in the world? I see beautiful arcs of pure, bright white light. They look like *white-fog rainbows*. The only words that come to my mind to describe them are *pure white rainbows* suspended in midair. Mystical, ethereal bows of glistening mist! Never in my wildest imagination could I have ever dreamed up such pure beauty!

When I arrive home, my research reveals I have seen the rare "fogbow."

These mystical arcs of white, in some ways, represent to me this great gospel of life about God's amazing maternal mercy, a truth migrating across the global landscape in all the mainstream faiths, from Jerusalem to Rome, from Geneva to Atlanta.

What is the implication of this for people of faith?

First, it opens a pathway for both men and women to develop a deeper, more meaningful relationship with the Creator. Second, this has the potential to make a positive global impact by vastly improving the way women feel about themselves.

Rev. Margaretha Hendriks-Ririmasse, for one, advises leaders to start teaching people that the love of God has a maternal side, metaphorically speaking.

And when this spiritual breakthrough becomes more well known around the world, she says, this has the amazing potential to bring about "a profound sense of dignity for half of the human race, currently marginalized."

That is a lot of people!

PART THREE

The Role of the Holy Spirit

CHAPTER 12

Elizabeth and Mary

I have seen my wife give birth to three children, and
I can tell you that there is nothing weak about a
woman.

Dr. James Shelton, Oral Roberts University

MOTHERS ARE DIFFERENT from fathers. They tend to have softer
hearts. In many ways, moms are *"Exhibit A"* for the heart of
God, while dads represent His strength.

Men may go to war conquering nations and planning grand
projects like the Great Wall of China, hydroelectric dams, and
space explorations. But it is a humble mother who gives birth to
new life—a Michelangelo, a Mozart, and a Marie Curie.

Mothers are their son's and daughter's proudest and loudest
cheering section.

Hannah prayed for a child and gave birth to Samuel who became a great prophet. Eunice taught her son Timothy to be a
faithful servant of God, and he grew up to be a powerful leader
and wrote two of the epistles in the New Testament. Rachel and
Sarah are among the women of the Old Testament who quietly
shed tears and pleaded and prayed for God's favor to bless their
children.

Since the Holy Spirit blesses babies even while they are unborn in their mother's womb, Dr. James Shelton believes the
womb of a woman is a most sacred place.

"Holy women are the temple of the Holy Spirit, and they are
cherished in the eyes of God," explains Shelton.

"Anyone who says that women are not created in the image
of God is not facing the facts," says Shelton, the author of such
books as *Mighty in Word and Deed: The Role of the Holy Spirit in
Luke–Acts*. He is professor of New Testament and Early Christian
Literature at Oral Roberts University in Tulsa, Oklahoma, and
he is also Senior Fellow at the St. Paul Center for Biblical Theology.

Shelton explains that Luke, the Gospel writer, gives greater in-
tricate details about the pregnancies of Elizabeth and Mary than
any of the other authors in the Bible.

The wondrous display of God's power in the lives of both the
mother and her unborn child makes a serious statement about
the sacredness of human life right from the day of conception,
Shelton says.

Jesus gave women and children "a voice" as people who
should be listened to and respected. He startled the religious culture of His day when women were not even considered good
enough to be witnesses in a court of law, says Shelton.

He gives my question about the possible gender of God some
deep thought.

The professor notes that the Holy Spirit exhibits comforting,
protective behavior which may be understood as feminine. However, that would be too narrow a definition of femininity, since
men also protect and comfort their children.

One must not get too hung up on stereotypical gender
roles, he says, because each person exhibits both feminine and
masculine features. Though men are generally regarded as the
stronger gender, women exhibit great strength in their own
right.

"I have seen my wife give birth to three children, and I can tell you that there is nothing weak about a woman."

𝒵

I turn again to some of my favorite stories in the New Testament.

Luke is a Greek doctor with an observant eye, a listening ear, and a passion for writing. He is awestruck by the power of mothers to deliver babies. They inspire him and make him smile, and his writing shows it.

We don't know his last name, but he writes one of the most gripping human-interest stories of all time, giving a preview of the birth of two boys who will change the world. The other three Gospel writers focus on the well-known events leading up to the birth of John the Baptist and Jesus, the angels and the shepherds—you know the story—but Luke does not stop there. He takes us on another journey.

The physician is fascinated by the grand entrance of the Holy Spirit who gives a life-altering visit to two humble women, Mary and Elizabeth.

It happens during the vilest days of the Roman Empire while an elderly priest by the name of Zacharias is praying in the Jewish temple. When an angel appears to him, he almost faints with fear. The angel tells him not to be afraid, but gives him the staggering news that his elderly wife, Elizabeth, will soon carry a child.

"Say what?"

He is speechless and cannot speak again until the baby is born.

The angel tells him that his son, John, will be a delight, will never drink wine, and be filled with the Holy Spirit. The child is blessed with the promise of the Spirit of God before his first human cells start multiplying.

Elizabeth is the cousin of Mary, the soon-to-be mother of Jesus.

Fast-forward a few months. When Mary walks into Elizabeth's house to visit her, her unborn son John suddenly does a free-wheeling summersault inside her womb when he hears the sound of Mary's voice. Immediately, Elizabeth is filled with the Holy Spirit (see Luke 1:41). The electrifying connection between the Spirit, the babies, and the mothers can hardly be lost. The unborn child's leap is a fascinating detail reported only by the good doctor Luke.

The attentive devotion of God to mothers is everywhere in this story about the two pregnant women as Elizabeth expresses how thrilled she is that Mary has come to visit her. During the outpouring of the Spirit, she praises her sweet cousin Mary:

> "But why am I so favored, that the mother of my Lord should come to me? As soon as the sound of your greeting reached my ears, the baby in my womb leaped for joy."
>
> *Luke 1:43–44 NIV*

What emotion! Heart-stopping emotion! Earlier, the angel Gabriel informed Mary that God had chosen her to miraculously conceive the Son of God. He is to be named *Emmanuel*, which means *God with us*. Though she is confused and fearful, she immediately submits her life to the will of God. And Doctor Luke gives full attention to the enthusiasm in her prayer:

> *"My soul glorifies the Lord*
> *and my spirit rejoices in God my Savior,*
> *for he has been mindful*
> *of the humble state of his servant.*
> *From now on all generations will call me blessed*
> *for the Mighty One has done great things for me—*
> *holy is his name.*

His mercy extends to those who fear him,
from generation to generation."

Luke 1:46–50 NIV

Mary's poetic tribute highlights the power of the *Mighty One* who "has done great things" and balances this with praise for God's "mercy" which, as we know from our earlier study, is protective and "womb-like" in the original Semitic languages.

It is clear that women fulfill an important role in God's plans.

Dr. Daniel Ayuch puts it beautifully: "Mary—the mother of Jesus—is a woman *par excellence*. She totally gave herself to God, and she is the pattern for women."

One of my dear friends, Ingrid Haines, the busy mother of five little children, recently wrote me an e-mail with some of her insights about Mary. How would you answer some of the meaningful questions Ingrid asks about the mother of Jesus?

Mommy of the Messiah
By Ingrid Haines

What faith Mary had!

Mary was given direction from the beginning about the "Mommy-dom" in her pregnancy when the angel said to her: "The Lord is with you" (Luke 1:28).

The challenges she faced in her pregnancy prepared her to be the Mommy of the Messiah. While she was pregnant, did she ever think about how to bring up Jesus? Once he was a little boy, did she ever ponder if he should play with all the children around their hometown, or just with the children brought up with good morals?

Was she concerned about picking the best heads of wheat to grind for her children to eat, and later on, did Jesus help her pick the wheat and learn to grind it too? Did she think it was important for him to have a set bedtime, so that his body had lots of time to heal, refresh, and grow? Or did he go to bed whenever he felt like it?

Was it a pleasure to teach him to do chores around the house, sweep the floor, and make his bed? I wonder if she planted a garden so she could teach her children spiritual applications in life. Did she talk to Jesus about the things of God all day long as they did the simple things of life? Did she ever struggle with anger, frustration, lack of patience or control, or act holier-than-thou, just because she knew she was the Mommy of Yahweh?

Probably not!

Would Mary think in her mind, I can't wait until he is off doing his ministry so I can have my life back? *I doubt it. She would know "this is my purpose on Earth, to be the Mommy of the Messiah." I am sure she also realized, like I do, that I am human, a broken vessel!*

She would pray, as I must pray each day, that the love of the Father will shine through my brokenness, my imperfections, my frustrations, my lack of patience with my five little children as I get down on my knees and say "Lord, I can't do this on my own. I need your help to be the best Mommy for my little ones."

Mary was a simple woman just like the rest of us. Yet she found favor with God! God handpicks each of us to be Mommies! And handpicks each child we are to influence!

Pregnant Teen

I (Trudy) am a skinny eighteen-year-old teenager when I return home from a whirlwind three-day honeymoon—happy, hopeful, and very much pregnant. Within weeks, I cannot sleep, I cannot eat. I am ill, twenty-four hours a day. Repelled by food, I grow weak in my first pregnancy. Dry crackers become my staple.

Life grinds to a sudden halt. To carry this child, I am rendered so sick I can hardly sit, stand, or walk. Often all I can do is crawl. My life revolves around this thing called pregnancy with my body supine on the couch and moaning. Even looking at the wallpaper makes my head spin! Disoriented and discouraged, I ask myself a thousand times a day: *What was I thinking when I wallpapered this wall bright red brocade?*

I am a teeny-tiny teen woman at 105 pounds. A few weeks later, the scale drops to 95 pounds and I tremble in a hospital bed, dehydrated and hooked to an IV drip.

I cannot believe I feel so awful!

Finally, my body adjusts to this thing called carrying a child. And soon I start reading human development books with a passion, studying carefully the pictures of unborn babies. By Week Four, I learn that my child's little brain, her skin, the blond hair on her little round head, and her ten teeny-tiny fingers are already perfectly forming.

Everything in my body aches, yet deep within me—my baby's heart starts beating at only Five Weeks gestation. I am so proud to discover that her brain will ultimately develop more than 100 billion neurons.

"She is already a genius, I am absolutely sure," I tell my husband.

I touch my tummy. I can't believe the skin around my belly will swell and my uterus will stretch to one-thousand times its original size. "Yikes!" I say as I rub my stomach with Vitamin E oil. I worry about all that stretching to come, but I guess if my mom did it when she carried me, I must be able to do it, too.

My little girl is at the Two Month mark today, and she is dancing already.

At Nine Weeks, she is sucking her thumb and fascinated by her fingers. This seems so incredible to me. She is barely one inch long, yet she is forming her own set of unique fingerprints. By Week Ten, the beautiful irises in her eyes are dazzling greenish-blue. Even before I feel her move inside me, her vocal cords are forming, and I imagine what her voice will sound like when she cries the moment I deliver her.

By the eleventh week, my baby is almost perfectly formed with organs starting to function. She is beginning to produce hormones as her ovaries move from her abdomen to her pelvis. She is so much a female already! If I had been carrying a boy, his little prostate gland would now be developing, so much a little man already.

> *For you [God] created my inmost being;*
> *you knit me together in my mother's womb.*
> *I praise you because I am fearfully and wonderfully made;*
> *your works are wonderful,*
> *I know that full well.*
> > *Psalm 139:13–14 NIV, bracketed word added*

My belly swells with kicking child around the fifth month, and my baby's emotions are tender. By Week Thirty-Five, she is soothed by my conversations with her.

"Sweet baby, I can hardly wait to see you."

I gently circle my fingers around my soft tummy, just like I did as a child when I used to caress my mom's fur coat as I sat with my family in church. Without really thinking about it, I spontaneously start singing to my unborn child.

I decide our delivery will be natural and practice my coping skills in advance. "Breathe in, breathe out, concentrate, breathe in; breathe out." The way I look at it, God is unfolding a dramatic feminine gift in me, giving my body the ability to give birth—a process I know will be mired with agony, yet also indescribable ecstasy.

Waddling clumsily to my bedroom at nine months pregnant, the contractions begin as I try, unsuccessfully, to sleep that night. Oxytocin, the hormone of love, and beta-endorphins give me a few scattered moments of reprieve, moving me into an altered state of consciousness to counteract the grinding muscle-bending cramps.

My husband and I go to the hospital as I approach the delivery, and I breathe rhythmically as practiced. Prolactin, the mothering hormone, washes in with a rush, and a sudden spike in noradrenaline and norepinephrine trigger the "fetal ejection reflex." It feels like my feminine prowess is finely tuned like a NASA rocket about to leave the launching pad (well, not quite, but sort of). I am in an adrenaline state of alert.

My mouth is paper-dust dry, and I groan. Ten overwhelming contractions! Then my baby slips into the safety of the doctor's hands.

New life! My child is alive! As I am!

I hold my little girl in my arms as we make eye contact. I cry with happiness as I hug her. I'm in love with her soft pink skin, her light blond, fuzzy-fuzz hair, pretty heart-shaped red lips, and round delicate face.

"You are so, so beautiful. I love you so very, very much."

This is amazing! So amazing!

Jesus uses the analogy of a mother giving birth to describe the emotions when He welcomes us home to heaven to live with Him forever. He assures us that the anguish we experience in our short life on this polluted planet will one day turn to supreme joy.

> "A woman giving birth to a child has pain because her time has come; but when her baby is born she forgets the anguish because of her joy that a child is born into the world. So with you: Now is your time of grief, but I will see you again and you will rejoice, and no one will take away your joy."
>
> *John 16:21–22* NIV

In one sense, it defies logic to explain how a mother can "forget" the grueling pain of labor and delivery. But I know as a

Mom that the nine months of self-sacrifice and the suffering of the delivery are more than worth going through—for the overwhelming joy and ecstasy of bringing another child into the world.

As I hold my daughter, all I feel is love—indescribable, unending love.

Seems to me, God does the same and infinitely more.

CHAPTER 13

Born of the Spirit

The wind blows wherever it pleases. You hear its
sound, but you cannot tell where it comes from or
where it is going. So it is with everyone born of the
Spirit.

John 3:8 NIV

THE STORYTELLER SEARCHES for words.

Her family and friends lean forward in their chairs, wide-eyed
and straining to hear more of the story. They are spellbound as
she cleverly carves colorful words into their imagination like a
sculptress designs an exquisite art form.

She has them glued to every word.

"My mother had the spiritual gift of communication. She
was the ultimate storyteller," says Tony Campolo, a well-known
American author and speaker. "My mother could hold an audi-
ence in total rapture."

Yet the church fathers never allowed his mother, an incredibly
talented storyteller and communicator, to speak publicly in the
church pulpit.

He never forgot that injustice.

Campolo is professor emeritus at Eastern University in Pennsylvania and the author of more than thirty-five books, such as
his seminal title *Carpe Diem: Seize the Day*. He and his wife Peggy

have two children, and he is among the most popular Christian speakers today in North America, the United Kingdom, and Australia.

He is also a compassionate humanitarian. As founder of the Evangelical Association for the Promotion of Education, he develops schools and social programs in Third World countries and cities in North America.

The author sometimes causes a public stir with his theology and his passionate quest to achieve justice. A featured guest on such TV shows as *Nightline*, *CNN News*, *Larry King Live*, and *The Colbert Report*, he is not afraid to go against the religious grain.

When Campolo speaks, the world tends to listen.

He says he is intrigued by the ministry and the work of the Holy Spirit, whom he believes is the essence of the feminine dimension found in God.

"The Holy Spirit is the nurturing and mothering force of God, just as females are in the world," he tells me without a moment's hesitation, noting that the masculinity and femininity in the nature of God's love relates to healthy human development.

God certainly has a feminine side, explains Campolo, adding that he found this to be true as he studied the life of Jesus Christ. In fact, he wrote about this topic in his book *Carpe Diem* in chapter 12, called "Embracing the Feminine Side of God."

He elaborates on this controversial topic during our interview.

Jesus came to reveal the "fully actualized human being"—the only one who has ever lived on Earth in a perfectly balanced way. He never married and was a sensitive spiritual healer, yet he was a strong dynamic leader at the same time.

Do cultural influences affect the way we express our gender qualities?

Campolo believes that cultural biases tend to make boys suppress their feminine qualities because society teaches them that only females are allowed to express emotions in public, while girls suppress their so-called masculine qualities.

Promoting healthy gender development in both boys and girls is one of the greatest benefits of authentic Christianity, says the author.

Christianity is expansive enough to embrace progressive Western thinking, like the teachings of Carl Jung, and also to utilize the best in Eastern philosophy.

Jung was an influential (Swiss) psychiatrist who popularized the notion that the spiritual life is essential for the human soul. He said Western culture tends to create skewed personalities because boys and girls are taught to suppress a part of themselves and their true personalities. Chinese philosophers, meanwhile, believe people may experience holistic well-being in life as they balance the Yin (feminine) and the Yang (masculine) within themselves.

True Christianity, in fact, blends the best in these two worldviews.

"This is essentially what Jesus Christ teaches. He achieved perfect balance!" says Campolo, who discovered this for himself when he was teaching a course on existentialism and asked university students what they wanted to get out of life.

One of the students blurted out that he wanted to become "fully human."

The professor asked him what he meant by this comment. The student answered that a fully actualized human being is an infinitely loving, kind, and forgiving person. The class nodded in agreement. The comment struck a nerve with Campolo.

This is exactly the kind of life that Jesus led!

The class then discussed how Jesus Christ revealed the love of God to the world by treating everyone as worthy of the utmost respect. In sharp contrast, the end result of hatred, violence, racism, and sexism is to dehumanize people.

"When you get together with people, how do they make you feel? This can tell you if they are treating you like a human being or not," explains Campolo. "When you go to a party and someone starts telling filthy jokes, something of your humanity is lost because sexism diminishes females as human beings."

This is not as it should be.

"When you become like Jesus, you not only become human, you become more Christlike and totally loving," he says, adding that listening to the Spirit inspires us to be considerate and kind to one another.

"When you love someone, you are kind and thoughtful to them, uplifting their dignity and nobility as children of God," he says.

"Being like God means being totally loving!"

U2, Grandma, and Butterscotch Pies

When Brennan Manning shares his life story in public, the Spirit of God often moves people to tears and to their knees. Upon rising from prayer, many people, including members of the legendary rock group U2 are never the same.

Manning, author of *The Ragamuffin Gospel*, is renowned for his down-to-earth manner of comforting people with the good news about God's love.

We sit down together during our interview, and he tells me a couple of great stories.

One day he was asked to meet personally with U2 guitarist Dave Evans, otherwise known by his stage name "The Edge," because he needed some spiritual advice. The guitarist was anxiously striving to be faithful to God, but was worried about how to have a meaningful prayer life. He told Manning he wanted to be the best guitarist in the world. But would that goal make him arrogant? This was not a characteristic he wanted to have as a sincere disciple of God.

"I assured The Edge that his heart's desire to be the best guitarist in the world was borne out of God's wonderful love and will for him and for his life," explains Manning.

The author gave him some practical advice.

God gives each one of us an array of talents and a burning passion to strive for excellence so that we may reflect glory and praise back to our Creator who formed us in our mother's womb in the first place, says Manning. As the guitarist contemplated Manning's advice, it transformed his prayer life and he experienced God's inner peace in a way he had never felt before.

This epitomizes the ministry of the *Ragamuffin* preacher— straight-talking and matter-of-fact as he shares the gospel with others in great wisdom and compassion.

Manning once thought he would be a journalist when he was a young man in his twenties, but he felt a longing for a closer relationship with God so he chose instead to become a Franciscan priest. He was ordained in 1963. Driven by his quest to understand God better, he once lived in a remote desert cave in Spain for six months to contemplate the mysterious nature of God. The author even volunteered to be a prisoner in a Swiss jail where his identity as a priest was known only to the warden.

This is quintessential Manning—introspective and thoughtful.

But he also loves to be social and to connect with people. He is the first to admit he is not perfect. He tells me that a collapse into alcoholism once drove him into a six-month treatment program to overcome addiction, and today he certainly feels grateful for his recovery. His ministry to help people on their spiritual journey is even more meaningful as a result of overcoming his troubles.

He candidly explains, during several of our interviews, why he believes God has a tender maternal side, and he is a passionate teacher about this discovery.

"Since God made men and women—both of their gender qualities are from God. The Holy Spirit is the bond of tenderness between the Father and Son and has most of the qualities associated with a woman," says Manning. "I find it interesting that the Bible reveals feminine imagery for God."

This teaching does not always win him popularity contests,

and he receives some "very interesting responses" when he speaks about this in public.

"Women are usually pleased, and some men acknowledge that it's the truth," he says. "But others are hostile."

Manning first experienced the unconditional maternal love of God early in his life through the love he felt from his kindhearted grandmother.

"She would delight in my presence," he explains with warmth in his voice. "She always made me butterscotch pies because she knew I loved to eat them."

This generous woman loved her grandson with all her heart. One day she took him, at five years old, to the St. Patrick's Day Parade in New York City and hoisted him on her shoulders so he could watch the colorful floats roll by. That epitomized her love for him—always making sure he was not lost in the crowd. When he was a young priest, his aging grandmother desperately wanted to see him dressed in his new priestly garb with her own eyes. Her doctor, however, strongly advised her not to travel because of the risk to her health. She decided to go anyway.

Dressed in his new habit, Manning was overjoyed when his mom and dad walked into the room with his grandmother walking beside them, carrying a butterscotch pie in her hands. She flashed him a big smile.

He will never forget that magical moment.

They visited for three happy hours, talking, laughing, and reminiscing about the good old days, and then they tightly hugged each other as they said good-bye.

She died on the train ride home.

"The Beautiful Side of God"

A mother and a grandmother may exert an enormous influence for good in the family just as Brennan Manning's grandmother did for him when she comforted him with something as simple as baking him a sweet butterscotch pie.

It brings to mind the Bible story about Timothy and his mother, Eunice, and his grandmother, Lois, who inspired his faith. A woman's encouragement creates a positive ripple effect in the family and community as she passes on her faith to her children and grandchildren who one day may become priests and rabbis, teachers and writers.

The quiet faith of a woman creates a dynamic domino effect.

Who would have thought that a grandmother's homemade pies or simply taking a grandchild to a big colorful parade would one day be among the stories to encourage U2, Michael W. Smith, and millions of others to a closer walk with God?

Manning says the gift of maternal comfort originates with God, and this often-overlooked characteristic promotes spiritual healing in both men and women.

In the meantime, I am able to speak to a comedienne about this topic.

Chonda Pierce's stories generate more laughs per minute than many of her contemporaries. The award-winning comic takes her comedy act across North America to sold-out crowds and is often promoted as the indisputable Queen of Clean Comedy.

Laughter does a person good—just like good medicine (see Prov. 17:22).

Pierce is side-stitching funny, but she is also serious about following God. She explains that women were created to reflect the "beautiful side of God's image."

It helps her to attribute God's love to his "parenting nature," she says. Her husband David, for example, brings great strength, direction, and protection to their family and also gives her space to be creative and nurtures her independent nature.

"I feel cared for by him—God is something like that," she says. "God is nurturing and protective."

While her husband may not understand her struggles with

PMS, he loves her enough to try to understand her hormonal challenges. Her comedy routines touch people with the love of God because of her honesty about her own struggles in life.

"That's the power of the Holy Spirit," she explains.

The comedienne does not think about the nature of God in terms as being either masculine or feminine, but she is willing to explore the possibilities.

Has Pierce ever considered the Spirit as the possible maternal side of God?

"That's precious! That's a precious thought! When I think of the Holy Spirit, I immediately think of the Comforter," she answers. "Who do you run to when you're a kid and you've skinned your knees? You run to your mom. That makes sense to me because the Holy Spirit is the Comforter."

Luci Swindoll also shares some important ideas about the Comforter.

"The Holy Spirit seals our lives, confirming that we belong to Jesus, and helps us in our meditations, prompting us to live on this Earth to do God's work," she says. "Many people believe the Holy Spirit verbalizes the female side of God, and it's an easy thing to do because the Spirit plays the comforting role. There is an abiding presence of sweetness and joy in the Holy Spirit."

Does she believe the Spirit may personify a feminine side to God?

Swindoll is not committed to that particular viewpoint.

"I don't know. To me, the gender of God is not important; it's not the big thing."

It's what God does in a person's life that is important!

"The Spirit's role in a Christian's life is enormous—the Holy Spirit can change and soften hardened hearts that not all of the guns in the world can change."

Born Again: A Powerful Metaphor

With faith in God, all things are possible.

Sandra M. Schneiders has gone where few women have ventured before her as she broke centuries of church tradition by being the second woman in history to earn her Doctorate in Sacred Theology (STD) at the Pontifical Gregorian University in Rome.

This venerated Catholic institution is where fourteen popes have graduated.

With dedication, hard work, and asking God to be by her side, Schneiders earned her doctorate, summa cum laude (the highest honor possible) in 1975. In addition to earning a doctorate at the Gregorian, she is the recipient of five honorary doctorates.

"It wasn't easy," she says humbly.

The theologian says that she has ever been mindful to pray to God to help her find the spiritual resources in the Bible that will encourage men and women to know, without a shadow of doubt, the high value the Creator places on their lives.

Today the award-winning theologian is professor emerita of New Testament Studies and Christian Spirituality at the Jesuit School of Theology of Santa Clara University in Berkeley, California, and she is the author of a number of scholarly books, including *Women and the Word*.

During our conversation, she explains to me the importance of having faith and understanding how much God loves each one of us as His beloved children.

The Bible, in fact, speaks to the hearts and minds of today's generation, presenting the nature of God in a balance of masculine and feminine metaphors, but unfortunately, the feminine metaphors have long been ignored, says Schneiders.

"We need to address the imbalance."

In the Gospel of John, for example, there is a story about a meeting between Jesus and Nicodemus. During this conversation, Jesus reveals a profound feminine metaphor to describe the regeneration of the human spirit:

> One evening a Jewish teacher named Nicodemus is set to meet secretly with Jesus because he wants to know how to experience spiritual transformation.
>
> Jesus is blunt. You must be born again, He says.
>
> How can I do that? Nicodemus asks, rather surprised by the thought, and he replies, with no small amount of cynicism: What am I supposed. to do—go back into my mother's womb and start all over again?
>
> Jesus looks kindly at the man and explains that a believer must be born again by the baptism of water and the mysterious power of the Holy Spirit.
>
> "Very truly, I tell you, no one can enter the kingdom of God without being born of water and Spirit. What is born of the flesh is flesh, and what is born of the Spirit is spirit.
>
> "Do not be astonished that I say to you, 'You must be born from above.'
>
> "The wind blows where it chooses, and you hear the sound of it, but you do not know where it comes from or where it goes. So it is with everyone who is born of the Spirit."
>
> *See John 3:1–8, quotes from* NRS

This is one of the most evocative chapters in the entire Bible, and this astounding conversation should excite Christians everywhere with a sense of wonder.

"This is a remarkable statement of Jesus that should open our minds to richer, more gender-inclusive ways of imaging God," explains Schneiders. "When Jesus taught Nicodemus to be born again by the Holy Spirit, he used the most profound female experience in the world—that of giving birth—to explain spiritual transformation."

Jesus used plain language that was enlightening for His time and culture, Schneiders says. And His words still are! This conversation with Nicodemus opens up an obvious truth that has been overlooked for far too long.

"Christians have, for centuries, read this passage without realizing that John, the author of the fourth Gospel, gave us, through the voice of Jesus, one of the clearest New Testament feminine metaphors of God," the scholar explains to me. "We are reborn by the Spirit in the waters of baptism just as surely as we are born physically of our mothers through the waters of natural birth."

Birthing is a uniquely female activity. This is what God does in the spiritual realm when we are born again, using the analogy of coming forth from the womb, and this experience introduces us to a deep mystery about our spiritual origin.

"The Bible uses both parental metaphors of father and mother to describe the love of God," she notes. "So why do churches continually emphasize our heavenly Father, but not the motherly terms used for God?"

In fact, even Moses writes about the paternal and maternal attributes of the Creator when he lamented the waywardness and unfaithfulness of God's people:

> You were unmindful of the Rock that begot you, and you forgot the God who gave you birth.
> *Deuteronomy 32:18 RSV*

In this Scripture passage, God not only "begot" or fathered his people, but gave them "birth," which is what a mother does, Schneiders explains.

Of course, God is neither male nor female, God is Spirit, she says.

But we cannot ignore the personal nature of our Creator's love and grace. It is an absolute wonder that the Nicodemus story could have failed, all of these centuries, to teach us to recognize the maternal elements in God's love. For many centuries, the Bible scholar says, the feminine aspects of God's love, recorded in the Bible, have been either ignored or underemphasized by the religious establishment.

"We need to make the feminine metaphors for God more prominent. The feminine notions of God are in the Bible—and they always have been—so now it's time to fully accept it."

It is a new era for believers to be renewed, broaden their thinking and enlighten their imaginations. Unfortunately, there has been a distinct lack of balance for many years, due to patriarchal reasons, not theological reasons, she says.

But this imbalance, she believes, is starting to change.

My Mess, God's Miracle, and Being "Gamma"

What does it mean to be born again by the Spirit?

Maybe it's a little like this. I never expected to be a mom. Period! End of story. My life had been a big mess as a teenager, and I seriously thought I would be dead by the time I was twenty years old because of my wild living.

But something even wilder happened.

Unknown to me, God had other plans for me.

I start to read the Bible after my eldest daughter is born, and my life suddenly changes dramatically as I feel the love of God melting away years of pain and shame in a matter of moments. He gave me a new beginning, a chance to start fresh again.

Dedicating my life to Him at twenty-one years old, I decide to be baptized when I am four months pregnant with my precious second daughter.

I now have inner peace; life has purpose and meaning.

By the time I am twenty-three, I have three girls, each uniquely blessed by God as my life revolves around diapers, bottles, reading books, and forever picking up dolls and Fisher-Price toys. Every time I look at my girls, I feel such warm love for them. Each one of my experiences with my girls as a mom seems to me to be a magical moment.

They are teaching me to appreciate God's love on a deeper spiritual level.

And many times those treasured moments come out of nowhere.

One of my daughters is six years old as she washes her hands with Ivory soap in the bathroom. She suddenly gets the bright idea of smearing the soap on the mirror and proceeds to paint squiggly pictures in the white froth. She is so excited by her artwork that she is completely oblivious to the idea that perhaps Mom would not be quite as excited as she is to see the mucked-up mirrors. I don't have the heart to scold her. Long after she runs outside to play, I smile as I clean up her "pretty little white paintings."

"Dear God, may you always bless my little artistic sweet-heart."

I think to myself, *God, you see me messing up, day in and day out, and I am so often oblivious to the junk I leave behind for you to clean up in my own life. Just like my little girl, I am often unaware that you are sheltering me in your mercy just as my daughters cannot comprehend how deep my unconditional love is for them.*

My children thrill me, and sometimes, I admit, they baffle me.

God instilled in my three beautiful daughters a quality called independence and free will. And as I watch them grow up, this enables me to appreciate the enormous risks God takes by giving me the power of choice. I have learned to respect God's willingness to let me fall and to learn from my mistakes, even though it hurts.

When my girls are in their teens, they don't always appreciate my advice.

"Aw, Mom, you're just being old-fashioned. You're way off

base," I'd hear them say, more often than I cared to hear. Naturally I would feel hurt and rejected because all I want to do is protect them and help them to avoid needless pain and heartache.

It is really hard watching my precious children fall and get hurt. How much more does God's heart break when I reject His will for my life, due to my faulty human reasoning? Being a mom helps me understand that God is very patient and kind.

It has been said that when a boy or girl feels loved by Mother, he or she will be able to trust God's love. The influence of a godly mother lasts a child's lifetime.

One day my daughter Charlene, by now a mature young adult, comes in the front door with her arm covered with bruises. I am mortified by the sight.

"What in the world happened to you?"

She explains that she was donating blood when a nurse missed her vein. Char tugs at her sleeve to cover up the purple bruises forming on her arm.

I look at her, and it hits me how my eldest daughter is making the choice to give the gift of life and to donate blood to an injured or dying person, even though it causes her to suffer. I feel really proud of her.

After I sympathize with her, I think about the agony the Father must have gone through when He watched His only begotten son being struck over and over again by the Roman soldiers and then shed His precious blood to give us the gift of eternal life.

What indescribable love!

On another occasion, one of my daughters asks me to stay with her in the delivery room when she is in labor with her first child. I cherish those remarkable moments of closeness with her as we pray together in the hospital hallway. What a trouper! I am so proud of her. When she delivers her baby, I cry with joy.

Everyone cries. Another child is born!

My granddaughter Amie is two-and-a-half years old when she looks outside our living room window one cold winter night and spots millions of diamonds as the moon lights up the frost on the grass like shimmering sparkles on a blanket of crystal.

"Gamma, we go walk in the dark?" she says.

I am surprised. She is usually scared of the dark.

"Do you really want to go out there? It's pretty cold out there."

She pulls me toward the door, convincing me that she is serious.

Soon we are feeling warm and snuggly as we put on our jackets and mittens. Holding her little hand in mine, I assure her that it is wonderful to walk in the dark, the "magical world of sparkle," and to explore the outside world of intrigue where trees wave around us like latticework dancing in the sky.

The air is biting cold as we pull our scarves close to our eyes.

Soon we can see in the dark without using the flashlight because the moon is bright enough to light our path. The frozen grass squeaks with every step. We hike around with our eyelashes moist with tears and vapor blowing from our mouths.

We challenge the dark, she and I.

We laugh and brag about our courage and our audacity to walk in the night!

"Gamma, see the moon?" she whispers.

"Yes, it's nighttime," I reply.

She giggles. When she starts shivering, she begs me to pick her up. So I carry her, and she nestles her face close to mine. But only temporarily—she's a big girl now, big enough to walk in the dark and to laugh at the coyote and the owl.

And so the cycle of life continues in my tiny shelter of love.

Life feels "just right" for me as I face the cold wind, carrying my precious little granddaughter. It is too dark and cold for Amie to walk by herself, but "Gamma" will get her home—warm and secure in her arms.

As I walk along, I reflect on the mystery of maternal love, the seasons of being a mother and now a grandmother, and the ever-rolling cycle of giving birth and nurturing new life. I thank the Holy Spirit of God for giving us spiritual new birth and passing on to women the unique genetic blueprint of giving birth.

A sacred holiness glows within me.

Doing a bit of what God does.

Being who God designs me to be.

CHAPTER 14

The Comforter

The characteristics of the Holy Spirit are obviously maternal. Known as the Comforter, the Holy Spirit comforts God's people as a mother comforts a child.

Jürgen Moltmann, Bible Scholar

JÜRGEN MOLTMANN IS recognized as one of the world's leading theologians.

It is a title he doesn't wear easily as he shrugs off the many accolades.

"Talk to my wife," he says with obvious delight in his voice. "She's the leading theologian."

Elisabeth, indeed, is a major inspiration to Jürgen—as he is for her. As a team, they are unmatchable. In fact, to many believers, he and his wife Elisabeth Moltmann-Wendel, who live in Germany, are a rare example in Christian history of a married couple who are both known publicly as theological bright stars.

She is a leading scholar, and Jürgen is renowned as one of the most creative and most widely read Protestant authors of the past half century. In addition to his long-standing career teaching theology students at Tübingen University in Germany, Jürgen has written more than sixteen books. Together, the Moltmanns also cowrote a book called *Passion for God: Theology in Two Voices*—his voice and hers!

It is an honor to interview both of them one bright sunny morning.

Jürgen explains to me that he grew up in a secular home reading such intellectual literary giants as Goethe and Nietzsche. He was living apart from God when his life changed dramatically after he was drafted into the army as a teenager. He was devastated during the Second World War when his friend who was standing beside him was blown apart by a bomb and died.

He survived the explosion, but in the middle of his anguish, Jürgen looked into the dark face of death and mourned: "My God, where are you?" Then a heart-rending question erupted in his soul as he asked why he did not die too.

After he was confined as a prisoner of war in Belgium, he explains to me that he saw the inmates all around him collapsing in despair because they had no hope. He would have sunk into depression himself, if it were not for a kind army chaplain who gave him a copy of the New Testament.

He started reading his new Bible with deep interest.

Although he was surrounded in an atmosphere of hopelessness, Jürgen was shocked to feel the Spirit of God tenderly healing his soul. In this place of anguish and sorrow imprisoned in the POW camp, he says, he discovered that the God of love would answer every one of his many daunting spiritual questions.

He felt his soul being uplifted as he read about King David, the stories about Jesus Christ, and the victories of the early Christian church. He learned that the "hope" God gives to each of us is the foundation of faith on which to overcome evil with good.

"God gives us hope so we can start a new life!" says Jürgen.

As he searched deeper for spiritual truth, he experienced for himself the intensity of God's love in Jesus, who gives hope to everyone who feels forsaken.

Once freed from prison, he pursued his newfound Christian faith with passion and became a student of Karl Barth, a world-famous theologian. He also studied the writings of Reformation leader Martin Luther and war critic Dietrich Bonhoeffer. Along the way, he also found time to have a romance with a theology student named Elisabeth Wendel, and they married in 1952.

Jürgen was ordained in the Reformed Church and taught systematic theology at Tübingen University for more than a quarter century, from 1967–1994, where he is now professor emeritus. The alumni of this world-famous university include Johannes Kepler, Pope Benedict XVI, and nine Nobel Prize winners.[1]

He knows the reality of the existence of God.

"According to my experience, God gives people hope, inner strength, and the purest love in life," he says, adding that we all need to hold on to this vital truth during this particular stage of Earth's history when physical violence and rampant environmental destruction threaten our very existence.

"We see on TV today so much death and killing all around us that we've become accustomed to it," he says. "But we must live out our Christian faith and our belief that the destruction of the Earth and the killing of people is wrong and is not according to God's will."

He is also moved to take action on important social-justice issues. His wife, he says, challenged his male-oriented way of thinking when she wrote a book called *The Women Around Jesus*. Her ideas about equality prompted him to start thinking "outside the box" as he felt impressed by her good theological arguments.

At that point of his life, when he was younger, he says, he was feeling stymied by his one-sided, male-oriented point of view. But as the couple raised four daughters, Jürgen became keenly aware of the gender differences between males and females and how each gender relates to God in their own respective, complementary ways.

Out of curiosity, he started to look at the possibility that God may have feminine as well as masculine qualities, and his investigation turned into quite an adventure.

The evidence kept mounting, he says, especially after he studied the case made by certain theologians and one of his PhD students, who wrote a dissertation on Count Nicholas Ludwig von Zinzendorf, a dynamic leader of the Moravian Church in the 1700s.

Jürgen was shocked to learn the historical fact that Christians in Syria were well aware of the "motherhood of the Holy Spirit" and that the pronoun "she" was used for the Spirit in the earliest copies of the Old Syriac Gospels. In fact, the Moravian Church—which traces its roots to the Reformation—also proclaimed this doctrine.

The professor found this fascinating.

"There is no longer any doubt in my mind that the Holy Spirit operates with qualities that are feminine. It is a theology absolutely relevant for the twenty-first century," says Jürgen, noting how this issue has been misunderstood for many centuries.

The word for the Spirit (*ruach*) in the original Hebrew language is grammatically feminine, Jürgen explains. This was later translated into *pneuma* in Greek, which is neuter (*it*), and then the Latin word *spiritus* came to be used, which is masculine (*he*).

"These changes led to incorrect assumptions that the Spirit is masculine, and this has created serious difficulties about understanding the Spirit," he says. "The characteristics of the Holy Spirit are obviously maternal. Known as the Comforter, the Holy Spirit comforts God's people as a mother comforts a child."

He believes the evidence is abundantly clear.

"Believers are born again by the Holy Spirit," he explains, noting this is "a tremendous attribute of motherhood."

Moms are uniquely designed to bear a child and to provide nurture and comfort to precious new life, and they have a seemingly unending capacity for giving unconditional love to their children. These unique maternal qualities show us how God behaves toward followers who sometimes err and need reminding that God is love.

The scholar advocates a return to this great fundamental truth.

His expertise on the Trinity may be studied in his contemporary classic called *The Trinity and the Kingdom of God* in which he writes about the relative independence of the Father, Son, and Holy Spirit, though they share a perfect oneness in purpose.

He does not mince words about the need of the church to be more innovative in its outreach to contemporary men and women who are longing and hungering for God.

Sexism and macho-ism must be overcome, he says.

"It's time for people to experience the real presence of God."

The Moravians and the Aristocrat

I can't get over what Jürgen has just told me. This well-respected scholar instills in me an even greater desire to put the pieces together in this unusual spiritual puzzle. Who was Count Zinzendorf? Who are the Moravians? Is there more to the Holy Spirit than I have been taught in church? What have I been missing?

My next step leads me to speak to Dr. Craig D. Atwood, a historian of note.

He is an award-winning author and the Director of the Center for Moravian Studies at the Moravian College and Theological Seminary where he teaches history. He earned his PhD at Princeton Theological Seminary.

The US scholar confirms for me that a rich young nobleman in Germany discovered convincing proof in the Bible about the motherhood of the Holy Spirit.

"Count Zinzendorf believed that the reality of the Holy Spirit acting as a mother would help the community to understand God better because the family is one of the oldest ideas in history," Atwood explains. "Even a child can understand this."

What sparked the Moravians to put forward this controversial idea?

It is a fascinating story which goes back to an era when Moravia and Bohemia made up what is now known as the Czech Republic, says Atwood.

Many faithful Christians were being killed for simply following the teachings of the Bible in the 1400s and 1500s. Their faith and testimony sparked the Reformation, a great spiritual movement that grew more fervent and powerful with persecution.

The founders of the Moravian Church (also known as the Bohemian Church) were horrified when John Hus, a God-fearing priest, was burned at the stake in 1415 for opposing the social injustices of the Roman Catholic Church. As the flames engulfed Hus, he reportedly kept singing praises to God until his last dying breath!

His faith left an indelible impression on a group of devoted followers—known as the Hussites and then the Bohemian Brethren—to continue fighting against spiritual oppression. This movement later evolved into the Moravian Church, whose members were severely persecuted for their belief in the Bible— *sola scriptura.*

"In fact, they were almost driven to extinction," says Atwood.

Their Czech-language Bibles were burned because it was illegal to own them, and families masterfully hid God's Word from public view. Even though the Moravian Church was destroyed, a few families survived. They outlasted their enemies by living according to biblical principles and leading quiet, publicly secretive lives.

Three centuries after Hus was martyred, this little church group escaped Moravia in 1722 to find refuge at the estate of Count Zinzendorf in Germany.

The members appreciated the kindness and generosity of this nobleman, who advocated religious freedom and equality for all. The Count later became the leader of the Moravians. The aristocrat walked in the footsteps of the early Reformers, studying the Bible with an enthusiasm rarely seen.

The Moravians formed an innovative community under his leadership called Herrnhut, where families devoted themselves to daily communal prayer, Bible study, and worship of God. Under his leadership, the Moravians experienced a spiritual revival in 1727 with a great outpouring of the Holy Spirit. In fact, this little church started a worldwide missionary outreach and a remarkable twenty-four-hour-a-day prayer chain that lasted, with few breaks, for more than one hundred years!

The Count, meanwhile, wrote more than two thousand hymns during his lifetime.

He is recognized as a pioneer in global missionary work and is known in some circles as the "Father of the Protestant World Mission Movement," says Atwood. The Moravian Church was the first Protestant church to dispatch missionaries around the world to such places as the Caribbean Islands, Africa, and North and South America.

Their evangelistic work was nothing short of extraordinary.

"The Moravian Church had more missionaries per capita than any other church. At one time, one in ten Moravians was a missionary!"

When many of these believers emigrated to the US from Germany, the Count continued to travel around the world as an evangelist. Among his many friends were Frederick William I, King of Prussia, Benjamin Franklin, and John Wesley.

"Zinzendorf had a magnetic personality," says Atwood.

And women certainly fared well during the Count's era of justice for all. He was a vocal champion for women's rights, and the church became known as one of the most egalitarian communities in the Western world. Challenging the social norms of the eighteenth century, the church allowed women to be ordained as deacons and presbyters.

The charismatic noble had a reputation for being a controversial Christian leader, particularly when he started teaching about the "motherhood" of the Holy Spirit.

According to Zinzendorf, the clearest way to explain the nature of the Holy Trinity is the model of the family: Father, Mother, and Son. He took Reformation leader Martin Luther's teachings to the next logical level because the family is one of the oldest, most respectable and endearing metaphors for God, explains Atwood.

The New Testament perfectly harmonizes with the Old Testament.

When the prophet Isaiah wrote that God "comforts" us like a mother (see Isa. 66:13), this connects seamlessly with the statement by Jesus, more than seven hundred years later, when He asked the Father to send us the "Comforter" (see John 14:16 ASV) to be with us forever.

"Jesus, at the end of His life, wanted to comfort His followers who would grieve His departure, and that is why He promised that the Father would send the Comforter, the Holy Spirit, to comfort them," says Atwood.

The Moravians spoke of the Spirit as "mother" for many decades.

Atwood translated some of Zinzendorf's most famous litanies and observed that the Count sometimes weaved the idea of the maternal nature of the Holy Spirit into the Moravian songs of adoration and worship. The following is an example:

Te Matrem

> Lord God, now be praised,
> *You worthy Holy Spirit!*
> *You, the mother of Christendom*
> *The church honors in unity. . . .*
> *O Mother of all God's people,*
> *O wisdom archetypal!*

You are the informer of all hearts
And the purifier of body and soul!

This unique teaching gave positive missionary results for the Moravian Church in the US, attracting thousands of women to join their community, Atwood says, adding that this theology also inspired a great deal of success with Native people.

The Count, however, was frequently criticized by other Christian denominations for using the term "mother" for the Holy Spirit. But it made sense to him because he believed God always reveals new spiritual light to each new generation.

When he died in 1760, a huge vacuum was left in the church.

The new leaders were far more conservative than the Count, and they were embarrassed by his unconventional teachings, due to negative public opinion. They began suppressing his teachings, and the word "mother" in relation to the Spirit was systematically removed from Moravian litanies starting in 1770, Atwood explains.

Eventually women were excluded from church leadership as they were in the wider Christian community. By 1848, not one woman was listed in the Moravian General Synod.

The teaching about the matriarchal qualities of the Spirit was fairly well buried until researchers, like Atwood and Gary Kinkel, began digging around in the church archives, especially about the year 2000, which was the 300th anniversary of the Count's birthday (May 26, 1700). Atwood worked full-time for more than two years, poring over church records stowed away in dusty old archives. As he patiently read old hymn books, church diaries, and records, he managed to piece together the historical story.

"The church had covered up much of this material," he says.

He decided to write a major part of his PhD dissertation at Princeton on the subject and has found this teaching is sparking a lot of public attention today.

"People are very interested in this research," Atwood says.

"Many of us did not know how richly developed this theology was for Zinzendorf and that it was not a wacky idea. But that it actually makes sense."

The Moravians are starting to reclaim this once-hidden spiritual gem.

"I think it has good implications for believers in the future."

Maturing in the Christian Life

Karl Barth was one of the most influential Protestant theologians since the Reformation, and he was already known as a legendary Christian thinker in the twentieth century when Neill Q. Hamilton, a bright young theology student, walked into Barth's classroom at the University of Basel in Switzerland.

Barth once wrote that "the best theology would need no advocates; it would prove itself."[2] And when he examined young Hamilton's logic in 1956 in his dissertation on "The Holy Spirit and Eschatology of Paul," he passed the student with flying colors.

Hamilton, it turns out, was an original thinker.

He was ordained in the United Presbyterian Church, and he earned the respect of students and colleagues alike as a New Testament professor at the Theological School at Drew University, a Methodist graduate seminary in New Jersey.

"Neill had a keen mind, and he took his calling very seriously," says Doris Hamilton, his wife. "His students loved him because he truly understood God's grace and could communicate that love very well."

He and Doris both loved to share their faith in mission projects as they raised three sons who became highly successful in their careers; one a lawyer, the other a pediatrician, and the third a bioelectrical engineer seeking a cure for liver cancer.

Working at Drew University for twenty-one years before retiring, Neill wrote such books as *Jesus for a No-God World* and *Recovery of the Protestant Adventure*. He died on February 5, 1998, but not before publishing a powerful book called *Maturing in the Christian Life: A Pastor's Guide*. While the title did not excite the mass market, the content of the book was profound as he unveiled in rare detail the feminine personality of the Holy Spirit as documented in the Gospels of Luke and John and the writings of Paul.

The overemphasis of God as a father figure and lack of attention given to the maternal nature of God in contemporary Christian culture in effect "makes us deprived children of a one-parent family," writes Hamilton.[3]

The young student, who was once examined by Barth, went well beyond his mentor's spiritual legacy to pursue the next theological step in Christian maturity. For one thing, Hamilton notes that the more we learn about the maturing adult, the more we realize that each one of us—whether male or female—have the endearing capacity to exercise both masculine and feminine traits.

By studying the Scriptures with undivided attention to detail, Hamilton learned that the Holy Spirit displays the feminine dimension of God's love as our divine *Comforter*. But we should certainly not deemphasize the masculine nature of God.

"From now on, it will not be either masculine or feminine, but it will be both!"[4]

It is noteworthy that the language for the Spirit is typically feminine in the Hebrew Old Testament, he explains.

The pronoun became neuter in the shift to the Greek in the New Testament. But the Spirit of God will once again inspire believers to "undo this linguistic neutering" because our faith must be based on the truth.[5]

The likable professor listened to his students with deep personal interest during his tenure and encouraged every new seminary student who walked into class.

June D. Hewitt happened to be one of those anxious new students. When she entered Drew University seminary, she had two major strikes against her—first, her gender and second, her age. The woman, who was in her fifties at the time, was struggling to fit in when Hamilton showed her nothing but compassion.

Hewitt tells me that the professor's support for her was absolutely amazing.

"He was a unique theologian with a wonderful laugh and a deep love for life."

She eventually earned her Doctor of Ministry (DMin) when she was sixty-two years old—a personal tribute to the encouragement of her beloved professor. And Dr. June Hewitt went on to pastor five churches in her senior years!

Imagine the inspiration of such a faithful witness.

One Little Word

I reflect on the power of one word.

What do I mean by this?

As I interview many leaders of faith, I find one word makes all the difference in the world. If some people emphatically state to me that God most definitely does not have any feminine features, they almost always do a complete U-turn if I change that one word in my question to "maternal" or "motherly" qualities.

Suddenly the answer swings around to a definite *yes*.

"Maternal?"

"Yes."

"Feminine?"

"No."

"Motherly?"

"Yes."

"Feminine?"

"No."

This observation is puzzling to me at first, but in time it starts making perfect sense. It is important to make a clear distinction. The nature of God is not masculine or feminine in the biological sense, but in the spiritual sense of the word as a loving, nurturing parent!

Divine Comfort

Comfort comes to us in all shapes, sizes, and situations for every age.

I am eleven years old, feeling forlorn and freezing cold one winter day as I struggle to walk home against the howling wind in a snowstorm. My teeth chatter so violently my cheeks, my eyes, my entire face aches in pain.

As soon as I enter the house, my mom wraps a fluffy warm comforter around me as my whole body shakes and shivers. She holds me close to her, trying to make me feel calm. But my icy-cold, red, puffy fingers start stinging in painful pins and needles. I almost faint in agony.

"Here, put your hands under my arms," Mom says.

Wearing her soft pink dress, she takes my hands into hers and firmly places them under her warm, dry armpits (which always smell nice, by the way) and squeezes me against her. The warmth that radiates from her body to my own weak body is stable, evenly distributed, and just the right temperature for me to adjust from the outdoors. Covered by my comforter, I snuggle with her until warm.

Today I am a journalist and supposedly a mature woman of faith, but some days, to be quite frank, I am rattled by insecurity and anxiety.

One day I cannot stop worrying about one of my daughters.

I obsess about the serious problems she is facing and pray every morning for God to give her a solution. Receiving the answer, I am afraid to share it with her. I feel the Spirit of God saying to me: *Just trust me. The truth will set you free.*

But Lord, if I speak the truth, it is going to cause conflict. You know I don't like conflict, and I just want to live in peace.

Right, but sometimes you can't have it both ways. Sometimes you keep silent and there is peace in the room, but you have compromised my perfect will for your life and for others who need to hear my truth because you gave in to fear. Speaking the truth won't always bring peace. Just look at me. They hated me without cause. But I gave my life for you and for them.

I close my eyes:

My dear, precious Comforter, I comprehend so little of the depths of your wisdom. Help me to learn to trust you each moment of the day as a drop of olive oil lands in a jar of clay, as dry dust absorbs the rain. May your Holy Spirit spark a little of heaven's firelight to kindle within.

The Kindness of God

The maternal comfort and mercy of God is a golden thread running throughout Scripture. This topic has been the subject of study and devotional writings ever since the beginning of time, as seen in the following excerpt written in 1706 by Rev. Matthew Henry, a famous Bible commentator.

The manner in which the Lord comforts the saints, especially young converts, is the most kind, tender, and affectionate—as a tenderhearted mother comforts her child when it has fallen and hurt itself, and cries. She takes [the child] up in her arms, hugs it in her bosom, and speaks comfortably—to still and quiet the child.

The children of God often fall into sin, and hurt themselves, [they lose] their peace, and joy, break their bones, and lose the enjoyment of God, when, being sensible of their evils, they roar as David did, and weep bitterly as Peter.

Then the Lord speaks comfortably unto them, and bids them be of good cheer, for their sins are forgiven them. Or, as when a mother has an afflicted child—more so than the rest—her heart yearns most after it, and she does all she can to comfort the child.[6]

The mother heart of our Father God is also a contemporary religious issue.

It is a watershed moment for me to interview Sandra Schneiders and Jürgen Moltmann. These personable Bible scholars are brilliant in their own respective fields of study, Schneiders a confirmed Catholic and Moltmann a renowned Protestant.

Yet there is no polarization between them, but instead, amazing harmony.

The Father is unveiling the mystery of His maternal love to humble, teachable people of diverse faiths and then places them in positions of leadership to teach the world. A number of theologians say it is a sign that we are maturing in our faith as we rediscover the maternal elements of the third person of the Trinity.

Jürgen Moltmann echoes what many believers are starting to learn.

"There is no longer any doubt in my mind that the Holy Spirit operates with qualities that are feminine. It is a theology absolutely relevant for the twenty-first century."

This is an exciting breakthrough, yet so simple.

A friend of mine in her twenties is pregnant with her second child.

With long blond hair draped over her shoulders, she looks at me with her bigger-than-life blue eyes. She is so naturally beautiful, she could easily be a model on any contemporary fashion magazine cover, but that is not her goal.

Her biggest ambition in life is to be a great mom.

"I'm worried," she says to me as she hugs her first-born daughter.

"I don't think I can love another baby as much as I love her."

But a few months later, she gives birth to her second daughter and holds her second precious little newborn in her arms, as her heart melts in awe.

"Wow!" she says with excitement and genuine surprise.

"I can actually love another baby with as much love as I love my firstborn!"

It is interesting, isn't it?

No matter how many children a mother gives birth to, each child is as loved and as special to her as if there is not one other in the entire world.

How much more is this true for the heart of God?

CHAPTER 15

Honor the Father, Son, and Holy Spirit

> All three persons of the Godhead reveal both paternal and maternal qualities in their relationship with us. The paternal aspect of God is a combination of authority and care; the maternal quality is one of loving support.
>
> *Dr. J. I. Packer, Editor, ESV Bible*

DR. J. I. PACKER takes a long gaze at the dozens of unread books on his desk, stacks of books on the floor behind his chair, and even more volumes that overflow the shelves in his wall-to-wall bookcase in his office. He peers over his glasses and smiles.

"I'll never get through all of this reading material."

He probably won't, but I am sure he will try.

Packer is named, along with Billy Graham, as one of the most influential Christians in North America today according to *TIME* magazine. The general editor of the English Standard Version (ESV) Bible is known for his practical wisdom as the author of the best-selling contemporary classic *Knowing God* and twenty other religious books.

The Regent College professor says he has one purpose in life: to know God and to share with others the hope he has discovered in the great truths of the Holy Bible.

I am interviewing him today to learn more about the Trinity

of God, one of the most difficult challenges in Christianity for the human mind to try to understand.

Yet, thankfully, Packer takes my prayerful questions all in stride.

The revealed mystery about the divine Holy Trinity is an essential part of the Christian gospel, explains Packer, because God the Father, Jesus the Son, and the Holy Spirit all work together as a team.

"All three are involved in some way or another in whatever the other one does," says Packer, who is a devout Anglican. "The Godhead is truly plural and truly singular; the Trinity is a mystery—three persons, one God."

He then offers a unique analogy to illustrate his point.

"Imagine three dancers on stage involved in a dance with all three dressed identically alike. Sometimes you may see all three, but when all three are lined up exactly one in front of the other on stage, you may be able to see only the one in front. But, in fact, you know that all three are there."

So it is with the Holy Trinity. The three members of the Godhead do all things together, fulfilling a common plan of action and delighting in each other. The most mysterious member of the Trinity is the Holy Spirit, says Packer.

For ages, the Spirit was virtually ignored in Christendom, and this actually caused the author great distress when he was writing his book *Knowing God*. At that time, he wrote that "the Holy Spirit is the Cinderella of Christian doctrines."[1]

But, like Cinderella, the shoe is finally starting to fit in this century.

Today Christendom is alive to the Spirit's work, thanks to the inspiration of the Charismatic movement, a movement that is maturing to the stage of also emphasizing the important Christian virtues of obedience and holiness as well as the spiritual gifts.

We must worship God in Spirit and in truth, says Packer.

The Spirit was sent to Earth by the Father in the Son's name to teach spiritual truth to His followers, the author explains. And Jesus promised to give each one of us the gift of the Holy Spirit, the third powerful being in the tri-personality of God.

"The Holy Spirit is a remarkable person," he observes, noting how the Spirit is known as our Comforter, Counselor, Helper, and Advocate.

The Comforter gives us encouragement, support, and assistance, and Packer explains to me that the Holy Spirit is not an "it," but a divine personal agent who speaks to us, intercedes for us, and can even be saddened or grieved.

Is the Spirit related to any particular gender? I ask him.

Not in Packer's thoughtful opinion.

"All three persons of the Godhead reveal both paternal and maternal qualities in their relationship with us," he says. "The paternal aspect of God is a combination of authority and care; the maternal quality is one of loving support."

The Legacy of a Syrian Monk

Orthodox Christians also believe that God is three distinct, divine persons, but one in essence. The biblical evidence is that masculine and feminine qualities are incorporated in all three members of the Trinity, explains Daniel Ayuch, a biblical scholar at the St. John of Damascus Institute of Theology in the Middle East.

I have never heard of St. John of Damascus. Who was he?

He led an interesting life. A devout Arab Christian, this Aramaic-speaking monk was born in the seventh century in Damascus, Syria, surrounded by the false religious teachings of Islam. John was an expert in theology, music, law, and philosophy and served as chief administrator for the Muslim caliph of Damascus.

The Lord blessed John with an extraordinary talent for satisfying the inquisitive mind. Despite facing ongoing opposition to his faith, he wrote extensively about the truth of Christianity, including his encyclopedic book *The Fountain of Wisdom*. He leaves a lasting legacy for us to contemplate. Below is an excerpt from one of his writings on the perfect oneness of the Trinity, which I have arranged below as a poem:

On the Trinity

If you are curious about God, first tell me of yourself,
And the things that pertain to you.
How does your soul have existence?
How is your mind set in motion?
How do you produce your mental concepts?
How is it that you are both mortal and immortal?

But, if you are ignorant of these things which are within you,
Then why do you not shudder at the thought
Of investigating the sublime things of Heaven?
Think of the Father as a spring of life
Begetting the Son like a river,
And the Holy Ghost [Holy Spirit] like a sea,
For the spring and the river and sea are all one nature.

Think of the Father as a root, and of the Son as a branch,
And the Spirit as a fruit, for the substance in these three is one.
The Father is a sun with the Son as rays
And the Holy Ghost as heat.
The Holy Trinity transcends, by far, every similitude and figure.

So, when you hear of an offspring of the Father,
Do not think of a corporeal offspring.
And when you hear that there is a Word,
Do not suppose Him to be a corporeal word.
And when you hear of the Spirit of God,

Do not think of wind and breath.
Rather, hold your persuasion with a simple faith alone.
For the concept of the Creator is arrived at
By analogy from His creatures . . . [2]

The Trinity and Me

I have read and reread these insights by St. John of Damascus more than a dozen times, and it always seems fresh and enlightening to me. As he writes so eloquently, *the concept of the Creator is arrived at by analogy.*

This gives me a jumping board for new ideas to explore.

Meteorologists point out that H_2O is liquid, solid, and vapor—water, ice, and the mist on the hill. How can I divide the sum of the sun? Are the radiant particles exploding in the massive gaseous star, or the light rays travelling about 186,000 miles per second, or the blessed warmth I feel in the air separate entities or part of the same?

Another analogy comes to me as I take apart a large colorful red-and-yellow wooden Ukrainian nesting doll that features a big doll containing a smaller one, and within that one, an even tinier doll. All three fit together perfectly, into one.

It seems to me that I am in the most comfy of places in the center of Christ's love, surrounded by an even bigger circle of compassion in the arms of the great and awesome *God of Heaven,* who reigns over the universe by His eternal Spirit.

I am secure in the middle of His sovereign domain.

The Trinity is a mystery—yet wonder of wonders, this great and aweome God of infinite mercy also condescends to provide for all of my needs and to love and to console me!

I like how Charles H. Spurgeon puts it:

"It is something very delightful to consider that [thc] Father, Son, and Spirit all cooperate to give us comfort," writes Spurgeon.

"I can understand their cooperating to make the world, I can understand their cooperation in the salvation of a soul, but I am astonished at this same united action in so comparatively small a matter as the comfort of believers."

The *Holy Three* think it a great matter that we should be happy! And the Lord God commands us to be pure and innocent as His little children.

"Ah," you say, "that will do for children, but it won't do for men."

But God keeps His saints as children before Him, and may God grant us grace to be as little children, or we cannot enter the kingdom of heaven.[3]

✒

I continually seek to know God on a deeper level.

At times, like an innocent child, I feel very close to my heavenly Father. Other times, I'm ashamed to say, this so-called saint runs away, a sinful rebellious child. It is a particularly painful period in my life when I avoid coming close to God because of a personal struggle with a besetting temptation to be unfaithful.

I am attracted to someone I have no business being attracted to. Dealing with those impure thoughts is one of the toughest spiritual challenges I face in life. I sincerely want to be pure in body, soul, and mind. Yet my soul is divided. I feel obsessed by an unrelenting inner battle raging inside me.

Feeling tormented, helpless, and depressed, I do not know what to do.

I do not succumb to the temptation, but surely want to.

Reading Proverbs 7:27, I feel determined not to give in as I learn that the house of the adulteress descends into the chambers of death because of her sin. I am petrified that if I give in to this temptation, it will destroy my innocent family.

A trusted friend prays for me for many months, but still I walk around in a black fog. She tells me she believes God wants to take me into His arms and really hug me. But I hold back. I cannot move. Is it shame? Is it because I am too weak? I don't know. All I know is that I am oppressed by evil. I am stuck! Over my head, stuck!

One night I am in church singing the chorus: "Yes, Lord, yes Lord, yes, yes, Lord."[4] Somewhere between this song and the next, during a few moments of silent prayer, something happens as I close my eyes that I will never forget.

I feel like I am suddenly transported halfway across the world to another era in time. And for some inexplicable reason, I find myself in a three-dimensional diorama, kneeling in front of Jesus who is hanging on the cross. I feel like I am right there. At Golgotha, bowed down to the ground in front of the cross!

I look up and see Him suffering intense pain with blood rolling down His face and oozing from the crown of thorns on His head and the wounds on His body.

Suddenly, in one slow-motion, step-by-slow-step movement, He came down from the cross and crouched in front of me with His arms open wide, motioning for me to come close to Him. Like a kindhearted father beckons his shy guilt-ridden child, He gestures that He wants me to come forward so He can hug me!

It is as if I am the only person in the world.

I shrink back. I do not want to be touched by Him. No way! He is covered with blood. And I cannot stand the sight of blood! That is why I can never be a nurse. Despite my shying away and firm reluctance, these gentle inaudible words press into my mind: *"If you don't let me hug you and allow my blood to completely cover you, how can I ever heal you if you don't allow me to come close to you?"*

His eyes are full of compassion.

Without another moment's hesitation, I quit resisting His efforts to embrace me; I close my eyes and feel His blood wash over me. Not one tiny speck of "me" is left uncovered in that blessed fountain.

A feeling of heartbreaking love fills me.

No longer avoiding Him, I sink into His warm hug, covered with His lifesaving love. Suddenly I want to dance—a little girl happy dance, yet at the same time a relieved, mature-woman dance, a white-swan-twirling-on-a-lake dance.

Yes, Lord, yes, Lord, yes, yes, Lord . . . yes!

The weight of ten tons of torment gone, I am finally free!

The Holy Trinity is not some dry religious theory. God the Father, Son, and Holy Spirit work on my transformation in unexplainable ways—grace upon grace, as Dr. Packer commented earlier, "like a three-partner dance in a beautiful ballet!"

That agonizing temptation to be unfaithful, thankfully, is no longer part of my life. It is a long-distant memory. But am I now somehow perfect and sinless?

Absolutely not! I have other sins to battle today. I have in no way "arrived" spiritually. In some ways, the conflict with evil grows ever more intense as I move onward in my journey. The temptation to sin and countless moments of personal defeat remind me of my ongoing desperate need for God's mercy.

It is usually not very dramatic when God gives me victory over sin. Typically, I trip over my self-induced blunders and bloopers. I fall, I confess, God gets me up. I fall again, I confess, God picks me up again; and on it goes. My spiritual walk is nothing but a series of falling, getting up, and walking again. In fact, as I think about it, there is not one sin I have not been guilty of—whether in word, thought, or deed.

But when I confess my sins, I believe that *He is faithful and just to forgive my sins* (see 1 John 1:9). I practice the spiritual discipline of being honest with God, praying, repenting, and accepting His forgiveness, asking Him for strength and power to help me obey.

A man with leprosy once kneeled before Jesus and begged Him on his knees: "If you are willing, you can make me clean." Filled with compassion, Jesus reached out His hand and touched the man. "I am willing," he said. "Be clean!" Immediately, the leprosy left him, and he was cured (Mark 1:40–42 NIV).

How tenderly Jesus still reaches out His hand to touch each one of us.

Our gracious God is not surprised by our sins, nor does He recoil from touching us. When Jesus ascended to Heaven, He promised: *I will not leave you as orphans. I will bless you with my gift—I will give you the Comforter, the Counselor, my very own Spirit, my very power, presence and peace!* (see John 14:18, 26–27).

We are consoled by the healing ministry of Christ.

The mission of the Spirit and the Son are inseparable, one in purpose and complementary to help us honor the eternal Father because the Trinity is one—thus, the *Holy Three* create a comprehensive, never-ending circle of compassion.

And we, the motley crew of wrongdoers, are safe in the middle.

Nicky Cruz and the Cross

Our *Comforter* is not aloof, nor far away, but is closer than we often realize.

The Spirit of God blessed Jennifer Rothschild with the gift of playing music by ear when she was devastated by blindness and gave Anne Lamott victory over alcohol. The Spirit also miraculously transformed Nicky Cruz from a notorious gang leader into a world-renowned peacemaker after he was deemed hopelessly beyond rehabilitation.

God delights in healing shattered lives.

Cruz is an internationally acclaimed public speaker, and his story is featured in the movie *The Cross and the Switchblade*.

During our interview, Cruz tells me that he does not know the answer to the so-called gender of God. The question is of no great concern to him compared to the importance of knowing and experiencing the power of God. He makes a key point: *"Just let the Holy Spirit's power change your life. That's what really counts."*

The spiritual experience is a total inside revolution, he says.

God reached into "a New York ghetto to save me," he explains, and God will do the same for you because the Lord is seeking a relationship with each one of us.

When God touched his heart, the transformation was dramatic. Raised by parents who practiced witchcraft, Cruz says he suffered severe physical and mental abuse. His own mother called him the "son of Satan" and other despicable names.

Growing up to be a hardened gang leader, he lost himself in the nightmare world of drugs and violence. One of his saddest moments, he says, was holding a friend in his arms as he died, bleeding from stab wounds.

Police arrested Cruz countless times, and a court-ordered psychiatrist once stated he was "headed to prison, the electric chair, and hell." Instead the warlord met the Lord of Lords, who unshackled him from the chains of darkness and set him free to walk in peace.

How did this happen?

A street preacher named David Wilkerson loved him with such relentless compassion that even though Cruz spit on him, hit him, and even threatened his life, he only treated him with kindness in return. Wilkerson courageously told Cruz, "You could cut me in a thousand pieces and lay them out on the street. But every piece would cry out, *'Jesus loves you.'* And you'll never be able to run from that."

Love melted the gang leader's heart as he devoted his life to God.

Today Cruz works tirelessly to help hurting youth.

Author of seventeen books, including his best-selling autobiography *Run Baby Run*, which sold 14 million copies, he is a world authority on youth violence and a popular speaker appearing before television audiences, legislators, and the general public.

"To think I came from a witchcraft home. How in the world would you connect a big-city ghetto and a warlord [me] with no concept of God to a country hick [David Wilkerson], who wasn't even of the same race as me, to bring the love of Jesus to me?"

He pauses in quiet contemplation.

"There is an important secret here," he says.

"The secret is the presence of God."

How to Invite the Presence of God

Get ready for an action-packed life because faith works.

God is not wishy-washy or illusive, He is present everywhere at the same time, personally convicting us of our deep need for Christ, our only hope in life. No one wants to live a life based on lies; therefore, the Spirit of Truth comes to us.

During His final sermon, Jesus spoke winsomely to His followers before returning to His former glory in heaven. *It is actually better for you that I go away. I will send you the Comforter. Thus, I will always be with you, wherever you are, to the end of time* (see John 16:7 amd Matthew 28:20).

Jesus ensures the fullest blessings of the Holy Trinity as He promised:

In fact, whatever you ask for in my name, I will do; so that the Father may be glorified in the Son. If you ask me for something in my name, I will do it. If you love me, you will keep my commands; and I will ask the Father, and he will give you another comforting Counselor like me, the Spirit of Truth, to be with you forever.

John 14:13–16 CJB

How should we invite God to come into our lives?

"Unfortunately, we often block ourselves from this experience," says Sebastian Brock, a Bible scholar at Oxford University. "We must be self-emptying. By emptying oneself of the negative aspects of our personalities—our anger, our ideas, and our ambitions—we make space for the Spirit to act in our lives."

How can we best experience this?

"Become a disciple of Jesus," explains Father Thomas Hopko, an Orthodox priest. "Take up your cross daily. Suffer patiently what you must suffer in this corrupt world for the sake of what is right, good, true, and beautiful."

It starts by being faithful in the littlest things of life. "Try not to do evil in even the smallest way. And you will know. There is no other way," says Hopko.

The "image" of God is recreated in our heart, as the divine spark of God's law of love operates within the soul of every human being. This is what makes us human in distinction from all other creatures in the universe.

J. I. Packer summarizes how the Spirit of God helps us to listen.

"The Holy Spirit dwells within a Christian believer like a person keeping a house in order and helping people to aim for godliness," Packer explains, adding that it is important to read the Bible daily for instruction, inspiration, and spiritual growth.

"We must learn to meditate on God's commands because we will become wise if we learn to obey God's Word," says Packer.

The Comforter gives us courage to follow Christ despite the storms we encounter in life and gives us the perfect sense of belonging to him!

Helping us to weigh our circumstances, Packer explains that the Spirit leads us to take loving actions with "a sense of deep joy and hope for the future and the sense that we are loved and our lives are blessed!"

Growing in faith is not as hard as people fear. It is actually quite simple.

When Packer wakes up, he prays with a childlike greeting: *Good morning, Lord. This is your day; I am your child, please show me your way.* And God always delights to answer his humble prayer! The author may have earned a PhD in Philosophy from Oxford, but a university degree means nothing when it comes to practicing faith.

"All we have to do is be humble and teachable and stand in awe of God's holiness and sovereignty," he says.

The Scriptures reveal that each person's heart is a sacred temple where the Spirit of God longs to dwell. We invite the presence of the Lord by meditating on the stories in the Bible and saying a simple prayer such as: *Please, God, fill the spiritual void in my life.*

And the peace of God moves quietly within.

As we submit to the sovereign will of God, His indwelling is accomplished "not by might nor by power, but by my Spirit" (Zech. 4:6 NIV). So we are privileged to live in the presence, the power and the pity of the Lord God Almighty.

This is how we may pray:

Dear God, thank you for the gift of life and shedding your blood to forgive my sins. You have promised that if I confess my sins, you are faithful and just to forgive my sins. So I confess my sins and trust that you are faithful and just to forgive me. Please, Father God, write your law of love on my heart so that I may honor you and live according to your will, as David once wrote: "I delight to do your will, O my God; your law is within my heart" (Ps. 40:8 ESV).

No god in any other religion comes anywhere close to the compassion of the God of the Bible, so loving, kind, and just, all-powerful, all-holy, and all-wise.

In my humanity, I (Trudy) will never fully comprehend the Holy Trinity.

It's like jumping to the moon. All I can do is imagine, and

in my dumb imagining, jump one foot into the air in the direction of the moon, but land so far short, it's laughable. Did I land on the moon? Hardly! I spring up so pathetically, gravity pulling clay back to muddy gray as I strain for the white globe in the velvet sky.

Dare I jump again?

The Father, Son, and Holy Spirit somehow carry me across the desert and the wilderness to a far-off country of coriander wafers and honey. The metaphor of God as a comforting mother is reassuring, but the analogy of a kind father is more common in Scripture. In Deuteronomy 1:31, for example, it is written that "the LORD your God carried you, as a man carries his son" (ESV). So He carries me today.

The Holy Trinity is a timeless paradox, explains Gay Lynn Voth.

"We worship one God; it's not like we have three gods," says the Bible instructor. "We have one God who represents Himself in three ways, the Paternal Creator, Maternal Wisdom, and Incarnate Christ."

The paradoxes in Christianity are difficult to understand, especially the spiritual concepts of *"both/and"* instead of the typical black-and-white logic of *"either/or,"* which is easier to figure out. Here are a few divine *"both/and"* propositions to consider:

Walking in faith, believers *lose* their lives in order to be *saved*. When we are *humble*, we are *exalted*, and we become *fools* for God and thereby grow *wise*.

There is a paradox and a sacred balance in the so-called gender of God.

"For example, Christ is both human and divine," says Voth.

"And God is both maternal and paternal."

PART FOUR

Ancient Words, Relevant Today

CHAPTER 16

Wisdom Calls Out

Wisdom calls aloud in the open air
and raises her voice in the public places;
she calls out at streetcorners
and speaks out at entrances to city gates . . .
"Repent when I reprove—
I will pour out my spirit to you,
I will make my words known to you."
Proverbs 1:20–21, 23 CJB

C. S. Lewis would inform his readers when he was about to lead them into a deep Bible study and offer the suggestion to skip the next section if they might not be enthusiastic for the subject. I think I will offer the same advice here.

I am about to delve into some controversial issues that even long-time theologians are struggling to understand. I invite you to find a quiet place with the Bible, pray for wisdom, and read Proverbs 8 in its entirety. May God grant you the thrill of discovering for yourself the mystery that unfolds in this unique creation story.

Proverbs 8 is a precious jewel set in the center of God's Word.

A Hidden Library

There is a pathway in the woods at Westminster Abbey appropriately called "Jacob's Ladder," a challenging slope where I love to hike and then head to the library to study. Father Boniface is in charge of the library at the monastery where the windows open to the panoramic view of the valley below with pastoral dairy farms and green pastures interspersed by the vibrant burgundies of the fields of blueberries.

Walking slowly and slightly stooped, Boniface wanders around his library admiring more than fifty thousand books, like a proud father adores his favorite children.

"It's a good library," he says in barely a whisper.

He has spent more than five decades in charge of the library, and it is obvious he is passionate about the power of words. From Harvard classics to contemporary religious titles, the elderly monk finds no shortage of noble ideas to contemplate here.

"Your feet should only be long enough to reach the ground." He smiles as he sits down and quotes Abraham Lincoln on the virtue of humility. He is not a tall man.

I follow Father Boniface as he climbs down the staircase and holds tight to the railing. Reaching the basement, he turns a key to unlock a yellow door that leads into a secret library. Turning on the light in the small hidden room, he looks at me.

"Well, what do you think?" he asks me in anticipation.

A musty scent permeates the shelves of leather with rows of humungous rare Bibles and religious books—some more than 450 years old. I look around the room in quiet awe. Some of the books are three inches thick, protected by covers of ornately carved wood with dark metal clasps holding the gilded pages together.

The books face the walls as if they guard ancient secrets.

"Father Boniface, I really appreciate being here."

As the custodian of thousands of rare books, Boniface is following in the long tradition of venerated monks and scholars in the Western world who have safeguarded the keys of knowledge to philosophy, history, language, science, and religion. He knows where every single book is located in this sacred vault of knowledge.

I feel honored to be on this side of the yellow door where few people are invited.

Will any of these sacred books add another link to the golden thread that connects the past to the present about the missing maternal features of God's love?

Countless famous religious manuscripts are preserved in monasteries across the world. It feels mystical to be here as I consider how the first movable type printing press in the mid-1400s made way for the very books and Bibles I will study today. This hidden library seems an appropriate place for me to seek the wisdom of the ages.

"This library is very special to me," says Boniface.

He picks up a tiny book called *The Life of Jesus* written in 1552 by a monk who plainly set forth the foundational doctrines of Christianity. This mini-book is only a few inches wide and fits easily in the palm of his hand.

"Can you imagine the work that went into setting the tiny type for this book?"

The chatting ends. Boniface knows I have research to do. He leaves a small silver key in my right hand and asks me to lock the yellow door when I leave. I nod. As I walk around the bookshelves in solitude, my thoughts are racing as I ponder the choices.

Where in the world do I begin?

I start to read a humungous ancient Bible that is two feet long. The Old English type is imprinted on coarse white paper, and the verses have no paragraph breaks. The texts read as stiff and awkward as the physical pages themselves. I return it to the shelf.

A Latin concordance, published in 1615, piques my interest.

No, it is not my favorite choice I decide after ten minutes.

A large black leather Douay Holy Bible placed high on the bookshelf catches my eye. This is a copy of a translation first published in 1609. I estimate this rare Bible to be three inches thick. Carefully, I put both of my hands around it and gently balance it out of the shelf. It is so weighty I bend my knees and brace my whole body to move it from the shelf to the study table. Excitement jolts through me as I leaf through the pages.

What I have before me is a precious manuscript.

The source of the Douay-Rheims Bible is the Latin Vulgate, which was first translated by Jerome, a highly educated monk, around AD 405. He painstakingly translated the original Hebrew Old Testament (OT) and the Greek New Testament (NT) into Latin. The (OT) Douay is the first Bible authorized by the Catholic Church.[1]

I am curious what I'll find as I turn to Proverbs 8. Immediately, I am intrigued by a divine person, mysteriously named "wisdom," who is exuberant during the creation of the Earth in a rarely revealed scene going back to the beginning of time:

> I [wisdom] was with him [God] forming all things and was delighted every day, playing before him at all times. Playing in the world and my delights were to be with the children of men. Now, therefore, ye children, hear me: blessed are they that keep my ways. Hear instruction and be wise, and refuse it not. . . . He that shall find me, shall find life, and shall have salvation from the Lord.
>
> *Proverbs 8:30–33, 35* DV, *bracketed words added*

The energy in these texts takes my breath away.

Who in the world is this person who accompanied God when He was *forming all things*? Interestingly, the pronouns "*she*" and "*her*" are used to describe this divine feminine persona named *Wisdom*. And she is definitely having fun enjoying the Father's newly created world, especially feeling great delight in the company of the children!

This is amazing. Who is she? Where does she fit into the creation story?

I quickly turn to Genesis 1 to find the Spirit *hovering* over the waters during creation, which in the Hebrew language is a feminine verb. Could *Wisdom* be another name for the Spirit? Other hints lead me to dig deeper.

I reflect on what I observe every day in life.

Who is the first to get up and dance when the music starts? Who is usually the first to crouch down to play with children? And, typically, who loves to create adventures in the middle of the loud, happy shouts of dozens of preschoolers?

It is more often than not a woman.

Whoever this divine feminine person is—and I am in a complete state of shock over this—it appears we share our femininity in common.

Many years go by. . . . My daughters leave home, they get married; grandchildren arrive to play in my family room. And still I ponder the meaning of wisdom.

I have questions to ask as I arrange to meet a well-known rabbi.

Who in the World Is *Wisdom*?

Rabbi Laura is a slender, high-energy woman with a radiant smile.

Whether lecturing on the environment or on the positive aspects of having faith in God, Rabbi Laura Duhan Kaplan is known for her wise insights. She grew up in New York to become a well-respected American philosopher, and she was named Professor of the Year in 2001 by the Carnegie Foundation for the Advancement of Teaching.

Today she relaxes in a bright blue chair in her library, which is located upstairs in the balcony of the Or Shalom synagogue in Vancouver. A quote from Isaiah 30:15 is set prominently on the wall above her study area.

"In quietness and in confidence shall be your strength" (KJV).

Looking over the balcony, the rabbi admires a handcrafted wooden chest at the front of the sanctuary containing a copy of the Torah. Carved into the wooden chest are the Hebrew words *"Eitz chaim hee,"* meaning: *"She—the Torah—is a Tree of Life."* This reminds the faithful to nurture themselves "in the light of the Garden of Eden and to thereby live holy lives."

The Torah[2] is filled with stories that are rich in meaning for women.

"Abraham, Isaac, and Jacob weren't the only ones who had a close relationship with God," explains Kaplan. "Sarah, Rebekah, Rachel, and Leah all had wonderful conversations and interesting relationships with God, all in their own right."

New light continues to shine from the ancient texts as the rabbi begins a Bible study on the possible maternal qualities in God. First, she notes that the divine feminine being in Proverbs named *Wisdom* is an intriguing character study.

Here is a biblical excerpt in a modern English version:

Doesn't wisdom call out?
Doesn't understanding raise her voice? . . .
I was there when he [God] set the heavens in place.
When he marked out the place where the sky meets the sea, I was
     there.
That was when he put the clouds above.
It was when he fixed the ocean springs in place.
It was when he set limits for the sea
so that the waters had to obey his command.
When he marked out the foundations of the earth, I was there.
I was the skilled worker at his side.
I was filled with delight day after day.
I was always happy to be with him.
                    Proverbs 8:1, 27–30 NIRV, bracketed word added

Who is this feminine skilled worker, who continually tells us she *"was there"* when the Creator formed the clouds above and fixed the oceans in place?

Kaplan explains that the Hebrew language implies that *Wisdom* has a love relationship with God. The "skilled worker" in Proverbs 8:30 is translated from the Hebrew word *amon*, which means a craftsperson, a nursemaid, or a nanny.

Of course, a nursemaid is a woman who takes care of children.

This story, therefore, paints a lovely picture of a female who is excited with childlike exuberance, wonder, and happiness. The word *amon* may also mean that *Wisdom* was like a friend rejoicing in the presence of God, says Kaplan.

In other words, explains the rabbi, this divine being, who was by God's side during creation, was filled with delight, day after day. She is a mystery, yet the Scriptures disclose a number of clues in an interesting chain of connections.

In the beginning, during the formation of the world, according to Genesis 1:2, the Spirit was actively partaking in creation by "hovering" over the waters.

"The Hebrew word for hovering, *mirachefet*, is the same word used to describe a mother bird hovering over her nest. This is very much a motherly image and is similar to other Scriptures which show God as a mother bird taking care of her brood."

This concept that the Spirit of God is feminine is "a beautiful and a very nice image," Kaplan says, noting how this fits nicely with the matriarchal metaphors in Isaiah 49:15 when God proclaims: *"Can a mother forget the baby at her breast and have no compassion on the child she has borne? Though she may forget, I will not forget you!"* (NIV).

"This verse clearly shows that God loves us like a mother loves her babies."

A poignant Hebrew prayer speaks of God as *Av Harachamim*, which means compassionate Father, and the Hebrew word *rechem* means "womb," explains Kaplan.

So this beautiful prayer teaches us that God is like a father and a mother.

Proverbs 8: Focus of Debate

Wisdom is not easy to categorize. Known as *Sophia* in the Greek language and *Hokmah* in Hebrew, she stirs no small amount of debate among scholars today.

I have questions. Lots of questions! And so do many other people.

First of all, I don't understand who she is, although the rabbi has given me some good clues to start thinking about. Now I am curious to find out what leading Protestant scholars might have to tell me about this subject.

Dr. Jürgen Moltmann of Germany is forthright in his summary.

Wisdom is basically another name for the Holy Spirit, he says.

The dual role makes logical sense to the famous Reformed theologian.

"There is a direct correlation between the feminine divine being named *Wisdom* and the Spirit. . . . *Wisdom* in Proverbs 8 is the Spirit who helped create the world!"

The book of Proverbs unveils details that are not disclosed anywhere else!

"She is speaking to God in Proverbs 8, on her own, and God is working through *Wisdom* in the creation of the world. They are one!" explains Moltmann. "The Father created the world through the Son, in the power of the Spirit."

His explanation is succinct in its simplicity. Beautiful! Powerful!

But, as with most theological debates today, not everyone agrees.

Dr. Robert Hiebert, the Director of the Septuagint Institute, for example, cautions against equating *Wisdom* with any member of the Godhead or reading too much into her feminine personality. He asks the following questions:

How do you explain the fact that there is also a feminine character named *Folly* and a *"foolish woman"* in the other chapters of Proverbs? Does that mean females should be identified with the character of *Folly*?

Hardly!

He believes it is better to understand *Wisdom* and *Folly* as personifications of two abstract concepts, both of which happen to be feminine nouns in Hebrew. The main role of wisdom is to instruct people on how to live well, rather than to reveal some aspect of the divine essence.

Wisdom, he explains, is the "personification of the principle of order," by which God accomplished His creative work and continues to sustain the cosmos today.

Dr. J. I. Packer, general editor of the English Standard Version Bible, concurs.

The writer of Proverbs was simply embodying the gift of wisdom by using feminine metaphors. The emphasis in Proverbs 8, Packer agrees, is that God is ready to give wisdom to all who desire this gift and will take the steps necessary to obtain it.

Scholars on both sides of the issue give many good reasons for their positions.

So what is a believer to do?

Dr. Rowshan Nemazee, an assistant professor at Champlain College in Vermont, says she finds it helpful to view *Wisdom* as both a good virtue—and the divine cocreator.

"*Wisdom* is an attribute or a part of God, and she's also an interesting character," says Nemazee. "Steeped in mystery, *Wisdom* was present and filled with wonder at the creation of the world, and she is certainly referred to as female!"

The Oldest Protestant University

Jesus once told a story about ten virgins to illustrate faith in action.

When five foolish virgins neglect to fill their lamps with oil, the door to the Kingdom is forever closed to them. Meanwhile, five other virgins, pure in heart, with lamps full of oil, live in expectation of the return of Christ. Though they fall asleep, they are ready for the Master to return with sweet fragrant oil in their lamps aglow.

The five "wise" virgins enter the door to the Kingdom.

I set my eyes on Marburg, a small, medieval town in Germany.

Steeped in religious history, Marburg is one of the towns where Martin Luther, one of the legendary founders of the Protestant faith, among other famous Reformers in the 1500s stood their ground in their allegiance to the Creator God of the Holy Bible.

The Protestant faith is very much alive and vibrant today.

A grand medieval castle stands like a mighty fortress on the hillside above the town of Marburg where Dr. Christl M. Maier, a world-class Lutheran scholar, is making the Holy Scriptures the focus of intense study.

She once taught at the Yale School of Divinity in the US and in 2005 was one of only seven scholars in North America to receive the highly celebrated Henry Luce III Fellows in Theology award. Maier now lives in Marburg and is a senior-ranking Professor of Old Testament at the Philipps-Universität, the oldest university in the world, established on Protestant principles in 1527.

"The Bible is relevant for people today," Maier tells me.

I enjoy interviewing her because, in my opinion, she brings a global perspective to the Christian faith as the sure foundation for true peace and inner happiness.

The professor graciously shares her extensive knowledge as the author of a scholarly book in German called *Die "Fremde Frau" in Proverbien 1–9*, which is based on her research in biblical wisdom literature.

Maier shares some important insights that I did not know before.

According to Proverbs 8, *Wisdom* was with God from the beginning of time, she rejoiced in God's creation, and the Israelites were certainly well aware of her feminine qualities. Secondly, the feminine profile of *Wisdom* and the Holy Spirit, unfortunately, were rejected by Philo, a Jewish philosopher in Alexandria, who was most influential on the early Christian traditions. He identified the Spirit of God with the *logos* of God; therefore, the spirit *could not* be feminine and thus became masculine. Subsequently, in many Christian texts, as they now stand, most of the feminine traces of *Wisdom* and the Holy Spirit have basically been toned down, explains the professor.

Revisiting this issue is vital today, says Maier, because to retain the status quo of the "all-male God" is no longer an option for believers.

"We have to reclaim the feminine imagery of *Wisdom* and the Holy Spirit," she explains because many people have been uninformed in the past about the maternal metaphors of God that have been beautifully preserved in the Bible.

"It is time to celebrate these spiritual truths!"

"Wise Adviser"

I decide to interview one last theologian to finish my study.

Students enjoy the lively teachings of Rev. Dr. James M. Lindenberger as he presents a powerful conclusion to the apparent controversy over Proverbs 8.

He is an expert on the Hebrew Bible and is professor emeritus at the Vancouver School of Theology, a large stately building set high above the waves of the Pacific Ocean. This is a long-standing seminary for the Presbyterian, United, and Anglican churches in Canada.

The theologian offers valuable context to the study on Proverbs.

Speaking in his office, he thoughtfully explains that the divine female persona named *Wisdom* is stirring considerable theological debate among scholars in the present generation. But these biblical passages were also heavily discussed in the past.

There was a great debate in the fourth century between interpreters who, on both sides, were misinterpreting the texts in Proverbs 8, believing the passages referred to Jesus, the second person of the Trinity—which the texts *do not*, explains Lindenberger.

"Who, then, do these biblical passages refer to?" I ask.

Wisdom was present when God created the Earth. This personified divine being was beside God as an *amon*, a rare word that is translated as "a master worker, an artisan, a craftsperson, or a highly skilled worker," says the scholar.

He confirms what Rabbi Laura had summarized to me earlier.

In the Akkadian language—a close relative of the Hebrew language spoken in ancient Mesopotamia—the word *ummanu* means "a wise adviser." While there are various interpretations of *amon*, the most likely one is a "master builder" or an "adviser to God," according to Lindenberger's study.

"The passages about *Wisdom* in Proverbs 8 very clearly personify a feminine aspect of God," he says with no hesitation.

Discussions need not be dogmatic about the feminine dimension of God, but certainly this divine being named *Wisdom* has personality and showed inexpressible delight and a sense of wonder during creation, says the scholar.

"*Wisdom* is personal and profoundly real—*she is who she is*."

Theologically, *Wisdom* is the centerpiece of the book of Proverbs.

Lindenberger agrees with other theologians who believe it is not right to teach the traditional view of an all-male God because scholars, from the earliest times, have acknowledged that God transcends the categories of male or female descriptions.

It is reasonable for theologians to use a balance of masculine and feminine biblical metaphors when referring to God, he says.

"It is important for our community of faith."

"I Love Those Who Love Me"

While the subject is controversial, clearly a number of mainstream theologians believe the Spirit of God operates in the divine personal role of *Wisdom*.

And there is more to contemplate. Not only is *Wisdom* depicted in the Scriptures as a feminine personality who delights in the eternal Father's creative works, but the Bible also reveals she hates sin and evil and is passionate about honesty and purity.

She has personality—plus!

Wisdom guides us to live a life of integrity, to be faithful in marriage, and to have good morals. These attributes are much needed in our materialistic, ever more godless Western culture. Ethics and morals are crucial to a spiritually fulfilled life.

Just listen to the voice speaking to us in Proverbs 8:

My mouth speaks what is true.
My lips hate evil.
All the words of my mouth are honest.
None of them is twisted or sinful. . . .
To have respect for the LORD is to hate evil.
I hate pride and bragging.
I hate evil ways and twisted words.
I have good sense and give good advice.
I have understanding and power.

By me kings rule.
Leaders make laws that are fair.
By me princes govern.
By me all nobles rule on earth.
I love those who love me.
Those who look for me find me.
With me are riches and honor.
With me are lasting wealth and success.
My fruit is better than fine gold.
My gifts are better than the finest silver.
I walk in ways that are honest.
I take paths that are right.
I leave riches to those who love me.
I give them more than they have room for.
            Proverbs 8:7–8, 13–21 NIRV

In summary, *Wisdom* speaks what is true (v. 7), indicative of the Spirit of truth (see John 14:26). And *Wisdom* hates evil, pride, and twisted thinking and converses with us as only a person with feelings and intellect can communicate. It is noteworthy that she loves us because we love her (v. 17), and she enjoys who we are (v. 31). Only a personal being can love us and feel happy spending quality time with us. Therefore, it makes sense that she is more than just a good characteristic.

Could *Wisdom* be a divine person?

What other characteristics are shared in common with the Holy Spirit?

Wisdom states that her "fruit is better than fine gold." Paul identifies the "fruit" of the Spirit as: love, joy, peace, patience, kindness, goodness, faithfulness, gentleness, and self-control (see Gal. 5:22). And James also writes that the wisdom from above *is full of good fruits* (see James 3:17).

In fact, *Wisdom* gives politicians the power to govern fairly

(vv. 15–16) if they ask for help. And she grants riches (v. 21) and blessings to those who "love" her, supplying financial riches in abundance—far more than we have room for!

It is obvious she wants to enjoy a personal relationship with each one of us. *Wisdom* inspires us to live a life of integrity and to walk in the ways of righteousness (see Prov. 8:20), just as in the New Testament we are instructed to "walk in the Spirit" (Gal. 5:16 NKJV). Then, amazingly enough, God gives us the strength and the courage not to carry out the desires of the flesh.

Wisdom is the source of power we need today to live an ethical life.

And she does something else that is marvelous.

When we seek her, we will find her (see Prov. 8:17). She gives us good advice to make the best possible decision in every difficulty in life because the *amon*, the *wise adviser*, makes this promise to us: *"Counsel and sound judgment are mine"* (Prov. 8:14 NIV).

And Jesus Himself identifies the Holy Spirit as our *Counselor*.

Returning home, I wash the dishes, scrub the floors, fold my laundry, and do other boring chores. I often do my best thinking when I'm cleaning, and when I'm worried, the floors get a really good shine. And so today I clean up a storm. I polish my worry into the cedar paneling in the family room with enriched Danish oil.

"There, that's done." I slowly lean myself down in the chair. I sigh.

Why me? Lord, this feels like I am getting in way too deep.

I look out the window and see the trees swaying in the wind on my hillside. I remember how happy I was when my husband and I bought our house in the country on 3.75 acres. My fondest prayers had come true. But my concept of what I owned was not at all what I expected! I thought our land ended at the top of the hill.

But that was not the end at all!

Imagine my surprise, years later, when a Realtor with a topography map in his hands showed me that my property was more than twice as big as I had thought it was. I *actually* owned two acres of rain forest, way past the top of the hill!

The landing over the ledge had been far beyond my eyesight.

How much more is this true of the spiritual realm? I see through glass darkly. I know only in part. I put down my dust cloth. *Who am I, Lord? That you have brought me this far, that I should write all of this? And listen to words from on high?*

Lord God, there is none like you!

Just as my little speck of Earth is so ridiculously small compared to the expanse of the universe, so my mind is so utterly minuscule compared to the atomic whisper of but one of my Creator's thoughts. When He vanquished the chill of nothingness and the morning stars sang together in concerto at the beginning of time, I cannot imagine the warmth of the luminous light that dispelled the darkness!

Let there be light! The command shone from the sight of God's great mind. And yet this great and awesome God condescends to warm and light my own little heart! I know so precious little. I need to be quiet, not argue, let God lead.

I fold up my dust cloth and wrap up my thoughts.

In the timeless thunder of the Trinity, *in the beginning*, the Father made the heavens and the earth. And *in the beginning* was the *Word*, Jesus, the Son of God, who was also present. And *in the beginning* the Spirit hovered over the waters as the eternal Father inscribed the circle of our planet on the face of the deep.

It was then that *Wisdom* declared: *I was there.*

Just as the *Word* is another name for the Son of God, could *Wisdom* be a sacred subtitle for the Spirit, both as a virtue and a cocreator? Might this quiet whisper *I was there . . .* be one of those mysteries God wants to unveil to believers today?

I put away the dishes. I avoid thinking about the obvious implications.

I don't know if I should write this. Who am I, Lord? Couldn't you choose someone with a PhD in religion?

A new granddaughter is born. It is a busy year. I hang up a new calendar with a picture of a hot-air balloon; I read the advice:

Believe. To accomplish great things, we must not only act, but also dream, not only plan, but also believe.

Anatole France

From my kitchen window, I cannot see the forest over the top of the hill. But I know it is there because after I walk up the pathway that leads almost straight up, I find peace among the tall cedar trees where I kneel, pray, and believe.

Word upon word, precept upon precept, like a treasure hunter follows the next clue in a complicated hand-drawn map, I press onward, drawn to the unfading beauty of a gem of great worth.

Will the next link in this golden chain be among the priceless tomes of the Magna Carta and the famous Gutenberg Bible at the British Museum in London?

My journey leads me now to speak to an esteemed Oxford scholar.

CHAPTER 17

The Spirit of Truth

The Syriac writers followed the example of the
Hebrew scribes who used feminine imagery for the
Spirit. This was widely understood in that era.

Dr. Sebastian Brock, Oxford University

HE EXPLORES GOD'S Word like a modern adventurer pursues
priceless treasure.

Dr. Sebastian Brock is one of the world's leading experts on
the Holy Bible in the old Syriac language, which is similar to the
Aramaic dialect spoken by Jesus.

Why is this scholar's expertise in such high demand?

The original language of the Old Testament was written in
Hebrew, and the New Testament was written in Greek. But
many people are not aware of the "Syriac factor."

Copies of some of the earliest biblical manuscripts were
painstakingly translated and handwritten in the Syriac language
by faithful scribes in Mesopotamia.

In fact, the first people to be named Christians lived in Antioch, Syria.

What does this have to do with today? Everything! The old
Syriac Bible is a virtual mother lode of spiritual gems—as close as
we may get to the original Aramaic language and words spoken
by Jesus to his twelve disciples.

Brock has spent decades studying the Syriac Bible.

He regularly reads portions of the oldest Syriac translation of the Gospels in the two remaining manuscripts, which date to around AD 400. These are priceless records of even older biblical manuscripts, originating in the late second or early third century. One of these precious tomes is preserved in the British Library in London; the other is stored at St. Catherine's Monastery at Mount Sinai in Egypt.[1]

When I speak to the Oxford professor, he is personable and approachable.

His scholastic knowledge on the Bible has earned him the worldwide reputation of being the "Father of the Renaissance in Syriac Studies," and he is frank about Christendom's long-lost feminine imagery of the Holy Spirit.

Brock rediscovered this for himself as he studied ancient biblical manuscripts which clearly use the pronoun "she" for the Holy Spirit. He was amazed. But no more than anyone else who reads these ancient texts for themselves. In the Old Syriac Gospels, Jesus made a well-known statement in the book of John which should be translated, according to Brock, into English this way:

"The Spirit, the *Paraclete*, which my Father will send you in my name: She will teach you everything."
John 14:26 Old Syriac Gospels

Brock says "the feminine pronoun is quite emphatic here."

For him, it was like finding a pearl of great price, and he was excited when he first read it about four decades ago. It certainly piqued his scholastic interest. The Oxford professor began breaking new ground in his research as he continued to explore the most ancient texts of the Syriac New Testament and found other references that also reflect the Holy Spirit in grammatical feminine language.

This was common in all the Semitic languages, explains Brock.

The Syriac writers followed the example of the Hebrew scribes who used feminine imagery for the Spirit, and this was widely understood in that era. But then, inexplicably, these references fell off the pages in later translations.

Only recently has this issue commanded greater public attention.

Many theologians in the past did not bother to pay too much attention to the possible feminine aspects of God. But today it is a different world due to the popularity of fictional blockbusters such as *The Da Vinci Code*. Serious biblical scholars like Brock, however, discount the allegations raised in *The Da Vinci Code* that there ever was a cover-up of the "divine feminine," or a so-called conspiracy.

"The feminine activities of the Holy Spirit have never been a secret," he says.

The truth may have been ignored. Some attributes may have been denied. Some features forgotten. But they were never a secret! Theologians have always known this.

Indeed, feminine imagery is used for the Father and the Son as well, says Brock.

Today these ancient facts are flooding into the religious mainstream.

Why now?

In the past few decades, women began to enter the field of theology which had formerly been reserved for men only, he says.

This new generation of scholars is pursuing investigations into the Bible, searching for clues about the maternal aspects of God. They're looking for solid facts, and they have discovered anew these spiritual gems. A number of well-respected male theologians, like Brock and others, are also at the forefront of biblical discoveries.

The Oxford professor says the "divine Spirit" was treated grammatically as feminine in the early Syriac writings from about the third century AD until the fifth century with the words *ruha qaddishta*, containing the *t* as the feminine indicator.

In later texts, however, one starts to find *qaddisha*, the masculine form.

It is interesting that the Holy Spirit was specifically referred to as "mother" in the sacred Syriac and Greek writings of Mesopotamia, Brock said. When he researched the early Syriac religious literature, especially the poetry of St. Ephrem, he found matriarchal imagery used for all three persons of the Trinity.

This soon started to change with time.

The Syriac writers became wary about addressing the Holy Spirit as "mother" near the end of the fourth century, no doubt because of the abuse of this maternal imagery by groups which worshipped false pagan triads with a father, mother, and son.

The church pioneers did not want Christianity to be confused with surrounding false religions. Therefore, they rejected the feminine pronoun for the Spirit.

Unfortunately, the concept of the once well-respected motherly qualities of the Spirit were practically wiped out. The feminine language for the Spirit started to disappear in the Syriac sacred writings as well as in various Bible translations, Brock explains.

Why did the changes occur?

It is a mystery, but one may surmise that the changes occurred because the majority of translators in the church were men. Therefore, they tended to think theologically as males, he says. In other words, gender bias may have influenced them. In addition, there was a backlash in Christianity, rightfully so, against the false worship of goddesses practiced in the Roman and Greek religious cultures.

The Greek authors who translated the Hebrew Bible (OT) referred to the Holy Spirit in neuter language (*hagion pneuma*). Then the Spirit was rendered masculine (*spiritus*) in later Latin translations. The pronoun changes continued unabated over the course of time. Translators of later Syriac versions of the New Testament made the pronoun masculine starting around the fifth century.

Thus, the feminine references to the Spirit started to disappear from the Syriac translations of the Gospels and were eventually "harmonized" to come into line with the Greek text of the New Testament, Brock said. These revised texts were included in the Peshitta, which became the official biblical version of the Syriac church. [2]

The public's awareness of the maternal aspects of the Godhead, unfortunately, has largely been lost over the centuries, says the professor.

Dr. Brock believes a balance is now required.

"It would be inadequate and misleading to confine any description of God solely to masculine or feminine imagery. On the other hand, we deprive ourselves of the richness of our rich spiritual heritage by ignoring the sacred gender attributes," he says.

"It is important today for faithful believers to correct the imbalance."

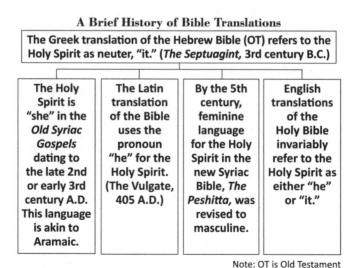

A Brief History of Bible Translations

The Greek translation of the Hebrew Bible (OT) refers to the Holy Spirit as neuter, "it." (*The Septuagint,* 3rd century B.C.)			
The Holy Spirit is "she" in the *Old Syriac Gospels* dating to the late 2nd or early 3rd century A.D. This language is akin to Aramaic.	The Latin translation of the Bible uses the pronoun "he" for the Holy Spirit. (The Vulgate, 405 A.D.)	By the 5th century, feminine language for the Holy Spirit in the new Syriac Bible, *The Peshitta,* was revised to masculine.	English translations of the Holy Bible invariably refer to the Holy Spirit as either "he" or "it."

Note: OT is Old Testament

The Lord God, "He" Is Righteous and Holy

The oldest Syriac Gospels can cause quite a stir among Christian scholars.

Are these sacred books considered trustworthy?

Dr. Richard A. Taylor has researched this topic at length because Aramaic studies and Syriac literature are among his specialties. He is well respected for his in-depth biblical knowledge as the director of the PhD program at Dallas Theological Seminary in Texas, as well as his work as professor of Old Testament Studies.

Taylor explains that the "inspiration and inerrancy of the Bible" are theological categories that should be restricted to the original Hebrew/Aramaic writings of the Old Testament and the original Greek text of the New Testament. Since the oldest Syriac Gospels were translated from the original Greek texts, they do not, based on this principle, meet the strictest standard of biblical inerrancy.

Dr. Sebastian Brock, meanwhile, has this to say:

"For the actual content of the words of Jesus, the Greek is obviously the oldest and best witness," says Brock. "But if one wants to go behind the Greek to the original Aramaic words of Jesus—which several scholars have tried to do, trying to reconstruct it in Palestinian Aramaic of the first century AD—then it is helpful to look at an early translation from Greek into a related Aramaic dialect, such as the Old Syriac Gospels."

How do other theologians consider this contentious question?

Dr. Robert Hiebert is the Director of Trinity Western University's Septuagint Institute, the only research center in North America that specializes in the ancient Greek version of the Jewish Scriptures. He, for one, admires Brock's scholastic research.

"In the world of scholarship he is highly respected, not only among Syriac specialists, but also among biblical scholars in general," he said.

Hiebert also appreciates the old Syriac Gospels as the product of one of the early Christian communities in which the original Greek texts were translated.

"They are part of the rich tapestry that constitutes the history of biblical interpretation and theological reflection," says Hiebert. "One may agree or disagree with aspects of that community's thinking, but it remains part of that history."

Pronouns to Ponder

Can there be peace among pastors over the pronoun puzzle?

In Syriac literature, adjectives or pronouns with "spirit" as the antecedent are feminine, agrees Taylor. The word for "spirit" is also usually feminine grammatically in the Aramaic and Hebrew languages. In Genesis 1:2, for example, the participle for "hovering" modifies the "Spirit [or wind] of God" and is therefore feminine.

But at times the "spirit" is regarded as masculine, explains Taylor.

The word is neuter in Greek, and the King James Version translators, on occasion, carried this gender-neutral feature of the Greek text over to their English translation, referring to the Spirit as "it," as in Romans 8:26, for example.

How should we understand these points in regard to the nature of God?

"It is helpful to keep in mind that in language, gender is a grammatical phenomenon that is not necessarily linked to sexuality at all," says Taylor.

This is purely a grammatical distinction. It would be a mistake to draw out of it anything more than that. Nonetheless, the Syriac writers sometimes developed theological conclusions from the fact that the word "spirit" is grammatically feminine. Such teachings are of great interest in the history of interpretation of the biblical texts. But one should not draw theological conclusions from this, explains the professor.

There is a sense in which human language is inadequate.

In the book of Ecclesiastes, the writer refers to himself as *Qohelet*, which is often translated "preacher" or "teacher." This Hebrew word is feminine, though the author goes on to call himself the "son of David, king in Jerusalem" (Eccl. 1:1 NIV). That is why we need to be careful about interpreting biblical language, cautions Taylor.

"In other words, the fact that the word *Qohelet* is feminine in gender is entirely a grammatical matter; it has nothing to do with whether the referent is male or female."

The Relevance of *Ruach*?

Another biblical expert, Rev. Joseph Fitzmyer, professor emeritus of Biblical Studies at the Catholic University of America, agrees with Taylor's conclusions.

The translation changes in the pronouns for the Spirit are not germane.

"You can't tell anything about the sex just because of the pronoun," he says, adding that it is "not relevant at all" to know that *ruach* is grammatically feminine.

Taylor concurs that ships and cities in the Hebrew Bible are typically feminine in gender, but this is a grammatical category, not an ontological one. Think of it this way: Hurricane Hannah is not a storm with female traits; nor is Mother Earth a feminine planet. These are simply nuances of language—figures of speech.

Is that the end of the discussion?

My research indicates that it is not.

Numerous scholars believe it is noteworthy that the author of the creation story in Genesis chose to use a feminine noun to depict the Spirit of God.

As many as 75 out of 84 references to the Spirit in the Old Testament are grammatically feminine or indeterminable (due to a lack of a verb or an adjective). Only nine occurrences are construed as masculine, according to theologian R. P. Nettelhorst.[3]

Meanwhile, Dr. Christl Maier, an Old Testament professor at Philipps-Universität, is on the cutting edge of twenty-first century biblical research, and she has this to say about the topic:

The Spirit, the divine *ruach* in the Old Testament, denotes a divine wind, the breath of God, a supernatural creative force. In Ezekiel 37, the Spirit of God, like a divine wind, miraculously breathes new life into a valley of dead bones, a metaphor for the restoration of Israel. In the New Testament, the Greek equivalent *pneuma* (a neuter word for breath) mainly denotes the Holy Spirit as a creative force or the life-giving presence of God.

The role of the Spirit seems to grow more personal with time.

Becoming known as a close, trustworthy, personal friend, the divine "Helper, Comforter, and Counselor" guides us in the path of righteousness (see John 14:15–26). And since the Spirit is *ruach*, a feminine noun, this adds weight to the growing amount of biblical evidence about the maternal qualities of God, says Maier.

It is interesting that the Latin word for the Spirit became masculine (*spiritus*), Maier says, because this change has created serious misunderstandings about the Godhead.

"It is important to say that God is neither exclusively male nor exclusively female, but an understanding of God must be understood in the light of both genders."

While that may surprise many people, she says it is scripturally sound.

"The problem is not that the images of God as a caring mother are not in the Bible; those verses of Scripture are certainly there.

But those images were largely ignored by men, which led to a one-sided perception of God," Maier explains.

There is now a major shift to a more holistic view and a deeper appreciation of the Spirit. As Neill Q. Hamilton points out: *This presence of the Spirit within each believer—bringing with it mystical union with the Father and the Son—empowers the believer beyond anything that was possible before!*

CHAPTER 18

Pronouns, Metaphors, and Names

This, then, is how you should pray: "Our Father
in heaven, hallowed be your name, your kingdom
come, your will be done on earth as it is in heaven."

Matthew 6:9–10, NIV

I LOVE READING and writing stories, but confess to becoming
somewhat bored by the topic of sentence structure, dangling par-
ticiples, and haggling over pronouns.

Yet language is as critical to truth in religion as data is to science.

In learning the language of heaven, we are commanded to
worship and serve the Lord God; therefore, I believe that making
sense of the precious ancient words that have been handed down
to us from the patriarchs and prophets is crucial to living true to
our faith. The following chapter is short as experts explain the
basic difference between pronouns, metaphors, and the names of
God. I tried to make this easy to absorb and created a simple
graphic at the end of the chapter to wrap it up.

Pronoun Puzzle

Although the Bible typically uses the masculine pronoun "he"
when addressing God, most scholars agree that God is not like a

man any more than He is like a woman—even though He was often addressed in the Bible in masculine terms such as *Lord* and *Father*, says theologian Jürgen Moltmann.

Human language falls desperately short in trying to describe God.

The pronoun for God presents a good case study.

The word "it" exists in the English language. But in many languages, including Hebrew and Arabic, a pronoun simply does not exist to depict a gender-neutral entity.

Therefore "he" or "she" is used at the discretion of the writer even though a noun may not have gender.[1] God is typically addressed as masculine, but theologians say this is due to language limitations, not a biological description.

Praying in the various names of God, on the other hand, such as *Father, Yahweh, King of Kings, the Lord Jesus Christ* and other titles, are not only sacred and holy, but are key to enjoying the Lord's gift of salvation. In Proverbs 18:10, we are told "the name of the LORD is a strong tower; the righteous run to it and are safe" (NKJV). And in Romans 10:13, the apostle Paul emphasized: "Whoever calls on the name of the Lord shall be saved" (NKJV).

Pronouns, on the other hand, are a human-devised communication tool, subject to the limitations of language.

Goddess Worship Forbidden

A word of caution is necessary to avoid any possible confusion.

Daniel Ayuch, an Orthodox scholar in the Middle East, explains that believers in the God of the Bible are clearly instructed to reject all forms of goddess worship. He notes that the Canaanites had worshipped El, Ashtoreth, and their son Baal. The Greeks revered the triad Zeus, Hera, and daughter Athena while the Romans were in awe of Jupiter, Juno, and Minerva.

We are forbidden to worship false god triads.

During the prophet Isaiah's era, carpenters and blacksmiths were making statues out of cedar and metal that looked like little human beings to bow down to. Isaiah defines the idol worshipper as "a person with a deluded mind, feeding on ashes" (see Isa. 44:20). The second commandment strictly forbids idol worship. When the Lord spoke to Moses, for example, He did not see what God looked like:

> You saw no form of any kind the day the LORD spoke to you at Horeb out of the fire. Therefore watch yourselves very carefully, so that you do not become corrupt and make for yourselves an idol, an image of any shape, whether formed like a man or a woman . . .
>
> *Deuteronomy 4:15–16* NIV

Words Are Not Idols

Idols are inanimate things. *Words and language, however, are not idols.*

The second commandment does not apply to images in speech. Using metaphors, parables, and analogies to try to imagine the wondrous nature of God are perfectly acceptable, explains Moltmann.

"We must not create physical images (statues, etc.) to depict God," says the Reformed scholar. "But figures of speech are very useful for conceptualizing the characteristics of God because this is how people think and imagine!"

Oxford scholar Sebastian Brock agrees, noting how God's compassion, metaphorically speaking, is comparable to a father hugging a wayward son and to a kind midwife rescuing an abandoned baby.

"The feminine and masculine metaphors in the Holy Scriptures represent aspects of God's nature that are beneficial for us to understand," he explains.

Words inspire us to experience the divine presence of the *Unseen.*

"God allows us to use our language, metaphors, and similes to try to understand and imagine God's character. This is how the writers of all faiths and eras have used these literary forms, without exception!" says Brock.

Fulata Mbano Moyo, a leader with the World Council of Churches, concurs:

"The Bible shares feminine imagery for God, and most people can accept that there are aspects of God's characteristics which are nurturing, protective, and highly relational, like a mother."

Rowshan Nemazee, a Catholic theologian, is candid: "When the church made the masculine pronoun the norm for God, we left our spiritual world half-souled."

And Christl Maier, a Lutheran scholar, agrees with many other mainstream Christian theologians: "The Bible does not teach an all-male God."

Christian and Jewish leaders today are calling for a balanced approach.

"Acknowledging the maternal and paternal elements of the love and compassion of the one true living God has absolutely nothing to do with goddess worship. In fact, this is a healthy way to view our Creator," concludes Daniel Ayuch.

And Eliezer Segal, a professor in the Department of Religious Studies at the University of Calgary, is pragmatic: "I doubt that any serious Jewish thinker has ever taken literally the notion that God is biologically masculine. A monotheistic God who is biologically male doesn't make much sense."

More about Metaphors

Metaphors help us to imagine the nature of the Creator, says Richard A. Taylor, director of the PhD program at Dallas Theological Seminary.

"The Bible reflects the use of analogy, borrowing from what is familiar to human beings to describe things that are otherworldly and unfamiliar to us."

How far should these figures of speech be taken to define what God is like?

In Isaiah 66:13, the prophet likens the Lord to a comforting mother, not a father. Yet the New Testament refers to God as Father, Son, and Holy Spirit with the second member of the Trinity as "the man, Christ Jesus." With this in mind, Taylor says it is appropriate to refer to God as *He*, which is what biblical writers generally have done.

"With regard to gender, there are aspects of God's personality that are best illustrated by using feminine imagery," Taylor explains. "And there are other aspects that are best illustrated by using masculine imagery."

Both should be embraced for the insights they provide to the faithful.

"By using the analogy of a comforting mother, we come to understand divine compassion, tenderness, and love in a way that we might not otherwise grasp."

Christl Maier agrees:

The Scriptures link mercy to the maternal qualities of our loving God because *rechem* means womb, thus God is like a tender, caring mother showing mercy and compassion to her children, explains Maier.

Charles H. Spurgeon, a famous Baptist preacher, once painted the following word picture to help us comprehend the immeasurable patience of God:

"We have heard of a good mother who wanted to teach her child something. And when it was complained that she had to repeat the same thing twenty times, she answered: *Yes, I did that because nineteen times would not do.*

"So God perseveres. . . .

"Oh, those mothers of ours! They never do grow tired when we are sick and ill. They seem to be up all night and all day long.

And if a nurse comes in for a few hours, they are up then, too, looking after the nurse, so that I do not know that much ease comes with the helper," writes Spurgeon.

Our mothers are so untiringly kind. . . .

For those passing through a severe trial, Spurgeon encourages the faithful to remember: "Your mother will not forsake you, and do you think God will?"[2]

Our Father in Heaven

The righteous *Almighty God* declares that He is the *Lord our God, and there is no other*. And we should worship only *Him*! He is the *Lord of Lords*, not the *Lady of Ladies*. Only He is worthy to be glorified and praised.

All of the holy names used for God in the Scriptures are masculine. With the exception of an interesting debate among some leaders about the title *El Shaddai*,[3] there is a fair degree of consensus that no name for God is feminine.

Jesus taught us to humbly approach heaven in the trusting demeanor of an innocent child by praying, *"Our Father (Abba) in heaven, hallowed be your name, your kingdom come, your will be done . . ."*

This is who God is, up close and personal.

Dear Dad: A Personal Story

Fathers fulfill a unique role in our day-to-day lives, and I am reflecting on a particularly poignant moment with my own dad. My father, a gentle, kind man, was my mother's primary caregiver for the last two years of her life. He faithfully washed her hair, made her meals, clothed her, patiently buttoned her sweaters, steadied her shaking hands, and calmed her paranoid fears. He never left her side.

"I've sure missed Mom since she died," my dad says to me.

"Me too." I look at him. I don't know what else to say.

We are walking out of the Cannon Clinic where Doctor Collingridge has just diagnosed him with Alzheimer's disease. I am shattered. Mom died of this very same terrifying disease! All I can do is walk quietly beside Dad with my emotions reeling. *Oh God, this is such a cruel disease. First Mom, now Dad too! Our family has suffered so much already. I don't think I can go through this again.*

Dear God, my dear, sweet dad.

I am silent as we get in my car. Dad gazes blankly into the parking lot.

"The only thing I hope is that I never lose my ability to play my harmonica," he says quietly. He used to play drums in a family band when he was younger, and music is his passion. With that simple comment about his harmonica, he accepts his diagnosis.

Not once does he ever complain—this calm gentleman with quiet strength.

"I'll do my best, and God will do the rest," he says. This is no cliché for Dad, who finds a deep reservoir of strength by praying to our kind heavenly Father.

My brother and his wife had earlier asked him if he would like to live with them on their twenty-acre flower farm. Dad and I discuss this idea as a realistic possibility. He says he wants to help them pick daffodils and tulips and tend their garden.

"That would be so nice for me to move in with them," he says. "I really love my family. But, Trudy, that means I won't be able to ride my bike to your house anymore."

He only lives about five miles away from my house, and one of our greatest pleasures is to ride around Matsqui Prairie and check out the dairy farms and the berry fields that spread across our magnificent valley surrounded by mountains. My brother's flower farm is too far away for him to ride his bike to my house.

A single tear rolls down Dad's cheek. This is rare for him. I never see him crying. I can't believe it. He didn't cry when he is diagnosed with one of the cruelest diseases on earth. Yet he cries when he thinks about not being able to ride his bike to see me!

That's what really gets to him.

Me!

He just wants to continue living close to me. That's my father's love. My composure starts wavering. Dad is generally always happy—stoic—never down or depressed. His blue eyes are misty as he rubs the single tear rolling down his face.

"Dad, don't worry, I'll come over to Pete's place and we'll ride our bikes together. Don't worry! You are very, very important to our family," I encourage him.

He slowly smiles. "Well, without me—you would not have any family!"

"Uh-huh, that's right, Dad," I laugh.

"I really love my family," he says once again.

Just in case I didn't get that. . . .

We get out of the car at my house and walk around the flower beds. He planted most of the flowers in my garden—and he knows each one by name. He even dug out some of my grandma's ivy in Holland, stuck it in his suitcase, and flew it halfway across the world so he could plant it on my retaining wall. I hug him tightly and don't let him go for a long time as we stand in the garden.

I kiss him. I think to myself: *He's like a sweet, vulnerable twelve-year-old boy in a man's suit.* He gently rubs my face. He smiles and relaxes a little.

We go into the house where he sees my African violets in the kitchen. He shakes his head, picks them up, and goes outside. He places them on the patio table by my front door. They look smart on top of the orange-checkered tablecloth.

"They'll do much better outside," he assures me. "You'll see, they'll get more blooms out here." He takes a bucket of fertilizer, puts the gray grains in his hands, and nimbly spreads his fingers to fertilize all of my potted flowers.

"Where did you get these orange flowers from?" he asks as he examines them.

"A woman named Regina," I reply.

"Oh. What kind of a flower is it?"

He would have to ask me that question, wouldn't he?

"I don't know," I shake my head. "I forget things, just like you do," I say with a laugh. "But it is beautiful, isn't it?"

My father derives such deep pleasure in the simple things of life—the birds, the flowers, the fresh air, nature's bold colors and soothing sweet fragrances.

How do I measure male creativity, strength, and leadership? Is it the unbridled passion to dominate others by fear as practiced by some male leaders? Or is it a man who gives himself to others, using his strength to help those who are weaker, giving encouragement, love, life, and healing to those within his circle of influence?

That is my father—in heaven and on earth.

A Garden of Praise

For as the earth brings forth its bud,
As the garden causes the things that are sown in it to spring forth,
so the Lord GOD will cause righteousness and praise to spring
*   forth before all the nations.*

Isaiah 61:11 NKJV

Made in the image of God, men fulfill their divinely appointed role of being masculine, being a man's man, being our fathers, brothers, government leaders, judges, and numerous other important positions in society. Men are loyal and protective of others, yet they are strong and tender in their love for their sons and daughters.

I have decided I will continue to use the pronoun *He* for God, and not *she*.

That seems logical to me for all the reasons already specified.

To me, the holy names of God are sacrosanct. It is a wonderful privilege to pray to our kind heavenly Father. Earlier I shared one of my favorite stories in the Bible about how Jesus surprised Mary Magdalene after His resurrection. I've read this story countless times during the past thirty years, yet I never grow tired of hearing what Jesus said to her. *"I go to my Father and your Father, to my God and your God"* (see John 20:17).

I love that!

How precious it is that Jesus so eagerly welcomes each one of us into His very own family, the family of God! When I pray to the Father, He reassures me that I am His precious child. I am in an intimate relationship with the *God of All Comfort.*

Never again should I feel like an orphan or that I don't belong.

Jesus referred to the blessed name of the Father more than 170 times in the New Testament, exalting Him as righteous and altogether holy. As a worshipper, I resolve anew to honor the sacred names of the *eternal Father, King of Kings, and Lord of Lords.*

Does praying in the name of the Father imply God is biologically male?

I believe it is a blessed assurance to know that He loves me as a benevolent father. As I pursue my investigation into the mother heart of God, however, I am also starting to understand that the love in which God embraces me is a profound blend of both masculine and feminine. Why? The Bible depicts the personality of our powerful and gracious Maker metaphorically in the parental roles of both a father and a mother.

This idea upholds the dignity of both men and women.

It appears to be a new day for people of faith.

I am reminded of a historical occasion when I watch the first Western pilot get into the cockpit of a Soviet MiG fighter jet. The Cold War between the US and the former Soviet Union is starting to thaw. I stand, shoulder to shoulder, with reporters from the *Pravda* newspaper, who stare in silent awe as the Soviet fighter jet flies low over the tarmac and disappears into the cumulus clouds, breaking the sound barrier.

It is a world-changing breakthrough!

But that moment is nothing compared to what I believe is happening in churches and synagogues all over the globe.

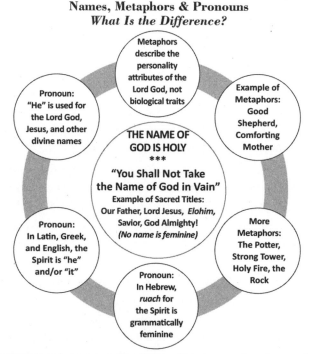

Names, Metaphors & Pronouns
What Is the Difference?

Metaphors describe the personality attributes of the Lord God, not biological traits

Example of Metaphors: Good Shepherd, Comforting Mother

Pronoun: "He" is used for the Lord God, Jesus, and other divine names

THE NAME OF GOD IS HOLY
***
"You Shall Not Take the Name of God in Vain"
Example of Sacred Titles: Our Father, Lord Jesus, *Elohim*, Savior, God Almighty! *(No name is feminine)*

Pronoun: In Latin, Greek, and English, the Spirit is "he" and/or "it"

More Metaphors: The Potter, Strong Tower, Holy Fire, the Rock

Pronoun: In Hebrew, *ruach* for the Spirit is grammatically feminine

In the Hebrew language, as with other Semitic languages, there is no gender-neutral pronoun. The Bible discloses more than 600 names and titles to express the majesty of Almighty God, who is so abstract and sublime that no definition or description, on its own, is able to sum up the essence of the one true Most High God. The Lord God is beyond gender. This is easy to understand. When we think of our own parents, we do not think of them in terms of gender, but in their role as our Protector, Provider, and Nurturer. Language is utterly inadequate in trying to describe our Creator.

PART FIVE

A Global Awakening

CHAPTER 19

The Shack, Father Thomas, and Ravi

The expression of the feminine or maternal personality of God's love is often very dramatic; and women
have the distinct privilege to reflect that sacred quality.

Ravi Zacharias, Evangelist

DURING THE EARLY stages of my journey, my friend Helen Grace
Lescheid, who is also a writer, phones me one day and insists that
I meet an unknown author who is going to share his story at the
House of James, a local Christian bookstore. "Why? Who is this
author?" I ask her, not in the least bit interested.

"His name is Paul Young, and he just wrote a novel called *The
Shack*. It's starting to really take off with the public," says Lescheid
with no shortage of excitement.

"Okay. But why do I want to meet him? What's his book
about?" I ask.

"Well, believe it or not," she says. "He has written about the
feminine side of God in his fictional book, and this is really starting to make people think."

Although I had planned to relax and read a book by the
fire that evening, instead I am meeting a quiet-spoken author
named Paul. As I shake his hand, I tell him I am interviewing
various leaders of faith from the Vatican to Virginia for a

nonfiction book on the controversial question of the possible gender of God.

He looks at me in a state of shock: "God's timing is amazing. . . ."

"It's really amazing, I know," I say to the author who is not yet famous.

Today, of course, *The Shack* has become a worldwide phenomenon, with more than 18 million copies in print. In Eugene Peterson's cover endorsement, he predicted Paul Young's novel may change the way our generation views God in the same way John Bunyan did with his spiritual classic *Pilgrim's Progress*.

He may be right.

The book is about a family that is on vacation when the couple's young daughter is abducted and brutally murdered in an old abandoned shack. What the father finds in that dilapidated shack turns his world upside down. Young takes the reader on a spiritual exploration about the nature of God in an unconventional manner and depicts the Holy Spirit, for example, with a feminine persona.

While the book has been controversial, Young says he has no particular religious agenda to promote.

He was a totally unknown writer when his book started riding a wave of popularity in 2008–09, and he was surprised when he was thrust into the public limelight. A resident of Gresham, Oregon, he calls himself an "accidental author."

The author shares his life story with me in his characteristically calm manner.

"I was a preacher's kid," he says. "I was born in Grande Prairie, Alberta, and moved with my missionary parents to Netherlands New Guinea (West Papua) when I was just ten months old. I lived among the Dani—a tribal people who were still technologically in the Stone Age and sometimes partook in ritualistic cannibalism."

Young was the first white kid on that part of the island, the first person outside this unique Stone-Age culture to learn to fluently speak their language. In fact, he actually thought he was a Dani child for the first six years of his life.

"The highlands of that island are beautiful; the most perfect climate in the world," he recalls, reminiscing about his life as an innocent young boy. In this veritable Garden of Eden, however, he was tormented by abuse in the Dani culture as well as in a missionary boarding school.

He faced a huge culture shock when he returned to North America.

During our interview, he explains that he had felt emotionally estranged from his parents who were focused on their calling as missionaries, and for some reason he truly believed that the life he experienced as a child was "normal."

But what is "normal" these days? he asks.

He had no idea his home circumstances were so unusual.

In fact, the abuse he experienced as a youngster caused him many years of distress, and he often felt lonely, confused, and ashamed. He describes his growing-up years as both "unbearable yet incredible" as he sank himself into schoolwork and hung on to the love of God as "the only safe place for me to be."

Eventually he earned an undergraduate degree in Religion at Warner Pacific College in Portland, Oregon, which is affiliated with the Church of God. While there, he met his wife Kim, and together they have six children.

For many years, the memories of the childhood abuse made him feel like he was tossed back and forth in a horrendous black tunnel of anger, anguish, and shame, he says. By the end of this horrific emotional roller coaster, he was healed through an arduous process of reconciliation.

He experienced spiritual peace in 2004 when God transformed his life.

Now, due to the popularity and commercial success of *The Shack*, he is a frequent guest on talk shows answering the public's toughest questions about the Creator God, although at times religious leaders do not always agree with his answers.

He still feels uncomfortable with all the publicity.

The Shack is not an autobiography, he says, noting that he just happened to stumble across many wonderful spiritual truths as he spent time reading the Bible. He is a relentless questioner of the religious status quo. After a lifetime studying the Scriptures, he has no interest in shallow forms of spirituality. The great truths which Jesus taught are far too valuable to ever be taken lightly!

And gender equality issues especially concern him.

"There is so much damage that happens when we use only male imagery for God," he comments, capturing in these few words how he and many other men have found it difficult to relate to the so-called all-male God.

"The key to truly understanding God goes back to Genesis 1. You will find the paternal and maternal characteristics of God at the heart of Christianity."

This biblical truth is healing to all who take the time to truly understand this.

"We are created in the image of God," Young says. "Since God created males and females, therefore it stands to reason that our maleness and our femaleness is derived from God."

Therefore, these attributes are found in the essence of the Creator.

He discovered the sacred balance in God when he was in his twenties as he studied the Bible and read books written by enlightened authors. When he questioned his theology professors, he realized he had more freedom to explore the wondrous nature of God than his professors did because they are often limited by the requirements and expectations of their profession.

"Many Bible professors are simply not allowed to teach outside the boundaries of the teachings of the church," he says. "Between job security and peer pressure, the male interpretation of the Bible has been dominated by that paradigm."

But the truth has a way of being brought to the light as Jesus described His love for us as a nurturing "mother hen" longs to protect her chicks, and the compassion of God is like a woman relentlessly searching for her priceless lost coin.

"These are extremely clear examples of the maternal love of God."

And just think, God actually pictures Himself as a midwife in Ezekiel 16!

God delights in shaking up our religious stereotypes. And so does Young.

He once conducted a thought-provoking experiment while he was teaching a Bible college class of about three hundred students. He listed one hundred personality traits for God on a sheet of paper and scattered within that list the fruit of the Spirit: *love, joy, peace, patience, kindness, goodness, faithfulness, gentleness, and self-control.*

Young then asked his students to describe which of these traits should be considered masculine, feminine, or both.

Can you guess the result?

The students identified most of the fruit of the Spirit as feminine, with the exception of self-control and long-suffering (patience). Innately, people are drawn to identify the personality qualities of the Spirit in feminine terms, Young said.

The so-called gender of God is a major issue today.

If Christians are hung up on the imagery of God with the traditional masculine traits of a father—which may well be marked in their own lives by the emotional distance of their own father and the hard line for performance—then they may feel that God is perpetually disappointed in them or separated from them, the author explains.

Once people learn to trust the maternal mercy and compassion God has for them, they can feel God's love wrapping around them, Young says, noting that men are awakening to this spiritual truth, and it frees them—just as it frees women.

"The concept of the maternal love of God breaks all of the past rules. And for many men, not just for women; it's like the whole universe shifts for them. God's love is like a mother's love and a father's love—only the love of God is even better than that."

"This Is the Issue of Our Day"

Everywhere you go, the public is raising questions about the gender of God.

"This is the issue of our day," says Father Thomas Hopko.

He is a respected Orthodox scholar and a prolific writer. He has written numerous books, including *Women and the Priesthood* and the theologically significant essay "God and Gender." As dean emeritus of St. Vladimir's Orthodox Theological Seminary in New York, Hopko is a popular speaker.

He is passionate about inspiring people to have faith in God because no one will ever find inner spiritual peace in our secular culture by pursuing materialism.

"In our times, we in the West are in danger of 'losing our humanity' as C. S. Lewis claimed in 1944 in his prophetic little book *The Abolition of Man*," Hopko says.

People are in danger today of becoming nothing more than "minds and matter, brains and bodies, computers and consumers, calculators and copulators, constructors and cloners who believe that they are free and powerful."

The truth is that they are not free!

Many people are actually becoming enslaved to themselves, and unfortunately they have lost their likeness to God, the scholar explains.

"When we realize how much God loves us, then we can love and worship God in return. Human beings cannot really be *truly human* without the God whom they are made to know, love, obey, and imitate in a growing relationship."

Our Creator gives us the answers to fulfill our deepest needs.

"I can tell you that being loved by God, and loving Him in return, is the greatest joy given to creatures and that without this, there is no real and lasting happiness for humanity," says Hopko.

The nature of God is beyond what people can imagine, beyond all created categories. Yet, thankfully, God may be spoken about because He has manifested Himself in our world. He has personality and is known by His personal names.

Not only is God's personality *like* a mother and a father, metaphorically, but God *is* the Father of Jesus and He becomes "*our Father*" relationally through Jesus.

"God can be named: His names are Father, Son, and Holy Spirit."

He is the *eternal Father,* and Jesus was incarnate on Earth as the *Son of God,* a carpenter, teacher, and healer, the one who died on the cross with a man's body, but who rose from the dead in His divinity.

Every name revealed in the Bible for God is a masculine term.

Metaphors, meanwhile, are helpful for understanding the personality of God.

"God is *like* a king and a friend. God can even be said to care for and comfort his people *like* a nursing mother."

That does not mean, however, that God has sexual or physical attributes. It simply means that God nurtures and comforts us and utilizes the word "mother" as an analogy to symbolize a dimension of His divine love.

"There is no possibility of renaming God as mother or calling God's son a daughter because this would render the Word of God meaningless," Hopko explains, adding that no person in the Trinity has a *name* typically used for females.

The attributes of God, on the other hand, are another matter. The Creator is pleased to be revealed in the metaphors of a mother, the theologian said. The metaphors of God giving birth, nurturing, feeding, and tenderly carrying a child, for example, may be applied to all three persons of the Trinity, in his opinion.

"The most central quality of God in the Old Testament, for example, his mercy or steadfast love (*hesed*), has definite 'feminine' connotations connected to womb-like protection, care, commitment, and compassion," Hopko wrote in his essay called "God and Gender: Articulating the Orthodox View."[1]

During our interview, he explains that Christian saints and writers throughout the ages, including Sergius N. Bulgakov, an eminent Russian Orthodox theologian, observed the special connection between the Spirit and typical feminine activities.

"The Spirit is the Divine Person in the Holy Trinity who in a special way is the Life-giver, Nurturer, Consoler, and Comforter."

All three persons of the Trinity work together in complete harmony. Yet the Spirit, in some mystical way, energizes God the Father and the Son in their particular Divine activities. Every action of the Trinity originates in the Father, is enacted by God's Son, and is fulfilled and accomplished by the Holy Spirit, explains Hopko.

In conclusion, God expresses Himself in parental metaphors, both as a father and a mother, for our benefit. But the *Almighty One* is far above any gender description.

"God is neither feminine, nor masculine—God is completely other."

It is very important to seek God for *who God is*.

"We are to seek after God without conditions. We are to want God *as God is*—not just to talk about Him, or discuss Him, or still less, to fight about Him," says the scholar.

"We are to know, love, and serve God!"

Moving beyond the discussion of language, grammar, and words—we need to encounter God as He relates to us in perfect love. There is nothing more important!

Living for God is a matter of life and death.

The Best "Forever" Love Story

The good news in the Bible erases the battle lines that used to divide people due to race, gender, religion, age, education, and economic or social status.

When the gospel is applied, it maintains our human distinctives without hierarchy, says Dr. Ravi Zacharias, an eminent US evangelist.

There are no favorites in the eyes of the Creator.

God's redemption story is the gospel of second chances for everyone.

The Lord redeems us with deep inexpressible devotion, and it behooves us to communicate this love to others with great diplomacy. There must be no extremes in speaking about the love of God. No going back and forth like a drunk who reels and staggers at wit's end (see Ps. 107:27), especially when discussing sensitive gender issues.

There has been enough of that already.

Mary Daly, a radical feminist theologian (1928–2010), so despised men that at one time she would not even allow them into her classroom. But God calls men and women to walk respectfully together in harmony so they may represent the splendor of God's salvation to the people of the world with wisdom, compassion, and balance.

That is the vision Zacharias has for our generation of believers.

The internationally acclaimed speaker has authored or edited more than twenty books, from *Walking from East to West* to *Why Jesus?*. Ordained by the Christian and Missionary Alliance, he has made a major spiritual impact on the lives of people around the world during the past four decades. As a spiritual mentor, his influence is felt far and wide. The evangelist has addressed the UN General Assembly, the White House, Oxford University, and such diverse audiences as the writers of the peace accord in South

Africa, military officers at the Center for Geopolitical Strategy in Moscow, and the president's cabinet in Peru.

Why are his teachings held in such high esteem?

It is because the Christian faith is a coherent worldview, says Zacharias, that answers the four basic questions we all have in life regarding:

- Origin
- Meaning
- Morality
- Destiny

And Zacharias can handle the toughest spiritual questions being raised by postmodern thinkers, including the controversy circling the globe about the gender of God.

"In what ways are women made in God's image?" I ask him one day.

The theologian explains that men and women are both made equally in the image of God. In fact, the Creator distinguished humankind above the animal world with the ability to make moral choices and with the power of self-determination.

"God gives us the privilege of living in community with one another, and it is important to note that no *one* individual can totally represent the image of God. There are many remarkable complementary aspects to the strengths and personalities of both the masculine and feminine genders that bring to light a reflection of *who God is*."

Then he pauses for a moment.

"We must keep in mind that God is the cause and we are the effect."

Neither gender is either good or bad because they complement the other.

"Is God's love maternal, as well as paternal?" I ask him.

The evangelist is quick to answer.

"Absolutely. God expresses His love in the metaphors of the family, both father and mother," he replies. "There are definite psychological and physiological distinctions between a man and a woman, and we must not rob the Sovereign Lord of the richness that is communicated to the world in the maternal metaphors about God's love."

The Scriptures reveal a number of parental metaphors to give us a glimpse into the character of God, he said, adding that one of the most profound stories in the entire Bible is the parable about the rich father and the prodigal son.

In this story, Jesus answers the unspoken questions of every skeptic and agnostic, and to anyone who may not believe the Creator is a God of love, this parable, found in Luke 15, satisfies the deepest needs of every soul and speaks volumes to people living today.

Here is the story that Jesus wants each one of us today to hear:

One day the son of a very rich man demands his father give him his inheritance and then he moves to a far country. Spending his money on riotous living, the arrogant son shames and humiliates his family. The Middle Eastern cultural norm of the day would have dictated that if the son ever decided to return to his father's house, he would have to beg and grovel for his acceptance and forgiveness.

But that does not happen, says Zacharias.

Unknown to the son who is busy drinking and carousing around and giving no thought to the aching void he has left in his father's tender heart, the father is praying and waiting for his boy to return. He holds no anger. No thought of punishment.

He dreams only of hugging his beloved son once more.

In the meantime, the young man does not give a second thought to his father, nor does he feel a moment of shame as he lives in frivolity and drunkenness, wasting away his dad's money. Then a famine strikes the land. He begins to be in dire need.

Destitute, homeless, hungry, and hurting, what can he do?

So he went and hired himself out to one of the citizens of that country, who sent him to his fields to feed the pigs. He would gladly have filled himself with the pods that the pigs were eating; and no one gave him anything. But when he came to himself he said, "How many of my father's hired hands have bread enough and to spare, but here I am dying of hunger!"

Luke 15:15–17 NRSV

The rich young man, so pompous and prideful earlier, now grovels for filthy grub. Yet no one gives him a thing to eat. Not even pig slop! Disgusted and miserable, the son recalls the wonderful home he had left behind, his father's unfailing love. What a fool he has been! Coming to his senses and feeling shame, he comes up with a plan:

"I will get up and go to my father, and I will say to him, 'Father, I have sinned against heaven and before you; I am no longer worthy to be called your son; treat me like one of your hired hands.' " So he set off and went to his father. But while he was still far off, his father saw him and was filled with compassion; he ran and put his arms around him and kissed him. Then the son said to him, "Father, I have sinned against heaven and before you; I am no longer worthy to be called your son."

Luke 15:18–21 NRSV

Overwhelmed with tears of joy, the father throws his arms around his boy, kisses him, and says to his servants:

"Quickly, bring out a robe—the best one—and put it on him; put a ring on his finger and sandals on his feet. And get the fatted calf and kill it, and let us eat and celebrate; for this son of mine was dead and is alive again; he was lost and is found!" And they began to celebrate.

Luke 15:22–24 NRSV

By covering his son with a magnificent robe, the father prevents others from seeing his tattered clothes. He has no desire to publicize the son's disgrace or point out the pain he has put him through for many years. Instead, he protects his child's dignity and feels nothing but joy at his return.

"Let's celebrate and have a party!" he says. "My boy was dead, now he's alive. He was lost, now he's found!"

The father's compassion is a radical departure from the cultural norm. This parable reveals for all time *the best "forever" love story.* It is your story, and it is my story. It is our Creator God's story. Instead of rejecting us, God redeems us. In His divine rescue mission, He covers us with the white linen robe of Christ's righteousness, cradles us in the arms of love, forgives us, protects us, shelters us, and upholds our dignity.

"The Lord redeems the fallen with deep inexpressible devotion, just as a mother's devotion never gives up on her children," Zacharias explains.

"In this respect, the father of the prodigal son was *maternal* in the way he related to the waywardness and rebellion of his son. That is because mothers will typically persevere and wait for their children to come back to them to the very last breath of their life. That is why God's love is sometimes compared to the love of a mother."

A favorite Bible passage proves this point:

Can a mother forget the baby at her breast
and have no compassion on the child she has borne?
Though she may forget,
I will not forget you!

See, I have engraved you on the palms of my hands;
your walls are ever before me.
                              Isaiah 49:15–16 NIV

Wherever we are, God is there! Just as a mother never forgets her child, our names are engraved on the hands of God. Every wall of our house is within view.

The story of the father and the prodigal son, and the metaphor of the mother caring for a child display the excellence of how each gender "completes and complements" the way God expresses His love to humankind, says Zacharias.

The evangelist himself learned to respect the complementary strengths of each gender as he and his wife, Margie, raised two daughters and a son.

Women may certainly be inspired by the Holy Scriptures, he says.

"The expression of the feminine or maternal personality of God's love is often very dramatic; and women have the distinct privilege to reflect that sacred quality."

God is appealing to each woman to live up to her special spiritual calling!

"Physiologically, and psychologically, a woman is made to bear a child and to hold and embrace and nurse her baby as only a woman can do," says Zacharias.

"Therefore, women of faith may find tremendous inspiration in the Bible because of the tremendous metaphors of God as a birthing mother and how the Holy Spirit regenerates us."

CHAPTER 20

Kneeling in the Presence of God

Come, let us worship and bow down, let us kneel
before the LORD our Maker.

Psalm 95:6 NASB

Amie is six months old on the day her eyes brighten with a
certain belief that she can get up in her crib and stand by herself. It is as if a spark of electricity suddenly ignites behind her
big blue eyes.

She does not know I am watching her.

I smile as she scans the white railing of the crib high above
her. In a flicker of thought, her eyes calculate in microseconds the
distance, the angle, and the thrust she will need to send herself
from her knees to her feet. She has never flown over this canyon
of space before. Suddenly, her hands flail high in the air, reaching
desperately for the railing in the same split second of raising her
chubby lead-weight body.

She did it! She is upright. Amie grabs the railing, hangs on
tight. She stands! Tall and proud! I savor her smile of triumph.
Then she sees me looking at her.

Look what I just did! she seems to say. *Next, I'm climbing over
and out!*

I pick her up and hug her as she presses her face up close to mine, and I tell her I am very proud of her great accomplishment. "You're a big girl now.

"Stand tall, sweetheart! There's no going back to the crawl."

ℒ❧

If we, who are imperfect, can feel so much joy over the baby steps of our children and grandchildren, how much more does God delight in our steps of spiritual growth?

"Remember the One who created you!" advises King Solomon (Eccl. 12:1 NIRV), once called the wisest man who ever lived. He notes how carefully we must weigh the evidence to discern the truth about our glorious, all-merciful Creator God.

Why is it important to carefully examine the evidence?

"The sayings of those who are wise move people to take action," writes Solomon. "Their collected sayings really nail things down" (Eccl. 12:11 NIRV).

It is time to take action. Here now is the conclusion of the matter. . . .

What is God really like? After spending five years pondering this question, I am not the same person I was when I started. My journey began as a fact-finding global investigation, but it ended up being a powerful spiritual experience for me as I felt the compassion of God on a level I had never thought possible.

Life is ironic.

Starting out a confident, award-winning journalist, it never occurred to me that as I pressed forward, I would end up suffering a broken heart, broken hands, and a broken spirit. Not me! No way! I never imagined I would crash into the soul-numbing roadblocks of an unwanted divorce, painful hand surgery, a car accident, one heartbreaking family crisis after another, loneliness and losses, too many to share.

Yet just as Amie learned to walk by aiming for the white railing, I flailed across this strange abyss of intense emotional and physical pain, typing at times with my right hand in a fiberglass cast, one finger, one letter at a time, sometimes overwhelmed by tears of loneliness, other times frozen in fear, yet I kept aiming for the goal.

Hang on. Trust God. Keep going. And when He wanted me to just sit still, kneel, and pray, then I learned not to argue. I kept reading the Bible and just listened.

I was brought back many times to the big question: *Who are you, Lord?*

I'd climb up the steep hill in my rain forest, sit on the fallen birch log, and meditate on the Scriptures and pray. And I'd feel the comfort and intensity of God's infinite embrace, the love that shelters, protects, and brings healing to every soul.

So this is who you are, Lord!

His love is more real to me today than my most intimate friend. And He is healing me! I've quietly slipped the fiberglass hand splints into the desk drawer, and symbolically I've put away the inflexible stereotypical ideas that I used to have about God into the archives of yesterday.

Like the patriarch Job, I now see God's mercy is everlasting.

When I meet people and share the maternal mercy of God with them, something miraculous always happens. Their eyes light up. They think a few moments. They pause. Their smiles grow wider and wider as their eyes sparkle. They *get it!*

Deanna, a health-care worker, for example, tells me that she is struggling with the teaching that God is all-masculine, and she feels a painful distance from Him. Suffering a lack of self-worth all her life, her experience speaks for millions.

More than one-third of the women in the world today have been physically or sexually assaulted. Deanna fits into that sorry statistic. Abused as a child, she suffers bouts of depression as an adult and admits she is responsible for the failure of her marriage. Like many women, she tends to view her femininity as a weakness.

When she heard about the sacred balance in God's love—it freed her!

"I feel so much happier and closer to God. It really helps me in a lot of ways." Her face brightens as she imagines the possibilities for global revival.

"Knowing that the maternal love I feel for my children somehow relates to the love of God is incredible; it gives me a real sense of belonging to Him," she says.

"I think this will help women all over the world."

When a woman discovers the truth that her maternal instinct to protect and shelter others corresponds to the *God of all comfort*, the insecurities she once suffered in her lack of self-identity are replaced by a quiet inner confidence that God created her with deep spiritual significance and dignity.

And it's not just women who benefit from this knowledge.

Many successful men, such as Jürgen Moltmann, Tony Campolo, Daniel Ayuch, and others, tell me this revelation also helps them to have a closer relationship with God. The nature of our Maker is unveiled in the Bible and in the majesty of creation:

> For what can be known about God is plain to them, because God has shown it to them. Ever since the creation of the world his invisible nature, namely, his eternal power and deity, has been clearly perceived in the things that have been made.
>
> *Romans 1:19–20* RSV

Since the God of all grace made men and women to mirror who He is, there are compelling logical reasons to conclude that His nature is not exclusively masculine.

It is quite simple. Just look at the way the world works!

Buffy Sainte-Marie describes her faith beautifully: *"The Creator may be discovered by the illiterate and the literate. When people are inspired by the Creator through nature—God's creation—there are no walls and no barriers."*

Women are not excluded from being identified with the Creator. Indeed, as daughters of God, they reflect a precious dimension of the personality of the *God of mercy and justice* that has been mostly missing for more than six millennia.

I had no idea that the root of the word "mercy" is *racham* in Hebrew, which means womb. In other words, the mercy of God is "womb-like," sheltering and protective.

I was amazed to discover that our Father God actually loves me as a mother comforts a child! This is life-changing. Deeply personal! Awe-inspiring and healing to my soul! I now experience the profound love of the *Father of mercies and the God of all comfort* at an intensity and at a deeper level I had never felt before.

This healing discovery is igniting on a global scale, perhaps on a magnitude comparable to the Spirit-filled days of Pentecost. The timing is right for this truth to be told as God sheds new light from the Bible for each new generation.

Let's move our faith to the next level of maturity, say many leaders of faith.

These spiritual gems can be hidden no longer.

God is not only our Creator and Redeemer, but our Comforter, giving us confidence and calm in the middle of the chaos of living on this planet.

After interviewing more than fifty leaders of faith all across the globe, from North America and Europe to Asia and the Middle East, the majority of leaders affirm that the compassion of God is like the love of a father and a mother. And the Spirit is the person of the Trinity who most profoundly exhibits maternal qualities and gives us new birth.

The Spirit of God is ever so kind, inviting each of us to a transformed life. Matthew Henry notes how God fulfills our spiritual needs:

> In a graceless soul, one that is not born again, there is disorder, confusion, and every evil work, it is empty of all good,

for it is without God; it is dark, it is darkness itself: this is our condition by nature, till Almighty grace works a change in us.[1]

"We are to seek after God without conditions. We are to want God *as God is*. There is nothing else. Living for God is a matter of life and death for all," advises Father Thomas Hopko.

The Spirit of God is inviting us to kneel and pray, to say *yes* to the *God of all comfort* who promises to give us life, hope, and a sense of belonging and to surround us in a warm, down-filled comforter of countless blessings.

Just as I was so excited to watch Âmie reach out her hands in faith, aim for the white railing, and to stand tall—God takes great delight in us. The mother heart of our kind, gracious, eternal Father is ready to wrap a big hug around us: *"Do not fear, for I have redeemed you. I have called you by name. You are mine! . . . You are precious in my sight . . . and I love you."*[2]

APPENDIX 1

A Holy Equilibrium

One of the greatest rewards of knowing God is inner healing.

If we want to know God, we must believe that we are treated much better than we deserve. The Creator does not ask if we are worthy of mercy, but takes the initiative to wrap us in the arms of an infinite embrace to make us worthy!

Mercy is often translated as "loving kindness" and "compassion" in modern translations of the Bible. Yet the original word "mercy" in the King James Version remains the most poetic.

The nature of God is a sacred balance.

Mercy is at the heart of His Divine justice.

Justice and mercy, law and grace, always go together—a sacred duality that cannot be separated as the Spirit of God writes the Ten Commandments, the divine moral law, on our hearts today.

> This is the covenant that I will make with them after those days, says the LORD. I will put my laws upon their heart, and on their mind I will write them. . . . And their sins and their lawless deeds I will remember no more.
>
> *Hebrews 10:16–17 NASB*

It is the kindness of God that leads us to repentance.

Into all eternity, the Creator will be praised for both His justice and mercy.

Moses, Paul, and John were each given a vision of the heavenly sanctuary where there is a majestic mercy seat, made of purest gold, set prominently above the ark, which is the sacred wooden chest containing the Ten Commandments.

The righteous law of liberty forms the very Constitution of heaven!

In the supreme order of the universe, the moral law and divine justice, therefore, are weighed in a holy equilibrium, perfectly balanced by the righteous Lawgiver who is also our benevolent *God of Mercy.*

What I Am Learning on the Journey

> Blessed be the God and Father of our Lord Jesus
> Christ, the Father of mercies and God of all comfort.
>
> *2 Corinthians 1:3 NKJV*

Many people ask me what I've learned during the past five years after interviewing numerous faith leaders and intently studying the Bible. They usually want a quick two-minute answer, but as Billy Graham once said, trying to understand the work of the Spirit of God is like trying to capture the "ocean in a quart jar." I love that quote. To be candid, I am just beginning to learn to appreciate the mercy, goodness and faithfulness of our Creator God. This is a life-long journey for me. Here are a few ideas from the Bible to consider in your own walk with God:

TWELVE POWER POINTS

1. God is love. As a beloved son and daughter of God, we find our true identity—and meaning in life—by being in close relationship with our compassionate Creator.
2. God created men and women equally to reflect His image in complementary design.
3. Men reflect the strength of God, women reflect the heart of God, but this is not exclusive. It is noteworthy that God designed men with the gift to lead and initiate grand new projects; while women excel in nurturing others and give birth to new life.

4. The metaphors of God relating to us as a devoted father and a kind-hearted mother are powerful revelations to help us appreciate the depths of His love.

5. The mercy of God is "womb-like," according to the original Hebrew word, *racham*; therefore, throughout our journey in life, the compassion and mercy of God is ever-sheltering and protective over us, tenderly nurturing us, as a mother comforts a child.

6. The "mother heart" of our Father God is an ancient biblical truth, relevant for today—and this is igniting a global spiritual awakening among people of various faiths.

7. The one true God expresses His love to us in three personal ways: Father, Son and Holy Spirit—a Trinity. He gives us life as Creator; forgives our sins as Savior; and transforms our lives when we are born again by the power of the Holy Spirit (*the Comforter*).

8. The Holy Spirit gives us spiritual new birth and is most closely identified with the maternal qualities of God—but all three in the Trinity always work together as one.

9. *Wisdom* appears to be a sacred subtitle for the Spirit, in Proverbs 8, and it is interesting that *ruach*, the Hebrew word for "the Spirit," is grammatically feminine.

10. Pronouns, however, are not definitive, because God is beyond gender. God is Spirit, immortal, eternal, and beyond description. His so-called masculine or feminine attributes refer to His *parenting personality*, not biology.

11. Like most people of faith, I will continue to pray reverently in the name of the Father, because it is biblical, and I use the pronoun *"He"* for God as most sensible.

12. The deity of the *all-wise and all-powerful God* is higher and more mysterious than the loftiest human thought; the extravagance of His love, beyond measure.

Biographies

(In alphabetical order)

Craig D. Atwood, Moravian. He is the author of three books on Christian history and editor of the *Handbook of Denominations in the United States.* Atwood holds the Charles D. Couch Chair in Moravian Theology and Ministry at Moravian Theological Seminary in Bethlehem, Pennsylvania.

Daniel Ayuch, Greek Orthodox. This Middle East theologian is a biblical expert on the book of Luke and Acts. He is professor of New Testament at the St. John of Damascus Institute of Theology in Lebanon and has published articles in Arabic, Spanish, and German and been published by *Biblica* in Rome.

Benedictine Monastery Monks, Roman Catholic. Three monks, Father Placidus, Nicholas, and Boniface, kindly allowed the author to interview them and to spend time at the monastery in prayer. Immersing herself in the daily life at Westminster Abbey, the author did research in a hidden library where a number of rare Bibles and sacred books are kept.

Sebastian Brock, Anglican. This Oxford professor is a world authority on the Old Syriac Gospels, a language similar to the Aramaic dialect that was spoken by Jesus. Brock is highly esteemed as an author and a scholar on ancient Syriac manuscripts.

Tony Campolo, Baptist. A well-respected sociologist and a popular Christian speaker, Campolo is the author of more than thirty-five books. He is a professor emeritus at Eastern University.

Recent books include *Stories that Feed Your Soul* and *Red Letter Revolution*, coauthored with Shane Claiborne.

Gary Chapman, Baptist. Chapman is well known for his best-selling book *The Five Love Languages*. In addition to his marriage conferences, sponsored by the Moody Bible Institute, the multi-talented author is a pastor and a popular public speaker.

Francis Collins, Christian. A physician-scientist of renown, he led the Human Genome Project and is now Director of the US National Institutes of Health. He has been honored with numerous awards, including the Presidential Medal of Freedom for his scientific contribution to genetic research and the Human Genome Project. He is the author of *The Language of God*.

Nicky Cruz, Pentecostal. This former notorious gang leader in New York City gained celebrity status when he gave his life to Jesus Christ and started working tirelessly to help hurting youth. Cruz is considered a world authority on youth violence. His life story is featured in the movie *The Cross and the Switchblade*, and he is a popular author.

Raymond Damadian, Baptist. The world-famous inventor of the MRI (magnetic resonance imaging) machine received the National Medal of Technology from President Reagan (1988) and was inducted into the National Inventors Hall of Fame in 1989. In 2007, he was granted the Inventor of the Year award for the upright MRI, among other accolades.

Danae Dobson, Nazarene. The only daughter of Dr. James Dobson, founder of Focus on the Family. Danae is a respected Christian speaker and author. She wrote her first book when she was only twelve years old and has written more than twenty books, mostly for children.

Stasi Eldredge, Nondenominational Christian. This engaging author mentors women on how to reach their potential. She leads the women's ministry at Ransomed Heart, a well-respected Christian organization in Colorado ministering to both men and women.

Ruth Graham, Presbyterian. As a daughter of the legendary evangelist Billy Graham, Ruth is a popular Christian public speaker and author of such books as *In Every Pew Sits a Broken Heart* and *A Legacy of Love: Things I Learned from My Mother.*

Viviane Haenni, Seventh-day Adventist. Based in Geneva, this gifted theologian founded the Christian Educational Center for Integrated Spirituality (CEPSI Pleroma) in Switzerland whose coaching section (CEPSI Coaching) is establishing the first Life Purpose Coaching Centers International® in France and French-speaking Switzerland.

Doris K. Hamilton, Presbyterian. She is the widow of Neill Q. Hamilton, an original-thinking Bible scholar who wrote a groundbreaking book called *Maturing in the Christian Life: A Pastor's Guide.* Doris, a violinist, passed away about a year after being interviewed by the author.

Margaretha Hendriks-Ririmasse, Protestant. A world-caliber theologian, she is Dean of the Indonesian Christian University in Moluccas, Indonesia, which was burned down by Islamic extremists. She is also a vice-moderator with the World Council of Churches (WCC) Central Committee, which represents more than 560 million Christians.

Robert Hiebert, Mennonite Brethren. He is Director of the Septuagint Institute, a research center specializing in the old Greek version of the Jewish Scriptures, the only center of its kind in North America. He is a Trinity Western University professor and translated the book of Genesis for *A New English Translation of the Septuagint*, published by Oxford University Press.

Thomas Hopko, Orthodox. Father Thomas is a well-respected theologian, speaker, and author. He was dean of St. Vladimer's Orthodox Theological Seminary in New York from 1992 until 2002 and taught dogmatic theology. He is now dean emeritus.

Elizabeth Johnson, Catholic. Sister Johnson is a nun and a renowned theological expert and author. She is a professor of theology at Fordham University, New York City, and is the past president of the Catholic Theological Society of America.

Laura Duhan Kaplan, Jewish. The rabbi is the spiritual leader of the Or Shalom Synagogue and a faculty member at ALEPH: Alliance for Jewish Renewal seminary. Kaplan received the prestigious US Professor of the Year award in 2001 from the Carnegie Foundation for the Advancement of Teaching.

Anne Lamott, Presbyterian. Lamott is a critically acclaimed writer and public speaker. She is a *New York Times* best-selling author of such popular nonfiction Christian books as *Traveling Mercies*, *Plan B*, and *Grace (Eventually)*.

James Lindenberger, Presbyterian. He was ordained by the Presbyterian Church in the United States in 1974 and was received by the United Church of Canada as a minister in 1978. As professor emeritus of Hebrew Bible at the Vancouver School of Theology, he is a scholastic expert on ancient Aramaic and Hebrew texts.

Father Federico Lombardi, Catholic. Spokesman for the Vatican and the Director of the Vatican Press Office. He shared documents with the author to illuminate the pope's insights. In addition, he translated into English a surprising statement made by Pope John Paul I.

Anne Graham Lotz, Nondenominational Christian. She is daughter of evangelist Billy Graham and an international Christian leader and faith speaker in her own right. This award-winning author wrote *Just Give Me Jesus* and a number of other inspiring books.

Christl Maier, Lutheran. The former Yale University scholar is now a senior theologian at Philipps-Universität in Marburg, Germany, the oldest Protestant university in the world. She received the Henry Luce III Fellows in Theology award in 2005–06 to conduct biblical research and is an expert who is respected on a global scale.

Brennan Manning, Catholic. This gifted speaker and writer is well known for his influential book *The Ragamuffin Gospel*. He was ordained as a Franciscan monk in the '60s and has written more than a dozen books including *The Journey of the Prodigal*.

Fio Mascarenhas, Catholic Charismatic. This Bible scholar is an internationally respected priest, speaker, and a best-selling author. He was living in Mumbai (Bombay), India, when he was interviewed. He helped form the International Catholic Charismatic Renewal Services (ICCRS) and is the chairman of the Catholic Bible Institute in Mumbai.

Fulata Mbano Moyo, Ecumenical. This world-class theologian works for global equity, justice, and unity as the program executive for Women in Church and Society with the World Council of Churches. She has applied for ordination with the Church of Central Africa Presbyterian in the Blantyre Synod.

Jürgen and Elisabeth Moltmann, Reformed. Living in Germany, they are known as one of the leading Protestant theologian couples in the world, and both are acclaimed as theological "bright stars." Jürgen has written a number of important books, such as *Theology of Hope* and *The Spirit of Life: A Universal Affirmation*. He and Elisabeth have coauthored *Humanity in God, God—His and Hers*, and *Passion for God: Theology in Two Voices*.

J. I. Packer, Anglican. Public accolades flow easily for this venerable theologian. He is named, along with Billy Graham, as one of the most influential Christians today. Packer is general editor of the English Standard Version Bible and the author of numerous outstanding books, including the contemporary Christian classic *Knowing God*.

Chonda Pierce, Interdenominational. A comedienne who wears her faith on her sleeve, she has won several Gospel Music Association Grady Nutt Humor awards and is a spokeswoman for World Vision and cofounder of the Branches Recovery Center.

Della Reese-Lett, Christian. A beloved singer and actress, she played the big-hearted angel "Tess" in the TV series *Touched by* *an Angel.* This was the only religiously based show to hit the Top Ten in the Nielsen ratings. She is in the Hollywood Walk of Fame.

Jennifer Rothschild, Baptist. A popular Christian singer, speaker, and writer, she is on the Billy Graham evangelistic team and has appeared on such TV programs as *Dr. Phil.* Her books include *Lessons I Learned in the Dark* and *Fingerprints of God.*

Sandra M. Schneiders, Catholic. A renowned theologian, speaker, and author, she holds the distinction of being the second woman in history to earn a Doctorate in Sacred Theology from the Gregorian University in Rome. Known for her expertise on the Bible, she was granted in 2006 the John Courtney Murray Award from the Catholic Theological Society of America.

James Shelton, Catholic Charismatic. He is a Senior Fellow at the St. Paul Center for Biblical Theology and is a highly regarded New Testament scholar at Oral Roberts University. He wrote *Mighty in Word and Deed: the Role of the Holy Spirit in Luke–Acts.*

Janet Soskice, Catholic. She earned her Doctorate in Philosophy of Religion at Oxford and is today Professor of Philosophical Theology at Cambridge University in England. Soskice has written such scholarly books as *The Kindness of God: Metaphor, Gender, and Religious Language.*

Luci Swindoll, Nondenominational. She used to work as a high-ranking business executive with Mobil Oil Corporation and also as an executive for *Insight for Living,* her brother, Chuck Swindoll's public radio ministry. Luci is a popular author and speaker.

Richard A. Taylor, Evangelical. A professor of Old Testament Studies, Taylor is the well-respected director of the PhD program at Dallas Theological Seminary in Dallas, Texas. Known for his academic acuity, his specialties include Aramaic studies and Syriac literature.

Gay Lynn Voth, Mennonite. At the time of the interview, Voth was teaching at Columbia Bible College. She welcomed the author into her classroom to observe the dynamics of the class and to interview students. She also shared her personal spiritual struggle to come to terms with who she is as a female in a culture that tends to favor masculinity over femininity.

Hyveth Williams, Seventh-day Adventist. She broke new ground as the first female black senior pastor in this denomination. She is a publicly acclaimed preacher, an author, and professor of homiletics at the Seventh-day Adventist Theological Seminary in Michigan.

William Paul Young, Christian. He was raised with a Stone Age tribe when his missionary parents were in (West Papua) Netherlands New Guinea. He thought he was part of the tribe for years and experienced major culture shock when he returned to North America. Young is the author of *The Shack*, a religious novel riding a wave of public popularity.

Ravi Zacharias, Christian and Missionary Alliance. An internationally respected evangelist, apologist, and author, Zacharias is a major Christian influence in the world. He has spoken to such diverse audiences as the UN General Assembly and to military officers in Moscow. He is the founder of Ravi Zacharias International Ministries.

Yair Zakovitch, Jewish. This leading scholar is professor of Bible Studies at the Hebrew University of Jerusalem in Israel and is an expert on the literary analysis of the Bible. Zakovitch is coauthor of a best-selling book in Israel called *That's Not What the Good Book Says*. He is former chairman of the Mandel Institute of Jewish Studies.

The following people also shared valuable insights with the author and are quoted in this book: Leslie Chambers, Joseph Fitzmyer, Christopher Foulds, Ingrid Haines, Lynn Ned, Rowshan Nemazee, and Buffy Sainte-Marie, as well as Rafael Zer and Eliezer Segal, who shared their expertise on the Hebrew language.

Notes

Chapter 1. The Journey Begins

1 "Lord Reign in Me," song written by Brenton Brown, Mercy Publishing, ccli #2490706.

Chapter 2. Benedictine Monks: Breaking the Silence

1 This interview took place before Father Boniface passed away on August 30, 2011.
2 Names in the stories were changed to protect the identity of the families.

Chapter 3. Science and Sex

1 Lewis, C. S., *Mere Christianity* (C. S. Lewis Pte, Ltd. 1952, New York, HarperCollins, revised 2001) 29.
2 Moltmann, Jürgen, *God in Creation* (Minneapolis: Augsburg Fortress Publishers, Fortress Press edition, 1993), 73.

Chapter 4. Dear Lord: Who Am I?

1 United Nations Development Fund for Women, "Violence Against Women World-Wide," Fact Sheet, 1997 study by the World Health Organization.

2 *The Simple Truth about the Gender Pay Gap*, American Association of University Women, 2012 edition.

3 Foulds, Christopher, "How Do I Answer My Little Girl's Questions?" Column originally entitled "On God, Baby Jesus, and Amen," is reprinted here by permission of the author and the publisher of *Abbotsford News*.

4 *Created in God's Image: From Hegemony to Partnership*, "Sense of Self," Felix Chingota, World Communion of Reformed Churches; World Council of Churches, 2010, 79.

Chapter 5. Jesus, Women, and Faith

1 Story is found in John 4:1–42. All statements in quotations are RSV.

2 *"My Father and your Father"*: Paraphrase John 20:1–17. All quotes RSV.

3 Sayers, Dorothy L., *Are Women Human?* (Grand Rapids: Wm. B. Eerdmans Publishing, 1971), 68.

4 Paul wrote about Junia in Romans 16:7, yet a number of translators later changed her name to "Junias," a man's name. *The Commentary: Critical, Practical, and Explanatory on the Old and New Testament* (1884) states that Junia was a female, "no doubt, either the wife or the sister of Andronicus." Also, see the *Matthew Henry Commentary on the Whole Bible (Complete–1706)*.

5 Column by Anne Graham Lotz (originally published in the *Washington Post*) reprinted here with the author's permission.

Chapter 6. Complementary Design

1 *"Daughter, your faith"*: Mark: 5:25–34, author's paraphrase. Quotes are ESV.

2 Lewis, C. S., *A Grief Observed* (London: Faber and Faber, 1961), 40–41.

3 *"My help [ezer] comes from the LORD"*: Bracketed word added. The Hebrew word *ezer* is identified in this verse according to the Brown, Driver, Briggs, and Gesenius Lexicon.

4 The Brown, Driver, Briggs, Gesenius Hebrew Lexicon explains that *tsela* typically means an entire "side" of something, as in the side of a tabernacle or the side of a chamber, etc.

5 "Caregiving in the United States," National Alliance for Caregiving in collaboration with AARP, November 2009.

6 Schaeffer, Francis A., *Trilogy: The God Who Is There* (Westchester, IL: Crossway Books, 1990) 340.

7 Yancey, Philip, *Reaching for the Invisible God* (Grand Rapids: Zondervan Publishing House, 2000) 118.

Chapter 7. Masculine, Feminine, and Beyond

1 *"If we follow Him, we will not walk in darkness"*: John 8:12 paraphrase.

2 Moltmann, Jürgen, *God in Creation: A New Theology of Creation and the Spirit of God* (Minneapolis: Augsburg Fortress Publishers, 1991) 223.

Chapter 8. The Mercy of God: Protective and Womb-Like

1 Bonnie [Penner] Witherall was murdered on November 21, 2002, at a maternity clinic in Sidon, Lebanon, which has been supported by the Christian Missionary Alliance Organization.

2 The disciples were first called Christians (Acts 11:26) in Antioch, Syria. The Antioch Church is part of the worldwide Orthodox Church, which has more than 200 million adherents.

3 Charles Spurgeon, from an essay titled "The Tenderness of God's Comfort."

4 In Hebrew *rehem* means "the mother, womb," and is translated to show mercy, to forgive and be gracious and kind, according to an article by Rabbi Kaufmann Kohler in the Jewish Encyclopedia. Variations *racham*, *rahamim*, and *rehem* are simply different ways of transliterating the word "womb," explained Dr. Yair Zakovitch, Bible professor at the Hebrew University of Jerusalem.

Chapter 9. God of Infinite Compassion

1 "Indonesia Flashpoints—The Moluccas," BBC news article, states that Christians and Muslims lived peacefully in their villages for many years, but economic and political pressures led to a crisis. Outside forces, including Islamic militant groups such as the Laskar Jihad and the army from Jakarta, exacerbated the carnage.

2 Hendriks-Ririmasse referred to a number of texts taken together in Isaiah 44, 49, and 66.

3 Catechism of the Catholic Church, Second Edition, Part One, Section Two, Chapter One, Paragraph Two, *The Father*, 239.

4 Pope Benedict XVI addressed priests and pastoral assistants in Loreto, Italy, on March 7, 1988, when he was known as Cardinal Joseph Ratzinger. Written translation is contained in an article called "You Are Full of Grace: Elements of Biblical Devotion to Mary." The Vatican provided copies of these texts to the author to reprint with their permission.

5 Passages from the *Jewish Encyclopedia* are used by permission from Josh Kopelman, founder of the online *Jewish Encyclopedia* at www.jewishencyclopedia.com.

6 The Complete Jewish Bible also uses exquisite language in this pas-

sage: "I keep myself calm and quiet, like a little child on its mother's lap—I keep myself like a little child" (Ps. 131:2).

Chapter 10. "As a Hen Gathers Her Chicks"

1 "Ducklings Fall into an Ugly Mess," Christopher Foulds, May 15, 1999, *Abbotsford News*.

Chapter 11. A Baker, a Midwife, and More

1 *"Yes, Lord, I believe that you are the Christ"*: John 11:27 RSV. Full story, John 11:1–27. All quotations RSV.
2 *Jewish Encyclopedia*, Biblical Data, Ezekiel 16, 1906.
3 *"Some are kissing mothers"*: www.goodreads.com/author/quotes/704.Pearl_S_Buck.
4 Pope John Paul II, sermon, Evangelium Vitae, presented at St. Peter's Square, Rome, March, 25, 1995, on the Solemnity of the Annunciation of the Lord.

Chapter 14. The Comforter

1 Tübingen University was established by Count Eberhard in 1477 and is renowned for its superb academics. A Protestant seminary was added to Tübingen in 1536, and a Catholic seminary was built later.
2 *Quotations from the Wayside*, edited by Brenda Wong (Unitarian Universalist Assoc., Boston, MA, 1998), 78.
3 Dart, John, "Balancing Out the Trinity, The Genders of the God-head," *Christian Century*, February 16-23, 1983, 147.
4 Hamilton, Neill Q., *Maturing in the Christian Life: A Pastor's Guide* (North Creek Press, 1984). Reprinted with permission from Doris K. Hamilton and son, Neill Hamilton.

5 Hamilton, Neill, Q, *Maturing in the Christian Faith,* subsection: "Holy Spirit—The Feminine Side of the Life of Faith."

6 Henry, Matthew, *Matthew Henry's Commentary on the Whole Bible,* published 1706. In some instances I changed the word *it* to *the child* as Henry would have meant it.

Chapter 15. Honor the Father, Son, and Holy Spirit

1 Packer, J. I., *Knowing God,* (InterVarsity Press, Westmont IL, 1973), 60.

2 Excerpt on the Holy Trinity, *Saint John of Damascus, Writings,* translated by Frederic H. Chase Jr., *The Fathers of the Church,* Catholic University of America, 1958, 162–63.

3 Charles H. Spurgeon, a Baptist minister (1834–1892), in a sermon called "The Tenderness of God's Comfort."

4 *"Yes, Lord, yes, Lord"*: A line from the chorus of "Trading My Sorrows," Darrell Evans, Integrity Music.

Chapter 16. *Wisdom* Calls Out

1 Facts cited are from the Douay-Rheims (DR) official website: www.drbo.org/index.htm. The DR is the first official Catholic Bible, OT published in 1609. The KJV (official Protestant version) was published in 1611.

2 The Torah, strictly speaking, refers to the first five books in the Bible (Genesis, Exodus, Leviticus, Numbers, and Deuteronomy), but may also refer to the entire Jewish Bible or what is known to non-Jews as the Old Testament, but to Jews as the Tanakh. This includes the law, poetry, and historical stories—from Genesis to Malachi.

Chapter 17. The Spirit of Truth

1 St. Catherine's Monastery is located at the foot of Mount Sinai, Egypt, the mountain where God handed the Ten Commandments to Moses. Its library contains more than six thousand religious manuscripts, including the oldest Syriac Gospels. Considered the oldest library in the Christian world, it preserves the second largest collection of early manuscripts in the world (outnumbered only by the Vatican Library).

2 The liturgy of the Syriac Orthodox Church continues to be in the Syriac language, an Aramaic dialect, one of the most ancient languages in the world. The word for "spirit" in Syriac, *ruho* (also "wind") is grammatically feminine. The Spirit is referred to with the feminine pronoun in almost all early Syriac writings. Later writings refer to the Spirit in the masculine form.

3 Statistics on *ruach* cited by theologian R. P. Nettelhorst, www.theology.edu/journal/volume3/spirit.htm.

Chapter 18. Pronouns, Metaphors, and Names

1 The most mysterious title for God since the beginning of time is *"I am who I am."* Sandra Schneiders notes that a verb has no gender. Neill Q. Hamilton, in *Maturing in the Christian Faith*, explains that the Spirit of God displays a "metasexual" role in the Godhead. The Greek word *meta* means *beyond*. Therefore, *metasexual* is not literal or physical, but means *beyond gender.*

2 Spurgeon, Charles, from a sermon entitled: "The Tenderness of God's Comfort."

3 *El Shaddai* is translated from Hebrew into English as *God Almighty.* The title is linked to mountain heights, power, and invincible strength. Some scholars believe the name has feminine connotations because the root of *El Shaddai* is *shad*, which means "breast" in ancient Hebrew. Therefore, in their view, an appropriate in-

terpretation might be "Breasted One" or "All-Nurturing God." Hebrew scholars in Jerusalem disagree. *Shadu* means "mountain" in Akkadian, and according to biblical evidence, they teach that *El Shaddai* means "God of great strength and invincible power," and in some cases even "violence or destruction."

Chapter 19. *The Shack*, Father Thomas, and Ravi

1 Hopko, Thomas, "God and Gender: Articulating the Orthodox View," *St. Vladimir's Theological Quarterly, God and Gender*, Volume 37, No. 2 and 3 (Faculty of St. Vladimir's Orthodox Theological Seminary, 1993), 153.

Chapter 20. Kneeling in the Presence of God

1 Matthew Henry's Commentary on the Whole Bible (Concise), Genesis 1, Verses 1–2, www.biblestudytools.com.
2 *"Do not fear"*: Isaiah 43:1, 4 NASB.

Acknowledgments

Talk about an explosion! When I first began to interview faith leaders in 2007 about the question of the so-called gender of God, very few people were talking about this controversy. But, suddenly, it became a "hot button" issue. By early 2011, Google was reporting 25 million hits on this question—and I thought, *Wow, that's certainly a decent amount of interest.*

But I was in for a shock. By the time my editor at FaithWords, Joey Paul, was in the final stages of editing *The Mother Heart of God*, public interest in this question had skyrocketed to 100 million hits. An electrifying increase, to say the least!

Where do I start in my acknowledgments?

First, I am humbled that God called me to write such a book as this. Stepping out in faith, I did not know how, or where, He was going to lead me when I took a sabbatical and started writing. It's been an adventure—turbulent and exciting, never dull. I am grateful for the privilege of interviewing scholars and celebrities who generously shared their insights and stories with me. I found these men and women kindhearted, wise, and passionately dedicated to serving God. They made a significant impact in my life. I hope they have in your lives, too.

I also want to thank my literary agents, Blair and Don Jacobson, at DC Jacobson and Associates, for seeing the value in my exploration of this contemporary topic, for their encouragement, and for their objective literary advice. I had no idea where the book would eventually land, but it's no overstatement to say it has been beyond my wildest dreams and prayers that FaithWords decided to be my publisher. I am over the top about this, and mere words cannot come close to expressing my gratitude for this amazing team of talented people.

Many heart-felt thanks to Joey Paul, my faithful and patient editor. In an era when editors tend to play it safe and comfortable, he took a risk, stepped out in faith, and prayerfully considered how this book would help fill some of the public's deepest spiritual needs.

To me, Joey's a man of great integrity. He came up with a wonderful title for this book, and in our growing friendship, I have to say, I could not ask for a more caring editor.

To Rolf Zettersten, thank you for your tireless efforts behind the scenes, for your passion for prose, and your dedication to excellence in book publishing.

In addition, I'd like to thank April Frazier for her detailed line editing and editorial assistant Laura Laffoon for her upbeat positive spirit, and the rest of the team at FaithWords for their tireless work and time in gently guiding this book into the hands of the public.

I also appreciate my many faithful friends who stood by me through moments of anguish and the proverbial insecurities that plague every writer. Thank you especially to Suzanne Ashley, Susan Janetti, Jules Johnson, and Helen Grace Lescheid, for your patience, your objective advice and analysis, years of emotional support, and most of all, your prayers.

I'd also like to pay tribute to my three beautiful daughters and my seven grandchildren for being the light of my life—the most precious people in the world to me.

Last, and most important, thank you, my dear reader. I pray you will be inspired to turn to the stories in the Bible with new eyes, and read these ancient sacred words as a precious love letter, from God, to you, personally. May you feel the comfort of His love and mercy to the very depths of your soul, and experience the blessed hope that will bring you healing and peace.

May the grace of God be with you!

About the Author

Trudy Beyak is an award-winning investigative journalist acclaimed by the North American newspaper industry for her compassion and tenacity in pursuing stories that help people to live healthier, happier, and more productive lives.

A journalist since 1989, publishers respect her as an original thinker. Her knowledge is well-respected on issues ranging from politics and the environment to science and religion. Many of her stories have inspired the public to take action in resolving issues of injustice. Trudy has earned thirty international, national, and provincial first-place writing awards and excellent-achievement awards. She was also nominated for the Order of British Columbia for outstanding work as a journalist and commitment to integrity and public service.

Trudy is a committed Christian, the mother of three beautiful daughters, and the grandmother of a growing number of adorable grandchildren.

She lives in Abbotsford, British Columbia, Canada.